THE GREAT BIKE RACE

THE CLASSIC, ACCLAIMED BOOK
THAT INTRODUCED THE WORLD
TO THE TOUR DE FRANCE

by
Geoffrey Nicholson

Introduction by
William Fotheringham

 velodrome

Praise for *The Great Bike Race*

impresses me that an Englishman, even one THE OBSERVER has
alled 'our resident cyclopath' has succeeded in a venture akin to ex-
laining Five-Day Test cricket to a visitor from Peking ... His de-
cription of the 1976 Tour is based on an honest eye and the careful
ssembly of *pointilliste* incident. It is interleaved with encyclopaedic
istoric flashbacks and is, as the French say of a decisive win, impecca-
ly 'lucide'. They ought to give him a special lap of honour.

Observer

If there were a *maillot jaune* for sportswriters, Mr Nicholson should
be wearing it.

Economist

... conveys the agony of the mountains, the exhilaration of the sprints
and the dull ache of the treadmill, as well as the tactics and mathemat-
ics involved in team racing ...

Times Literary Supplement

The smell of rural France pervades this lovingly written study.

Scottish Daily Record

A delightful and perceptive book ... his greatest success is in his won-
derfully vivid ability to describe the passing scene, whether witnessed
from the grandstand of a stadium, from a café terrace in a small mountain hamlet, or from the bedrooms of the participants and the armies
of their assistants ... Mr Nicholson is very good indeed.

The Sunday Times

The quality of his writing transformed the character of sports journalism.

Guardian

One of the first English language accounts of a Tour de France in
a book, and Nicholson is exploring virgin territory in his coverage
of the 1976 Tour de France. When you read about the Tour's iconic

places, they are often riffs on Nicholson's original descriptions. A real historical artefact.

Cycling Weekly

This is a gripping tale even for someone who doesn't know a bidon from a peloton.

Essex Weekly News

A thorough analysis of the Tour's background and history.

Sunday Telegraph

It is the best effort by a British sports writer for a long time. In THE GREAT BIKE RACE our erstwhile Guardian peddler has chronicled the sweat and spirit, drugs and dregs, intrigue and incest, clutter and clatter and wheel-whizz of the moveable feast that entrances all France for a very merry month in midsummer. Like the Tour itself, Nicholson's book is very special.

Guardian

An outstandingly attractive and exciting book, a coolly written and wry cliff-hanger. It is a virtuoso performance.

Economist

He is defiantly prosaic. His book is admirably lively.

New Statesman

For those who love a good read, from a pocket-size book, Mr Nicholson's effort is well worth while. The writing is impeccable, the allusions apt and inspiring and the whole a notable contribution towards present-day understanding of cycling.

Motor Cycle and Cycle Trader

He writes sports like Fielding wrote novels, good-naturedly, with a talent for revealing emblematic physical detail. Nicholson's Tour has plot, characters, complications, the narrative grip of a 'Tom Jones'.

Time Out

A Velodrome Book

First published in 1977

This new edition first published in Great Britain in 2016 by
Velodrome Publishing
A Division of Casemate Publishers
10 Hythe Bridge Street
Oxford OX1 2EW, UK
and
1950 Lawrence Road, Havertown, PA 19083 USA

www.velodromepublishing.com

Images courtesy Offside/ L'Équipe
Maps by David Gibbons

The publishers would like to graciously thank Mavis Nicholson, and the Nicholson family, for
their splendid support and assistance in the creation of this new edition.

A catalogue record for this book is available from the British Library

ISBN 978-1-911162-02-5

Printed in the Czech Republic by FINIDR s.r.o...

To receive regular email updates on forthcoming Velodrome titles, news and reader offers,
please email info@velodromepublishing.com with 'Velodrome Updates' in the subject field.

For a complete list of Velodrome Publishing titles, please contact:
CASEMATE PUBLISHERS (UK)
Telephone (01865) 241249
Fax (01865) 794449
Email: casemate-uk@casematepublishers.co.uk
www.casematepublishers.co.uk

CASEMATE PUBLISHERS (US)
Telephone (610) 853-9131
Fax (610) 853-9146
Email: casemate@casematepublishing.com
www.casematepublishing.com

This edition is dedicated to Geoff's three sons:
Steve, Lewis, Harry,
and to his five grandchildren:
Ben, Tess, Maud, Owen and Iris.

Contents

– Introduction –

It is one of the most evocative of opening sentences: 'In my case I came upon the Tour de France by way of Whitley Bay and Morecambe.' To paraphrase the late Geoff Nicholson's beginning to this book, in my personal case I came upon the Tour de France by way of *The Great Bike Race*. There are books that change your life and shape your life. This is one of those.

In my case, it is probably **the** one. I was thirteen when the paperback appeared in 1978 and my mother — who happened to be copy-editing for Magnum, the publishers — brought home a copy for me and my late father, a former cyclist who kept a close eye on his old sport. I don't know whether poor old dad even got to read it. He certainly never got hands on it again once it had found its way into my bedroom. That paperback is still with me thirty-seven years on, albeit read to pieces, lacking the front cover, and kept in an envelope so that the pages don't get lost.

The Great Bike Race arrived in my sweaty paws when I was at my most impressionable age — in the same way that Nicholson's sports editor at the *Observer* 'couldn't have picked a more susceptible reporter' to send to the Milk Race in 1959 — and it was after devouring his elegant, dryly witty phrases that I began hitting the Devon hills on a clunky old bike, COBs being what one had to ride as a teenager in the pre-Lapsarian days before carbon and aluminium. As I hauled the COB across Exmoor, it was Peter Post of Raleigh who I imagined driving up behind me waving a professional contract out of the window of his car. I knew just what he looked like thanks to Nicholson — 'a long, slim, elegant man with a silver scarab hanging from a thong round his neck and small blue scars like a miner's on his forehead.'

The Great Bike Race remains, in my eyes, the finest book ever written about the Tour de France. The blend of the four core elements of the Tour — travelogue, anecdote, *dramatis personae* and narrative — is perfectly balanced, presented with a perfect turn of phrase, the craftsmanship worn so lightly that a wry smile is ever present as you scan the page. Rightly, the book earned plaudits on publication in 1977 (£4.95, Hodder & Stoughton): compared to Henry Fielding's *Tom Jones* by *Time Out* magazine; 'based on an honest eye and the careful assembly of *pointilliste* incident,' wrote David Leitch in the *Observer,* 'as the French say, impeccably *lucide.*' Nowadays, there is less need to define *peloton* or *ravitaillement,* but in the 1970s — as remained largely the case until the advent of Team Sky in 2010 — there was a need to translate the Tour, to explain, to interpret, and one of the great strengths of *The Great Bike Race* was, 'making a rather foreign event perfectly intelligible,' as the *New Statesman*'s reviewer put it.

A stage race, Nicholson tells us, is 'a picaresque novel which each day introduced new characters in a different setting,' and his master-work is the tale of a Tour which 'was not one of those races dominated by a single rider' — for the follower in the 1970s, this meant one man: Eddy Merckx — 'it had a series of leaders . . . an elaborate web of sub-plots and a good deal more suspense than most.' The 1976 race was the first Tour of the post-Merckx era, won by his Belgian understudy Lucien Van Impe in a single Pyrenean attack which was the opening master-stroke in the distinguished career of his *directeur sportif* Cyrille Guimard, who would go on to direct Bernard Hinault, Laurent Fignon and Greg LeMond. It was the second of three Tours — two won by Bernard Thévenet — in the inter-regnum between the Cannibal and the Badger; often such Tours are more dramatic than those dominated by one of the greats. In that sense, Nicholson was fortunate, but his writing could have made any Tour spring to life.

* * *

One of the peculiar spin-offs of turning a personal passion into a career is that you are bound to encounter your heroes along the way; they go from being distant figures to human presences, warts and all. When, nervously, I first encountered Geoff on my first Tour de France, with a mere two years in journalism behind me, he was welcoming, in his diffident way, albeit a mite sceptical of my attempts to retain a cyclist's fitness in the face of France's culinary delights. For a quiet man, he was a distinctive presence in the press room; as his travelling companion Stephen

Bierley — my predecessor as the *Guardian*'s man on the Tour — put it, 'the abiding image for many was of him sitting in front of his portable computer with a precarious curve of ash [from his Gauloise] poised to drop on the keyboard.'

By a quirk of good luck — a hotel booking agency shared by our respective publications, *Cycling Weekly* in my case, the *Observer* in Geoff's — we spent evenings and mornings together. As Bierley wrote, 'to share anything with Geoff was a delight,' and it is an eternal regret that because the 'Comic' had me on a different schedule, I never took a seat in a car which had more than a hint of a journalistic High Table about it. Driven by the legendarily laconic ex-Tourman Graham Jones, with Bierley, Nicholson and Sam Abt of the *Herald Tribune* in the passenger seats, it is the English-speaking equivalent of the legendary vehicle that conveyed Antoine Blondin and Pierre Chany in the 1950s.

The time with that quartet on Tour sticks deep, and shows itself in present-day force of habit. The local *presse* has to be spied out on arrival at the evening's staging point so that *L'Équipe* can be analysed over the breakfast croissant and coffee. Dinner should be savoured slowly as a way of winding down from the stage, with the issues of the day chewed as reflectively as the rare steak. One of the marks of the true Tour journalist is his ability to recall a good locale for a decent dinner from years back; this was one of Geoff's fortes, be it the station buffet in Strasbourg or an obscure brasserie in the back streets of Grenoble. In his view, the entire experience of the race had to be savoured. If the *Observer* today features a Tour de France diary (now racily nicknamed The Backie), which takes a sideways look at the race and all that goes around with it, that format is entirely a personal homage to Geoff, who gave it his own erudite edge in the 1980s and early 1990s.

On Tour, certain books travel well, offering a gold standard to aim for, in the hope that a chapter or two in the evening will percolate down into your writing the following tea-time as you rush to hit the day's deadline. My original copy of *The Great Bike Race* has many Tours in its pages, with good reason. Geoff is English cycling writing's master, a Welsh wizard of the well-turned image. 'Relaxed but riveting,' to quote another great, Peter Corrigan; the similes leap from the page and stick in the mind. Freddy Maertens hoards points towards the green jersey — 'like a shopper saving trading stamps'; Paris-Plage in Le Touquet is 'a typically French high-production tannery'. My eternal favourite is the Col de l'Izoard — 'a rocky wilderness at 7,743 feet which needs only a few bleached skulls at the roadside to complete its image of desolation.' Like Gimondi contemplating yet another defeat by Merckx (who has 'the high-cheeked, graven image of a totem pole'), we fellow writers can only look on in admiration, tinged with a little frustration. The mark of the great in any field is that they make what they do seem simple; try as we might, writing with this consummate ease is so hard to match.

* * *

The Great Bike Race was one of ten books Geoff wrote during a distinguished forty years in sportswriting, hailed by his obituarists on his untimely death in 1999: 'one of a small team who transformed the character of sports journalism by introducing a quality of writing that matched, and was sometimes superior to, that on the foreign and arts pages,' wrote the former *Observer* editor Donald Trelford. Geoff was born on April 4 1929 in Surrey, and brought up in Mumbles, near Swansea, where he attended university; his first lecturer was the novelist Kingsley Amis. After an initial career in advertising, freelance work brought him to the *Guardian* and the *Observer* — then separate publications — where he became deputy to another legend, Chris Brasher, on the sports desk.

Rugby was an early mainstay, so too book reviews, but one early assignment for the *Observer* was the pivotal day when he was sent to cover the stage of the Milk Race — 125 miles from Whitley Bay to Morecambe, won by Bill Bradley from Brian Haskell — and he subsequently moved on to covering the race for *The Times*. In 1976, at the time of writing *The Great Bike Race,* he was appointed Sports Editor of the *Observer;* he filled the same role at the short-lived *Sunday Correspondent* although front-line reporting was his first love. By the eighties he was combining the role of rugby correspondent for the newly founded *Independent* with coverage of the Tour. Among the legendary figures of Fleet

Street sports writing such as Frank Keating and Hugh McIlvanney, he carved out his own niche with the 'spare, precise, evocative,' writing lauded by Trelford.

In Geoff's second cycling book, *Le Tour*, he pictures what the senior French Tour journalist he travelled with in the 1960s might have made of the race 30 years later and that raises an obvious question. What would Geoff have made of the Tour, now that his last race, 1993, is now as far-removed in time as the early Merckx years were back then? He would have regretted the Tour's expansion even since the nineties into the bloated event it is now and I can't see him being anything other than damning about the overweening status given to television cameras and the dozens who wield them, or the bland statements unwillingly offered at the press conferences which now form the bulk of the media's interaction with the riders.

Compared to the era of *The Great Bike Race*, stages on the Tour are shorter, the days more intense and less forgiving on those who report it, driven by social media to an extent that seems unfathomable to those of us who were on the race twenty years ago. It's a more instant world, offering less time for the reflection that came so naturally to Geoff, but it still should not be taken too seriously; I love to imagine what ironic comment he would have made on the fact that in 2015, in an attempt to emulate Formula One, the organisers designated the area where *suiveurs*, team personnel and riders congregate at the start as 'the paddock'.

The 'subtleties' of the racing have changed — teams are better organised, with better communication on the road with the advent of helmet radios meaning the fog of war has thinned — and there is a sophistication in the teams' backrooms that was lacking in the seventies. But the Tour retains the fundamentals that Geoff found so alluring: adventure and suspense, speed, physical stress and hazard, constant change of scenery, the element of the unpredictable and 'tactical variety . . . riders attacked and chased, flagged and rallied, formed instant alliances for instant ends and broke them without another thought.'

On the other hand, British cycling culture of the 21st century is a world away from the 1960s and 1970s when, as Geoff put it, the sport faced, 'the same kind of problem that soccer has done in the United States. How to promote a sport with no indigenous tradition?' It is hard to conceive of the situation that he found himself in in the 1960s, when, he writes, 'cycling was not the proper concern of a serious paper,' and sports editors were less than enthusiastic about covering the sport. Thanks to Sir Chris Hoy, Mark Cavendish, Nicole Cooke, Victoria Pendleton and Sir Bradley Wiggins, that tradition has been forged, to the extent that – incredible as it would have seemed back then – Great Britain has become a dominant nation in cycling worldwide, no longer the poor relation among the European cycling family. London and Yorkshire have staged *Grands Départs* which dwarf the Tour's 1974 visit to Plymouth. Back home, there is an expanding calendar of international races — sixteen days of UCI racing in 2015 watched by European-scale crowds — and a wealth of teams and lesser events. Cinderella has not merely turned up at the ball but is boogie-ing round her handbag, drink in hand, the life and soul of the party.

One by-product of that upsurge is a burgeoning of cycle culture, the full panoply from specialist cafes to designer clothing and exhibitions at the Design Museum. The canon of cycling writing has equalled or outstripped that in more established sports not merely in output but also in its literary quality and variety. Geoff has spiritual sons among the current crop, and it is only right that the father should take his place among his family. In sport, the greats rarely make successful comebacks long after their heyday, but great literature at least can outlast the mere humans who figure in its pages and shine time and time again. *The Great Bike Race* and its writer deserve nothing less.

William Fotheringham is the cycling correspondent at the Guardian, *covering every Tour de France since 1990 bar one, and is the author of best-selling biographies of Eddy Merckx, Fausto Coppi and Tom Simpson, while his latest book is a biography of Bernard Hinault.*

– La Grande Boucle –

In my case I came upon the Tour de France by way of Whitley Bay and Morecambe. On the morning of 29 May 1959 a caravan of sixty-eight cyclists, a dozen cars carrying organisers, time-keepers, judges and reporters, a St. John's ambulance and a mobile milk bar moved out of Whitley Bay on the north-east coast and headed west across the Pennines. It was the fourth stage of the 1,320-mile Milk-for-Stamina Tour of Britain cycle race. 'Another gruelling 125 miles today,' said the announcer. 'And do you know what the riders have in their gruel? Milk, ladies and gentlemen. They have milk.'

At that time cycle racing couldn't have been further from the thoughts of the heavy Sunday papers, but this particular event struck the *Observer* as having a certain gaudy appeal, and out of curiosity they sent me to have a look at it. They couldn't have picked a more appealing stage or, for that matter, a more susceptible reporter. The cyclists left the resort in a cloud of whirring silence. Motorcycle marshals ripped importantly past. Loudspeakers issued imperative warnings as if the race owned the road. The whole thing went off with tremendous urgency. Then, as the riders moved into the hills, two of them split away from the rest and played out for us the latest episode in the twelve-day serial.

One was Bill Bradley, a small, slight Lancastrian who worked as a Post Office engineer; he was the best amateur of his day, and already the race leader. The other was Brian Haskell, a solid Yorkshireman and a semi-professional who was set on becoming King of the Mountains, a title, handsomely endowed by the standards of that time, which went to the best climber over hills along the route. They were in different teams and therefore rivals, but this didn't prevent them striking up an alliance to gain their separate ends. Each took it in turn to set the pace at the front while the other tucked in behind his rear wheel, the two of them running a perpetual relay along unfenced, unclassified, unprintable roads until they were far out of sight of the main bunch of riders.

Climbing out of the patchwork of fields and over the open moors on a fresh summer day, the two men faced six hills with extravagantly rustic names which counted towards the King of the Mountains competition — Weatherlaw, Pawlaw Pike, Scargill, Pinseat, Crackpot and Deepdale. At the crest of each Haskell jumped away to take the points then waited for his friendly enemy, and once more the two would career downhill in tandem at fifty miles an hour. The partnership was briefly dissolved, too, at Barnard Castle when Haskell sprinted away from Bradley to pick up the £7.00 town prize. But it was Haskell who cracked three miles before the finish on the Morecambe promenade, and after waiting a moment to make sure that he would be able to struggle on, Bradley rode on to collect the return *he* wanted from his effort: the stage win and an extra two minutes lead in the race.

These six hours contained virtually all the elements that make cycle racing on the road attractive. The adventure and suspense of the long escape. The surprising speed — over twenty miles an hour over twisting roads that rose from sea level to 1,500 feet, and continually dipped and rose again. The blatant physical stress of climbing, the hazard of the downhill runs. The change of scenery. The unpredictable factors, not just of wind and rain (absent this day but easily imagined), but the common problems of competing on public roads instead of custom-built tracks: road works, newly-laid chippings, straying sheep and (in Britain anyway) other traffic. The tactical variety: riders didn't just put their heads down and their bottoms up and pelt from A to B; they attacked and chased, flagged and rallied, formed instant alliances for immediate ends, and broke them without another thought.

Even more compelling, though, was the strong narrative quality of the sport. A race was a rounded, self-contained story with complex relationships, sudden shifts of action, identifiable heroes, a beginning, a middle and an end. When it was simply a stage in a longer race, then it became another chapter in a picaresque novel which each day introduced new characters in a different setting.

In those summers I was reporting cricket, a game in which I could rarely be certain whether I had seen a batsman bowled, stumped or caught at the wicket — even if I happened to be looking at the time — and which took three days to reach a conclusion, or not, if it happened to rain. After that day in the Pennines cycle racing seemed to offer a far more coherent story to tell. As in cricket there was the problem of seeing the action; you couldn't be with every group of riders along the road. But cyclists were far more communicative than amateurs in the major sports. They wanted to tell you what had happened, and why. Feeling that their sport had been unfairly neglected by the Press they responded to any sympathetic interest. I took to covering the Tour of Britain for *The Times,* though they would only accept reports on alternate days and made no pretence of sharing my enthusiasm for the event. Over a report of a particularly melodramatic struggle on the stage from Cardiff to Aberystwyth, when there was a series of escapes and captures, punctures and crashes in the Black Mountains and along the lonely mountain road to Tregaron, they put the headline: Cyclists Traverse Welsh Valleys. Cycling was still not the proper concern of a serious paper, and it was 1965 before I saw anything of the Tour de France, following the race from its start in Cologne to Saint-Brieuc in Brittany. Or rather preceding it. I had hired a Press seat from the correspondent of *Le Progrès,* the Lyon paper, whose custom was to drive ahead to a quiet spot, type out the morning interviews with two rapidly prodding fingers, and at the first sign of the riders' approach, drive on again to the finish. I was briefly allowed to watch two nonentities on the attack, a tame parody of the Bradley-Haskell runaway win; otherwise I saw only the sprints at the stage towns. But even though the whole experience was like seeing the Second Coming from the top of a passing bus, I couldn't help noticing that, as sports events go, the Tour de France was a bit of a phenomenon.

By any kind of statistical measurement the Tour is the world's biggest annual sports promotion. Even among events held at longer intervals, it is overshadowed only by the Olympic Games and the World Cup (and these, of course, are visited on a different country each time). It lasts twenty-five days, spreading over from the last week of June into mid-July, covers some 4,000 kilometres (2,500 miles) along a different route each year, and has 2,000 people travelling with it. Of these only 120–140 are the professional cyclists — of probably a dozen nationalities — who compete in the race. The rest are camp followers of various degree — officials, technicians, reporters, publicity makers — who live off the country and at the smaller stage towns fill every spare hotel bed for thirty miles around. And this number doesn't include the task force employed at each resting place, or the 26,000 gendarmes, members of the Compagnie Républicaine de Sécurité and local *agents* who clear the way for the Tour. Nor, in themselves, do the figures convey the intensity of the national obsession with *la Grande Boucle*, the big loop, the great bike race.

If you have to separate one distinctive feature from the rest it is that the race goes out to the people; over a decade it will penetrate almost every corner of this enormous and enormously varied country. A farmer in the loneliest stretches of the Auvergne will one day find it on his doorstep. And since it takes place in front of the café terraces, it plays a far livelier role in café life throughout France than does, say, an England football game at Wembley in the pub life of Lancashire. Weeks before the start, the map of this year's route will have been pinned up over the bar beside those closely-printed warnings against public drunkenness.

Almost every region, too, will have a local rider in the race. As the race passes through a small hamlet in Normandy you will suddenly notice that the banners no longer mention the stars like Poulidor and Thévenet but one of the more obscure members of their teams. And if nothing of much importance is happening, this young novice or old, unsuccessful hack will be allowed to lead the column down the main street and gain enough seconds to stop and greet his family.

It's reckoned that around fifteen million people, one third of the population of France, come to the roadside each year to see the Tour pass. An unverifiable but perfectly credible figure, for especially on Sundays and on Bastille Day the crowds form an almost unbroken corridor for hundreds of miles. They arrive in time to push their Renaults into a gateway, set out lunch on the edge of the field and collect their paper hats and cracker gifts from the publicity caravan, then they stay to watch the Tour which passes like a mirage in a flash of chrome and colour. The more devoted go to the tops of the mountains where they can pass the time etching out the names of their favourites in last winter's snow, or spelling them out in stones and flowers, and then see the riders toiling up the slopes in ones and twos. But even they witness only a few minutes of a race which is spread over more than

115 hours. They turn up in the spirit less of football spectators, expecting to have the whole action laid out before them, than of rubberneckers at a state procession content to catch a glimpse of historic figures.

What feeds their interest for the rest of the three weeks is the saturation coverage of the Tour. By twiddling between France Inter, Radio Belge, Radio Luxembourg and Radio Monte Carlo they can hear an almost continuous commentary while the race is on. On television the final approach and the finish are covered live from cameras mounted on motorcycles and a helicopter; later there will be an abridged film of the stage and a post-mortem. Popular papers give up at least two pages to reports, analysis and background.

To give an example of Press devotion to the Tour, which presumably reflects its readers' wishes, in 1968 I travelled with the *Sud-Ouest,* a Bordeaux paper with a wide circulation area stretching south to the Pyrenees. In our car, apart from the driver, were the chief cycling correspondent and a reporter who gathered human interest stories; in addition to their work *Sud-Ouest* carried agency reports and two syndicated columns. In a second car, equipped for telex, was the operator and his driver. And while the Tour was in the southwest the paper also leased a half-share in a plane taking aerial photographs. All this for a single provincial newspaper, even if it was one of the biggest.

It's the sheer scale of the Tour that first impresses you. It moves around the country like a sovereign state. Ahead of it roads are closed to all but emergency vehicles for ninety minutes before the first rider is due; they are not reopened until ten minutes after the last Tour vehicle has passed. A column of motorcycle outriders from the gendarmerie provides a guard of honour, simply emptying its holsters when the race crosses onto foreign soil. Internally it has its own judiciary of commissaires and jury of appeal empowered to exact penalties as well as award prizes: £2.50 fine for taking pace behind a car; thirty seconds added to the rider's time for asking spectators to push him uphill. Medical services are provided by a group of doctors supported by two or three motor ambulances and a helicopter ambulance; another medical unit supervises the daily dope tests.

The communications system is just as elaborate. During the stage the private, short-range Radio Tour — fed information by motorcycle marshals travelling alongside the riders — relays the state of the race to the following team and Press cars. And at the finish a Press centre provides telephone and telex links for 200 reporters. The day's results and communiqués alone run to twenty closely-typed sheets.

Not everyone in France shares the general enthusiasm for the Tour. It is resented for its privileged position (an international call from the Press Room will be put through in two minutes, while a businessman waits in his office for two hours), for its disruption of normal traffic and its distraction from work. Recently, too, there has been a rising student protest against the number of police involved in the race and the weight of commercial interests behind it. According to a student broadsheet handed out at Lacanau-Océan in 1976, 'Thanks to the victory of Thévenet last year, the French cycle industry has sold an annual 2.5 million units. Bravo! Sport is neutral and disinterested.' But this sort of criticism simply washes over the Tour. The audience for its unsophisticated circus is larger than ever in the countryside, and there's a lot of countryside in France. Officially, too, it's an article of faith that the Tour is a Good Thing.

The Tour is promoted by two papers who provide the joint organisers. Jacques Goddet, director of the daily sports paper, *L'Equipe,* is the father figure in direct line from one of its founders; educated for a short time in England, he likes to wear khaki shorts and a pith helmet when the Tour is in the south. Félix Lévitan of *Le Parisien Libéré* is a small, dapper man who is astutely in charge of the commercial arrangements. Yet although the Tour is firmly in private hands it is now accepted as a national institution to be protected by the State. After the civil unrest and general strike of 1968, now benignly described as 'the events of May', it looked as though the Tour would have to be cancelled. It was the government who insisted that it should go ahead as a signal to the world that France was back to normal.

Over the years it has been gradually pushed off the national highways and onto minor roads as a concession to French business life, but government support is as enthusiastic as ever. In 1975 the Tour was allowed to turn the Champs-Elysées into a racing circuit for its final stage, and the President of the Republic presented the prizes. The following year the President of the Senate was on the rostrum. And if these were political gestures, there is little doubt that national sentiment approved them. In France cycle racing, not soccer or rugby, is the people's sport, and after more than seventy years, the Tour has become its most popular expression.

Whether or not they order things better in the Tour de France, they certainly order them wholesale. From the length of the cavalcade to height of the mountain passes, everything is bigger. In essence cycle racing may be much the same in the Pyrenees and the Pennines — Van Impe's win at Pla-d'Adet in 1976, a version of Bradley's win at Morecambe. But on a bigger stage and in a grander setting. And it is the size of the Tour de France, the size of the demands it makes on its riders, and the size of its rewards in money and celebrity, that make the difference. In these it is a world apart.

I thought the best way to describe the Tour was to tell, in alternate chapters, the story of a particular Tour, that of 1976. It was not one of those races dominated by a single rider: it had a series of leaders, one of whom lost control and regained it with an uncharacteristically bold attack; an elaborate web of sub-plots; the biggest stage win since the war; and a good deal more suspense than most. From that story I have moved off into the past to explain how the Tour developed its character, and its characters developed the Tour, how it is run, and how it has dealt with scandal and success.

One minor point. I have generally stuck to kilometres, since they are easy enough to convert if you want to do so, and since certain sections of the course are in precise metric measurements: the final kilometre, the last hundred metres, etc. On the other hand I've converted altitudes into feet, people's height into feet and inches, and their weight into stones and pounds, since that's the way most of us think. I've converted francs at ten to the pound, which gives a better idea of comparative value than the latest exchange rate. To convert back into francs and do your own sum, just add a nought.

– Le Vélo de mon Oncle –

There are many French cycling terms which are not defined at all in the standard French-English dictionary, or are not defined in the sense in which cyclists use them. If you read, for instance, that 'X failed to pick up his *musette* at the *controle de ravitaillement*', it is not particularly helpful to learn that *musette* means: 1. bagpipe, musette; 2. nosebag (for horse); 3. bag, haversack. The third meaning comes closest but still gives the wrong impression (see below). For that matter, what the hell is a revictualling control? What follows is a guide to some of the less self-evident terms.

bidon Plastic drinking bottle which fits into a holder on the frame (usually the down-tube) or the handlebars of the bike. Used for carrying water, cordial, cold tea, liquefied cereals. There is often a small hole in the cap with a plug which can be prised out with the teeth. This enables the rider to sip his drink as he goes along without it slurping all over him.

bonification Time bonus. This takes the form of a deduction of so many seconds from the rider's overall time, so improving his position in the race. Bonuses are most frequently awarded to the first three or four riders to cross the line at the end of any flat stage; for example, the winner will get twenty seconds deducted, the second man fifteen seconds, the third ten seconds, and the fourth five seconds. Bonuses rarely apply at the end of mountain stages, but occasionally they are offered at the top of a particular climb. They were dropped altogether in the 1975 and 1976 Tours.

car balai Broom wagon. Small coach or truck decorated with a besom or witch's broom beside the driver's cab. It follows the last man on the road 'sweeping up' any riders (and their bikes) if they abandon the race.

casquette Peaked cotton racing cap.

classement général General classification. The daily list of riders in the order of their overall position in the race. This is determined by the total time (with any bonuses deducted) which they have taken to cover the stages up to the present. The rider with the shortest time is — to offer a glimpse of the obvious — race leader.

classement par points Points classification. Ranking list based not on overall time but on the placings that riders have achieved at the stage finishes so far. The points system varies from time to time, but to give the general idea, the scale on any flat stage in 1976 was: stage winner, twenty-five points; second, twenty; third, sixteen; and so on down to one point for the fifteenth man. On mountain stages, half-stages and time trials fewer points were given. And for the first time the *Point Chaud* sprint was included on a points scale of three, two and one. The points competition was included as a special incentive to the sprinters in 1953, the Tour's jubilee, as the Grand Prix de Cinquantenaire. Today the rider who collects the largest number of points during the course of the race receives a prize of around £1,200; this is in addition to the money he has picked up from day to day.

commissaire One of a dozen officials whose job is to detect and punish riders' misdemeanours.

contre la montre Against the watch. A time trial in which the riders set off individually at intervals of one minute or two minutes and are timed over a set distance. The same principle applies to the team time trial *(contre la montre par équipes)* except that each team is sent away in a flying column, and its time is judged on that of the third man to cross the finishing line.

controle de ravitaillement Feeding station. A specified stretch of road, maybe a kilometre long, where team officials are allowed to hand up *musettes* of food to their riders. There are two feeding stations on a long stage.

controle médical Euphemism for the centre at which daily urine samples are taken from selected riders. These are analysed to check on the presence of forbidden drugs in the riders' system.

critérium Race over so many laps of a small road circuit generally marked out by barriers in the centre of a town or village. There is no standard length to the race, but since the object is to give spectators as much as possible to see, the circuit is rarely more than five to six kilometres long. A *critérium,* or series of *critériums* for different categories of rider, is often the centrepiece of local fairs and festivals. The same word, without the accent, is used in English.

démarrage An escape or breakaway by a rider or group of riders which gains an advantage on the rest of the field.

directeur sportif Team manager.

domestique The lowest-ranking member in the team. His job is to act as 'servant' to the leader and the other protected riders — filling and fetching *bidons* for them (hence his other title, *porteur d'eau),* giving up his bicycle or a wheel to them if they have mechanical trouble, pacing them back if they fall behind, and so on.

dossard Rider's identification number, which he must wear on either the right or left hip, depending on the position of the photo-finish cameras at the line.

en ligne (of a race or stage) With all the riders setting off together, as opposed to the staggered start of a time trial.

équipe de marque Trade team; that is, with a commercial sponsor.

étape Stage. Distinct section of the race, whether massed-start or time trial, and whether or not it takes the Tour on to a new town (time trials, in particular, often end where they began). When a day's racing is divided into two sections *(demi-étape)* or three *(tiers d'étape)* a victory in any of these counts to the rider's credit as a stage win. So, for that matter, does victory in the time trial prologue although it isn't listed in the programme as a stage.

extra-sportif (of a sponsor) From outside the cycle industry. Some cycle teams have just one *extra-sportif* sponsor, e.g. Frisol (petrol), Jollyceramica (chinaware). In other cases *extra-sportif* sponsors put up most of the money for running the team, while a cycle company provides the equipment, as in the combination of Peugeot (cycles), Esso (petrol) and Michelin (motor tyres) which makes up Thévenet's team.

Grand Prix de la Montagne Introduced as a special prize for the climbers in 1933, this is judged on the basis of points awarded to the first riders to cross particular summits. These climbs come in four categories according to their severity. In the first category are the great cols like the Galibier and the Aubisque where the first to grind to the top gets twenty points and a prize of £70, and even the twelfth gets a single point. In the fourth category are the little côtes, just ripples in a flat landscape with only £30 and three points to the winner. The top scorer at the end of the Tour, the King of the Mountains, receives £900.

lanterne rouge The last man on general classification, to whom someone usually donates a red lantern. Although the joke has worn thin, this booby prize has a certain cash value. Many promoters like to help the poor struggler by including him in their post-Tour races.

maillot jaune Yellow jersey worn by the race leader; the term applied to the leader himself. It was introduced in 1919 so that the crowds could identify their hero more easily. It is worth £120 a day to the wearer on stages 1 to 14, £50 a day thereafter.

maillot vert Green jersey worn by the leader in the points competition; the man himself. It is worth £100 a day to wear.

musette Cotton bag with shoulder strap in which the riders' food and fresh *bidons* are handed up to them at the feeding station. After they have transferred their rations to the back pouch of their racing jerseys the riders jettison their *musettes* at the side of the road where the spectators scramble for them. A *musette* containing a discarded orange or jam sandwich is highly regarded as a souvenir.

neutralisation Same word in English. Period when riders pedal along but may not race, for example, between the ceremonial start in a city centre and the real start on the outskirts. The race may also be neutralised when it is disrupted by a road accident or obstruction, a political demonstration or extremely bad weather.

peloton The main body of riders at any point in the race; what the British usually call 'the bunch'. Occasionally when the field splits into two or three groups of roughly equal size, these are referred to as the first, second and third *peloton* or, when they include important riders, the *peloton maillot jaune,* the *peloton* Thévenet, and so on.

pistard Track rider.

Point Chaud Hot Spot. One of a series of daily sprints held in mid-stage and judged on a line marked across the road. It does not interrupt the flow of the race, and in fact often speeds up the action. Its value is around £40, £20 and £10 to the first three riders. In addition the first five riders win points which count towards an overall prize of £600.

prime Prize to the first man past a given point in the course of a stage. There are mountain *primes* which make up the *Grand Prix de la Montagne, Point Chaud primes,* special *primes* like the prize in memory of Henri Desgrange which is normally judged on the col de Galibier, and *primes* spontaneously offered by the people of towns and villages through which the Tour passes.

routier Road race rider.

routier-sprinter Rider who is regularly in at the sprint at the finish of a road race.

soigneur Official attached to the team primarily as a masseur, but is also concerned with the treatment (or prevention) of minor physical disorders like boils, stomach upsets, chills, sunburn. *voiture balai.* Same as *car balai.*

1

– The Giants are in the Vendée –

Saint-Jean-de-Monts, 23 JUNE

According to a headline in *Presse-Océan,* the local morning paper, Saint Jean is 'a town in the grip of Tour fever'. But except at the entrance to the Palais des Congrès, a cool, marbled building on the seafront where the race has set up its headquarters, the fever appears to be comfortably under control. At the Palais the various painted wagons of the Tour are beginning to jostle and cluster like iron filings at the end of a magnet. Elsewhere the town goes about its summer business: the visitors applying themselves to their suntans, the residents making meals and beds and money out of them.

For tourist purposes the Vendée coastline, which curves south from the rocky promontory of Brittany in a series of long, sandy beaches, is known as the Côte des Lumières. Saint Jean is one of its leading lights. It is built on sand, a ribbon development along the dunes, and is not at all picturesque. For even a hint of quaintness you have to travel further south to the small port of Saint-Gilles-Croix-de-Vie or the older resort of Sables d'Olonne, a French Cromer or Tenby. Saint Jean is little more than a row of holiday apartment blocks facing the indivisible sea and sky.

Inland from the narrow town are the *campings* with names like Laugh at Life, Air and Sun, and Twisted Wood. Not the really primitive sites, the *campings sauvages,* where you dig your own latrine and wash by the stream, but at least with trees for shade and privacy and pine-needles underfoot. Then the *colonies des vacances* from which crocodiles of brown-limbed children on bicycles are led down to the beach by bearded pioneers. And beside the main roads, show houses for construction firms like Cottages de France, builders of the instant dream house.

With its apartments and rustic villas, wooded camp sites and children's holiday centres, Saint Jean is a working model of the French holiday system. It has few international hotels; it was designed for the domestic market. And it suits the French middle class with their passion for outdoor inactivity and, nowadays, the money to indulge it. The beach at Saint Jean is clean, the bathing safe when the sea is calm. As it is today. A cloudless sky. A temperature of 24°C (74°F). Between the swings and slides of the Scoubidou Club and the rows of buoys which mark out the supervised bathing area, the young mothers bask in a spray of Ambre Solaire, occasionally raising their heads to call a Jennyfair or a Patreeck to their sides.

The Tour de France has to start somewhere, but why this year at Saint Jean? The answer lies in a fanciful complex of tall, white villages with multi-coloured shutters which stretches from Saint Jean for nearly ten miles along the coast. It is called collectively Merlin Plage, and was built out of nothing by the Merlins, father and son.

In France a good deal of the sponsorship of sport still takes the form of patronage. English cricket has a John Player league, but not a man called John Player to thank for it. French motor racing has a Circuit Paul Ricard — and every reason to thank Paul Ricard himself for its provision, not just the company and fortune that he built out of Ricard pastis. It's not that corporate sponsorship, originating in the minds and budgets of the promotions department, is unimportant in France. Cycle racing would be lost without it. But alongside it runs a rich vein of private philanthropy (not to mention private interference, paternalism and all the other temptations of wealth). Where the rich Englishman will buy a racehorse, the French industrialist is as likely to buy — at least in the sense of picking up the bills — a rugby club, a *pétanque* tournament or a promising young sportsman. What the Merlins did was buy the start of the Tour de France.

The deal took several years to complete. It was in 1972 that Merlin Plage was first selected for a modest role in the Tour: host to a time trial which occupied just half a day's stage. 1973 was fallow. Then the following year, when the race briefly entered Merlin Plage on its way from Saint-Gilles-Croix-de-Vie to Nantes, the Merlins produced their grand gesture. They offered to make a millionaire of the first rider to sprint past a given point in their territory. True, the million was in *old* francs, but this wasn't a twist like paying in Confederate dollars; even today the older half of the population thinks and talks and conducts its country auctions in old francs. And since, on conversion, the prize still came to 10,000 new francs (£1,000) it made a favourable impression. Particularly, of course, on Patrick Sercu who won it. The relationship developed and in 1975 Merlin Plage was awarded not only a stage finish but also a time trial on the following day which was a complete stage in itself. This meant that the area had the Tour quartered on it for two nights. It was entitled to a production of the *Spectacle,* an open-air entertainment, and a generous forty hours of disruption.

Now, 'in apotheosis' as the official Tour programme describes it without false modesty, Merlin Plage has become the *Ville de Départ* — a privilege shared with only twenty other French centres, most of them large cities or, in the case of Evian and Vittel, at least familiar as brands of mineral water.

Exactly what the Merlins have paid to get their string of villages included in the roll of honour is impossible to discover. But presumably the largest single item is an apartment at Merlin-Plage-Aquitaine, a southern outpost of their empire, which is worth an estimated 100,000 francs (£10,000). This will go to the overall winner of the Tour and is, say the organisers, the most valuable prize ever offered in a cycle race. Precisely what the family business will get in return is equally hard to quantify. But at any rate they can count on four or five days of intense publicity up to the start of the Tour, and from there on three weeks' favourable mentions, a few minutes of television time at the prize-giving in Paris, and a permanent place in the Tour records. All that, and much more: the satisfaction of being on first-name terms with a national institution.

But back to the present. With just over twenty-four hours to go before the Prologue to the Tour, an eight kilometres time trial, no riders have so far turned up to have their machines examined by the commissaires and their physical condition by the doctors. So, accepting Hobson's choice, the spectators gather and stare in through the open doorway of the Press Room. After the organisation itself, the journalists form the second wave of arrivals. We have spent the morning collecting our passes and the plaques for our cars; the 112-page quarto-sized programme containing itineraries, town plans, contour cross-sections of the route and vibrant travelogues ('On the Côte des Lumières, caressed by the ocean, the desert-like dunes . . .'); the twenty-four-page rule book comprising the thirty-six articles of conduct peculiar to the Tour ('Assault on another rider, first infringement, fifty francs fine and one minute penalty'). From the Gan insurance group, which has taken the concession for helping the Press, comes a dark-blue plastic case to hold the programme, a spiral-bound exercise book with squared paper, and a ball-pen like a small microphone which hangs from a thong worn around the neck. From the police a card to ease our passage across the frontiers of Belgium, Switzerland and Spain — a card which, to my knowledge, no border guard has ever asked to see. From SCIC-Fiat an invitation to meet their team at a *buffet campagnard* this evening at the Casino. So, fully equipped, we begin work on our previews and forecasts. And although we are not yet up to our full complement of 200 newspaper, radio and television reporters and photographers, we're no doubt a fine, inspiring sight to see.

As a rough generalisation, cycling reporters on the Continent belong to the denim not the creaseless cotton school of roving correspondent. One-time athletes whose jeans and shorts and tee-shirts ripple with fat but who still engage their typewriters in prolonged bouts of formidable energy. A diffident writer, agonising over the choice of a word or the turn of a sentence, wouldn't live a day in their company. Their output is prodigious. It is nothing for them to turn out 1,500 words of comment on a stage, then add a verbatim interview with a rider and half a dozen *echoes,* those snippets of gossip and coincidence which wedge the sports pages together. To cope with this spate of words their papers employ a system of copy-taking little used in Britain. Where we dictate to a typist wearing earphones and mouthpiece, they declaim into a tape recorder back at base, so economising on phone bills and leaving a message which can be unscrambled at leisure. There are no sounds more evocative of the Tour than an Italian reporter shouting into a telephone at the speed of a horserace commentator, then bursting with fury as he finds that the line has been disconnected.

It doesn't take long to sort out the national groups since they like to sit together at the same tables. Only the French, guarding their secret and exclusive conversations with the riders, prefer to disperse and often handwrite their copy with a concealing arm around it like schoolboys sitting an exam. Individuals emerge more gradually, except for the Spanish journalist, Utrillo, said to be a grandson of the painter. A one-man commotion padding around in sandals, he squawks as he holds out a rubber chicken to the crowd and accosts us with the only words of English he knows: 'A May-ry Chreesmas and a Appy New Yeeer.' Us, I should explain, are the only three British reporters following the Tour. Our *chef* is David Saunders of the *Daily Telegraph* who has useful connections with the Belgians and Dutch. He speaks to them in simple, declarative statements, and as time goes on he lapses into pidgin English with his own kind too. 'Today,' he will tell us, 'I have to make television.' The lean and frequently hungry Phil Liggett of the *Guardian* does nearly all the driving. He is the only one of us to have ridden a bicycle in anger, and was on the point of turning professional when he was offered a job on *Cycling* magazine. I sit in the back seat, and since I am writing only for a Sunday paper, the *Observer,* in principle I am free to spend five or six days of the week making notes for this book.

The Press is not as solidly masculine as it used to be. Quite apart from the occasional pretty, braless girl with sunglasses in her hair who turns up at the Press Room and tends to be attached to a photographer or television man, there are two accredited women journalists. One is from a Dutch magazine, and will be leaving soon after the weekend. The other, booked for the whole Tour, is a serene Spaniard with patient eyes who walks behind her reporter husband carrying a portable typewriter labelled *El Pais.* On the whole we don't make a bad diversion until the action starts.

Which is almost at once. As we set to in the late afternoon, the cast of the twenty-five-day serial begins to assemble outside, 130 riders from eight different countries and thirteen teams filing in from their team cars. For the moment, though, the reporters are more concerned with the absentees. And first, by a street, in order of non-appearance, is Eddy Merckx, the Belgian *grand seigneur* of cycle racing. He has won five of the past seven Tours and so many one-day classic races that it has become pointless to pursue the argument that he is a greater rider than the Italian, Fausto Coppi, the Campionissimo, Champion of Champions, of the immediate post-war years. In any measurable terms, Merckx is the most successful, most versatile and richest cyclist of all times, in strength of character, the noblest Roman of them all.

Still, cycling isn't always a dignified profession, and in the Tour of Italy, which ended ten days ago, Merckx was disabled by a saddle boil (using saddle anatomically, as in saddle of lamb). He had the option of riding on in considerable pain and finishing a race which he had no hope of winning, or else abandoning, having the boil lanced, and giving himself three weeks' recuperation before the French Tour started. To nobody's great surprise he chose to continue. It may have suited Molteni, the Italian sausage makers who sponsor his trade team, that he should prolong his appearance in their country, even when he was riding at a disadvantage. But this was probably not the deciding factor. Merckx can make his own terms. It was just as consistent with his own stubborn nature that he should see the race through to the end. That it would probably cost him the chance of winning the Tour de France for a sixth time — so beating the record which he now held jointly with the Frenchman, Jacques Anquetil — only added to the element of worthy self-sacrifice.

Returning home to Brussels after the race Merckx went through further medical checks and a few days later announced that he was unfit to ride the Tour. This was accepted with a sympathetic understanding that did not extend to Molteni when it immediately withdrew the whole team. Merckx has as his principal lieutenant Josef Bruyère, who in his time has won classics and led the Tour. People were resentful that he wasn't now given his head. But they missed the real point. Merckx is like a feudal chieftain. He is the sole leader, and all the other members of the team are there to support and protect him. They have few complaints, for they live very well on the spoils he wins them. And they accept that when the chief is laid low, nobody goes into battle.

This is not to say that, had he been riding, Merckx would certainly have won. At thirty-one he is still impressively strong, but at an age when he can't be too lavish with his efforts. Last year he came into the Tour after a bout of tonsilitis. Mid-June; his rivals moving out onto the high plateau of their season's form; Merckx still grinding up the slope. The hot, heavy weather was against him. So were the physical contours of the race. After two weeks' gritty resistance Merckx lost to the only man who had both the capacity and the nerve to exploit his lack of stamina, the Frenchman, Bernard Thévenet.

Merckx talked about this set-back and its implications on Belgian television last autumn. He accepted that a rider had to know when to stop, but in his case it wasn't yet. (After all he might have lost the Tour but he was still outright winner of the Prestige Pernod, the pro riders' equivalent of champion jockey.) 'When the wind is favourable, that's not the time to stop sailing. I became a racing cyclist to express myself, therefore I must go to my own limits. The problem of money is secondary. But what I have to avoid, above all, is hitting a decline, the beginning of mediocrity. In a year's time I will go through a complete medical examination and, depending on the result, will continue or retire. I am optimistic, but in any case it will not be a matter of reducing my activities by cutting such and such a race from my programme. If I broke away from my normal schedule I would feel I was deceiving the others and deceiving myself.' For a man so unwilling to compromise, and unprepared to look further than a year ahead, renouncing this Tour can only have been a bitter disappointment.

There are other notable absentees, most of them Belgians and nearly all, to some extent, victims of the Tour of Italy. Patrick Sercu, better known as an indoor sprinter on the winter circuit of six-day races, has ridden only one Tour de France. That was in 1974 when, with a great deal of help from Merckx, he won the points competition. Happily for Merckx, a good turn to a friend coincided with his own tactical interests. Last year Sercu missed the Tour for the bizarre reason that the boss of the Brooklyn chewing gum company, which sponsors his trade team, was kidnapped earlier in the season. By the time the ransom had been paid, Brooklyn had to cut back on its racing budget. This time Sercu is convalescing from an accident at Ozegnia. He ran into a German television cameraman on the far side of the finishing line. He still gets spells of dizziness, and the doctors say he has to stay under observation for two months.

Two more Brooklyn riders crashed in Italy. One was Roger De Vlaeminck, another finishing sprinter and Merckx's personal gadfly in the classics. Their dislike for each other has been stirred up by the gossip writers for some years. When, on the eve of last year's world road race championships, *Les Sports,* the Belgian daily, ran a photograph of Merckx entertaining De Vlaeminck at his breakfast table it was as if the Pope had been caught supping with the devil.

The other casualty was Johan De Muynck, the most interesting discovery of the season, not least because he is already twenty-eight years old. A talented climber in either sense, he is the only man who has contrived, quite by accident, to get Merckx and De Vlaeminck working spontaneously together. It happened in May during the Tour of Romandie when De Muynck, supposedly employed as a *domestique* to De Vlaeminck, used his gift for riding rapidly uphill to stage a servant's revolt. This was too much for Merckx's conservative nature. He made common cause with De Vlaeminck — the cause of authority and discipline — to teach the upstart a lesson.

At least that was the idea. Instead De Muynck managed to hold them both off, won the race and then continued his rebellion in the Tour of Italy, finishing only nineteen seconds behind the winner, Felice Gimondi. More on the De Muynck case later, since it says a lot about the frustrations of professional cycling. Meanwhile, probably suffering less from their injuries than from wounded feelings, both De Vlaeminck and De Muynck have cried off; what remains of the Brooklyn team will be led by a rider of modest means, Ronald De Witte. Gimondi, doyen of Italian racing, has decided not to follow one arduous tour with another. So has his young pretender, Francesco Moser, a handsome downhill racer from the Dolomites who always carries with him, like a whiff of after-shave, a touch of the expensive glamour of winter sports.

Finally we won't be seeing that banana-shaped, Fernandel grin from Barry Hoban (of Wakefield and Ghent), the most adaptable of all the British cyclists who have tried, and generally failed, to make a living in Continental racing. After competing in ten Tours and winning eight stages, he had hoped, at thirty-seven, to ride and win at least once more. But this season he has suffered from a pinched sciatic nerve in the small of the back, and has now declined the place that Gan-Mercier hopefully kept open for him in their team.

All these riders will be missed, but none, of course, as acutely as Merckx. No race in which he is involved can possibly be interpreted except in relation to his current form and immediate ambitions. Even last year's Tour is remembered less as Thévenet's first victory than as Merckx's first defeat. Today at Saint Jean we can't even foretell who will try to control the race, let alone who will win it. But after all those years when we waited for Merckx to make up his own and everyone else's mind, perhaps it is no bad thing. At least this Tour is bound to break with the past.

The favourite, by right of conquest, is Thévenet. Even Merckx, as always doing the correct thing, has acknowledged this in a telegram of good wishes from Brussels. And certainly if he won a second time, no figure is better shaped by background and upbringing to slip into the legend of the Tour.

Road racing is a sweaty occupation. For every minute of heightened excitement and accelerating action in the sprint or the chase it demands perhaps an hour of pure drudgery, back bent under the sun, shoulders hunched against the wind and rain. And although there are ways of avoiding work, by and large those who don't put in the graft aren't there to share the prizes at the finish. The analogy with work on the land is only too obvious, and explains why so many professional cyclists, particularly in France, are recruited from the peasant smallholdings. They are used to the toil and monotony of jobs which have to be completed whatever the weather. In contrast, the shorter hours of work as a cyclist seem just as much a luxury as the restaurant meals, hotel beds and regular pay (instead of pocket money and keep).

Thévenet fits into this pattern perfectly. He was born in 1948 outside a village called Le Guidon ('the handlebar', which is not such a startling coincidence since the name is often applied to French hamlets at a fork in the road) near Saint-Julien-de-Civry in the Charollais district of Burgundy. And you don't get anything much more rural than that. At the time his parents were only one rung from the bottom of the peasant ladder; they were *métayers,* that is, as a form of rent they made over half their annual produce to the landlord. But shortly afterwards they inherited a nearby farm where Bernard was brought up. It had twenty-four acres, twenty dairy cows and four goats, a big advance, but still too small to pay Bernard more than a labourer's wages.

At fifteen he began competing in local races and within two years was doing well enough to attract a patron, a Lyon builder, who bought him a new bicycle and transported him to his races. Meanwhile he worked with his father and took an agricultural course at Charolles, but with no sense of vocation. As soon as he had finished his national service he signed a professional contract with Peugeot-BP for £100 a month.

A year later he came fourth in the Tour de France, and in 1973, after winning the national championship, second in the Tour to Luis Ocana. He was strong and self-willed, but not particularly adroit on a bicycle; he could climb efficiently, but on the descent lost time manoeuvring round the corners. In fact his team manager, Maurice de Muer, said that when he first arrived 'Thévenet rode like a postman'. So last year, although he had every right to a place on the short list of favourites, he was not expected to give Merckx any real trouble. Will and resilience, however, turned out to be more important than natural talent. Thévenet nagged away at Merckx's weakness, and on Bastille Day he at last took the road in the race leader's yellow jersey. With a showman's ride through the Alps that afternoon he won the stage at Serre-Chevalier to increase his lead by over two minutes. The parish priest at Saint Julien asked his congregation to pray that their former choirboy would wear the jersey into Paris, and so he did.

Thévenet's victory was clean and decisive — *lucide,* as the French like to call it — yet the man himself still gives the impression of engaging but baffling innocence. Enjoying his fame and liking to be liked, he turned down scarcely any of the social invitations that jam the letterbox of a Tour winner, and the effect on a man used to early nights and simple living was cautionary. He made nothing at all of the early-season races and so far has only one victory to his name. Still, for the moment, he is perfectly entitled to live on his ample credit.

Luis Ocana, a volatile rider of undoubted class but uncertain temperament, is the only other man in the field to have won the Tour. Also the only other man to have inflicted at least a moral defeat on Merckx, although it was not on the same occasion. That was in 1971 when he destroyed Merckx in the Alps only to crash in the Pyrenees while coming down from the col de Menté in a violent rainstorm. Acknowledging that he had regained the race lead only by accident, Merckx refused to wear the yellow jersey on the following day. Ocana crashed once again the next year, and it was only in 1973, when Merckx decided to give the Tour a miss, that Ocana gained it. Accident prone, and understandably anxious, he has done very little and suffers from what you could practically class as an occupational disease among cyclists: hypochondria.

A group of promising newcomers includes Freddy Maertens, a Belgian, who is currently the fastest sprinter in road racing but climbs as though he were pushing a barrel ahead of him; the young Italian, Gian-Battista Baronchelli, fifth in the Tour of Italy, and the man that Merckx has warned Thévenet to watch; and Hennie Kuiper, an intelligent, educated Dutchman who won the world road race championship in Belgium at the end of last summer. Kuiper is riding for TI-Raleigh, a team supported by British money but, for lack of able and willing candidates, not one British rider. Perhaps it's that we don't have peasants and sons of peasants.

Then the regular runners-up of previous years, the men who can't offer the excuse this year, 'But for Merckx . . .'. By far the most experienced of them is Raymond Poulidor, forty last April and riding in his fourteenth Tour. In the style of Nellie Melba he is making his second, and possibly final, final appearance, having been disappointed with his performance last year. He has three times been second, four times third in the Tour, but oddly has never worn the yellow jersey, an honour which has settled on the shoulders of many lesser riders. All the same he has grown rich on being France's favourite loser — rich, but not fat. His body is as slim, his hair as thick, his smile as shy and his face as unlined as it was fifteen years ago. Even now he can't be counted out.

Finally the Dutchman Joop Zoetemelk and the Belgian Lucien Van Impe who will have the most explaining to do if they fail. Both are far better climbers than men from their low countries have any right to be. Therefore, in principle, they are capable of making the kind of giant strides that trample down opponents. But they remain a little too careful of where they tread.

Zoetemelk's problem is his constant need for reassurance by telephone from home, his unwillingness to take the initiative. Last year the Belgian journalists, who feel as warmly toward the Dutch as the Dutch do toward them, concocted a heavy-handed joke (perhaps it sounded better in Flemish) which ran, *Question:* Why, with all this sun, will Joop end the Tour as pale-skinned as when he set out? *Answer:* Because he has ridden all the way in Merckx's shadow. But to be fair, the very same dig might have been made against their own man, Van Impe. He has been just as circumspect, never using his ability as a climber to do more than win the Mountain Grand Prix, the competition which goes to the man who leads the others across the summits. He has carried this off three times, and it was only last year that larger ambitions began to stir within his cautious mind. They were sparked by his success in the forty-kilometre alpine time trial between Morzine and Châtel when he beat Merckx by fifty-seven seconds and Thévenet by seventy-two. At last it got home to him that had he ridden more aggressively from the start of the race, then he, not Thévenet, might have been the death of Merckx. It was too late then to push the challenge any further (he finished third overall), but he is said to have nursed throughout the winter a new resolve to fight for the top prize.

At the moment I find it hard to take much interest in Van Impe himself or the prospect of him winning the Tour. And at the SCIC-Fiat buffet party in the evening I tactlessly mention this to a Belgian reporter. He looks at me severely. No rider, he says, is ever without interest if you have the patience to search for the true facts about him. In Van Impe's case it just takes a little more time.

Did I know, for instance, why Van Impe had been so assertive at the start of last year's Tour? (I had even forgotten that he had been, but later, when I look at the records, there it is: Van Impe third in the time trial prologue, fourth on the last section of stage I). Well, that was because Mme Van Impe and Mme Tierlinck are very close friends. So when Willy Tierlinck, Van Impe's teammate, won the Belgian national championship, Mme Van Impe, who didn't want to see her husband outshone, demanded that Lucien must win the Tour. Really? So perhaps that meant that Van Impe was overawed by his wife as well as by Merckx.

And did I know that a month before the start of this year's Tour, Van Impe put his watch on one hour? And whatever he did, whether it was going to bed, or eating his meals, or going out training, he did it an hour later than usual? In that way, when he came across the border, the rhythm of his daily life would not be put out by double French summer time. Well now, there was something interesting about a man who took such extreme precautions. Something curious, although not exactly heroic.

2

– A Drama in Three Acts –

The route of the Tour de France is different each year, but always based on the same two principles — tradition and solvency — and the same four landmarks: the Alps, the Pyrenees, the Massif Central and Paris. The Vosges and Jura mountains are optional extras, so are the frequent brief incursions into neighbouring countries, but a Tour which didn't pass through the three great mountain ranges would be unthinkable; and although the race has only once started from Paris since 1951, it invariably ends there. Tradition also requires that the Tour should encircle the whole country. Some outlying regions like Brittany are difficult to include each year, but the race feels an obligation to visit them every so often.

Otherwise the selection of the route — agreed in broad outline at least two years in advance, but only revealed in strip-tease instalments during the preceding autumn — is a nice logistical and financial exercise. In the first place it must conform to the limits laid down by the Geneva-based Union Cycliste Internationale: a maximum of twenty-two stages (plus Prologue) with one day's rest for every ten days in the saddle; a maximum overall length of 4,000 kilometres; a maximum stage length of 260 kilometres. All these are observed in spirit if not precisely to the letter. Naturally, too, each stage must bring the race to a town, or at least to a district, which has 2,000 hotel beds available. What yields optimum happiness all round is if that town also wants the honour and publicity of playing host to the Tour, and is willing to pay for the privilege. It isn't always the case. In order to join up the dots on the map the Tour may need a certain strategically placed city more than that city needs the Tour. But the presence along the route of so many small towns with large ambitions argues a high degree of reciprocal contentment.

The organisers are extremely sensitive to the charge that they are avid to make profits, though this doesn't stop an unworthy suspicion entering the riders' minds when a particular course has clearly been taken for commercial reasons. Félix Lévitan's reply is that money must be found in order that the riders can win it. The Tour's working budget is substantial — between £800,000 and £850,000 a year — 'We try to balance our expenses and receipts, without always managing to do so.'

The Tour is a free public show with a negligible income from paying spectators at the stage finish, so receipts must come from other sources. One of these is the group of companies listed in the programme as the Grand Supporters of the Tour; they come under the heading of Donations and put up cash for the prizes, or of Services and Concessions which means that they provide banking facilities, official cars, heavy transport, clothing, food, drink, or colour television for the Press Room. Another source is the publicity caravan, a procession of trick motorcyclists and cars got up to look like cigarette packets and vacuum cleaners which travels ahead of the race. The dozen or so teams also pay an entrance fee, in return for which they get their basic keep (see chapter 11).

Support for the Tour from the start town and stage towns is a grey area of negotiable and usually confidential deals although occasionally figures appear in print or can be deduced from prize lists. Angers, for instance, was reported as paying £9,300 to get the Prologue and start of the 1967 Tour, which doesn't seem excessive and is on much the same scale as the Merlins' apparent contribution nine years later. There have been bigger spenders. In 1974 the Tour crossed the Channel for the first time — the riders flying over while their equipment came by sea — to hold a 100-mile stage up and down the Plympton by-pass. The initiative for this came not from Plymouth, who were asked to provide accommodation and the basic needs for the stage, but from the vegetable growers and exporters of Brittany. To boost their sales of artichokes to England and promote the newly opened Roscoff-Plymouth ferry, they put up £180,000, financing the start at Brest, two stages in their region and the Channel crossing. Plymouth's share in this costly operation was only £40,000.

This was one obvious case of conflict between the organisers' and the riders' interests. It meant two early starts, one late night and a long unforeseen delay at Exeter airport on the homeward journey. The riders, who simply like to eat, ride, eat, lie on the massage table and then

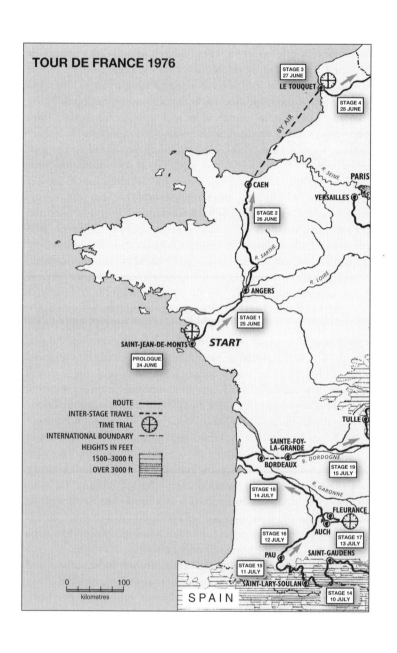

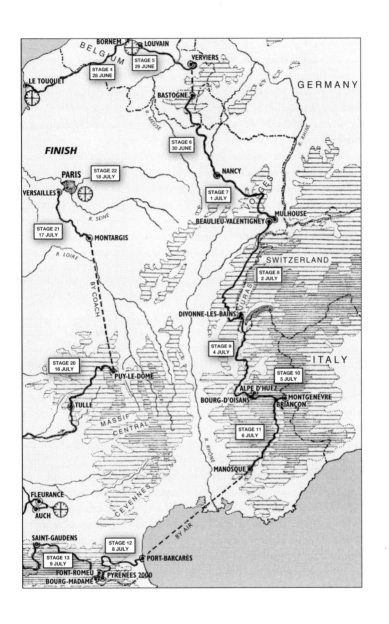

sleep for the duration of the Tour detested the whole business, and it was days before they were able to get back into the reassuring monotony of their routine. If there was to be an English stage, then clearly for the sake of the riders (as well as for the English public) it should have taken place at the narrow end of the Channel. But unfortunately the miners of the Nord weren't in a position to outbid the Brittany market gardeners.

Although the Tour has followed its nose for business along some curious paths, it generally begins with a series of flattish stages. These allow the riders to settle in and, since it's rare for any of the favourites to gain a big lead on the flat, they prolong the period of suspense. Some people find them intolerably dull. Most Frenchmen accept them with the stoicism of a Headingley cricket crowd watching the slow construction of an opening stand. As Lévitan puts it, 'The Tour must be put together like a stage play in three acts with the interest rising in a crescendo.'

Take the 1976 edition, which had most of the basic characteristics of recent Tours. It began on a Thursday with a brief time trial Prologue at Saint-Jean-de-Monts on the west coast and, circling clockwise, took two days to reach Caen. Then came the riders' first forty-five-minute airlift to Le Touquet for a second, more substantial time trial on the Sunday. A loop through Belgium brought the Tour back to Nancy on the Wednesday, and was followed by two transitional stages in the Vosges and Jura foothills — mountain scenery but no real mountaineering — which ended at Divonne-les-Bain on the Swiss frontier. There the Tour rested for twenty-four hours on the second Saturday with the first act completed.

The second act was divided into two scenes. It opened with two days heavy climbing in the Alps, the stages ending at the ski resorts of Alpe d'Huez and Montgenèvre. Uphill finishes have recently become a more regular feature of the Tour, and largely for financial reasons. Winter resorts, eager to encourage bookings for the following season or advertise themselves as centres for walking holidays in summer, are ready to pay for the publicity of a stage finish, and the only way to a ski resort is up. In this instance the demands of commerce ('We want to promote everything that contributes to the richness of our natural heritage') and of sport run more or less parallel since a summit finish effectively divides the flock of valley sheep from the individual mountain goats.

The gradual descent of the third alpine stage brought the Tour to its second airlift — across the south of France from Salon-de-Provence to Perpignan — and to its second rest-day on the coast at Port-Barcarès. This came unusually soon after the first, and was more unsettling than restful since Act II Scene 2, four days climbing in the Pyrenees with another summit finish at Pla-d'Adet, followed immediately.

The second act curtain came down at Pau, 'the belvedere of the Pyrenees', on the third Sunday, leaving exactly a week to kill in Act 3. It was mainly spent wandering through the low-lying province of Aquitaine, but to ensure that there was no steady diminuendo, another long time trial was included and, on the final Friday, a fourth mountain-top finish on the Puy-de-Dôme in the Massif Central. By then it was assumed that the real business of the Tour would have been settled. It just remained to board the train from Clermont-Ferrand to Montargis, make a quick dash by bike to Versailles, and take what was virtually a curtain call on the Champs-Élysées on Sunday.

If the contours of the route set the pattern for any Tour, there are any number of variable factors to upset it. Weather is the most obvious: high wind, prolonged rain, extreme heat all tend to exaggerate the differences between one man's resilience and another's. In the Alps after a late spring the riders may have to climb the passes through banks of snow after climbing in the sun, a bronchial nightmare; there and in the Pyrenees they are often treated to lurid electric storms and pelted by rain, which can be merely uncomfortable or thoroughly dangerous. It was during a cloudburst, remember, that Ocana crashed near Luchon and had to abandon a race which he seemed certain to win. Whether or not assisted by Acts of God, crashes occur almost daily, the most sickening of them in the sprints and in the mountains, the most frequent when the bunch is simply idling — concentration is lost, pedal touches wheel and a dozen men go down. Often they fall heavily since their feet are secured to the pedal by toe-straps (you will see them loosen these straps as a precaution just before any mountain descent); and although, in most cases, they ride on with nothing more serious than grazes and bruises, three or four disregarded incidents like this is bound to weaken and demoralise.

There is always the possibility, too, that they will not ride on. Two professionals died in 1976 as a result of racing injuries. Juan Manuel Santisteban was killed almost instantly in the Tour of Italy. Roger Rivière, a much-admired track and road rider of the 1950s, died at the age of forty having been disabled for seventeen years after a fall on the col du Perjuret in the Pyrenees.

Hostile intervention by spectators is less frequent now than it was in the early days of the Tour, but in 1975 Eddy Merckx was punched by a fifty-five-year-old Frenchman who came out of the crowd on the Puy-de-Dôme; seventeen months later his assailant was fined £60 by a Clermont-Ferrand court, and Merckx awarded the one-franc damages he had asked for. Nowadays riders suffer more at the hands of well-intentioned supporters. In 1966 a fan who knew that riders were grateful to have water poured over them in the heat of the day threw a bucketful over Jacques Anquetil — but at the top of the chilly Grand-Saint-Bernard pass. Anquetil immediately began to have trouble with his breathing, the recurrence of an old problem, and the next day retired from the race.

Then there are the inanimate outside agencies. That familiar old stage prop, the level crossing gate that closes between the pursuers and the pursued, doesn't cause as much disruption as it used to do either. Every year there were photographs of cyclists scrambling across the line as trains bore down on them, and the haphazard clash of the railway timetable with the schedule of the race was accepted as a rub of the green. But now, in the interests of safety and equity, runaways are obliged to stop for as many seconds as their chasers are delayed. For all that, there are still the normal hazards of the road which perversely single out one rider rather than another. Mechanical breakdowns for example, a broken spoke, a jammed gear, an unshipped chain. In 1968, on the opening stage from Cologne, Radio Tour announced with ceremony: 'Number 100, Such. First victim of the Fifty-second Tour de France. Number 100, Such . . . a puncture.' A bit portentous, but not as absurd as it sounded.

In normal circumstances when a rider punctures on the flat he just puts up his right hand, and the official car immediately relays the signal to his team car. The rider freewheels to the edge of the road, and when the team car barges its way through the convoy, the mechanic, ready to jump from the doorless back compartment, will normally change a front wheel in twenty seconds, a rear wheel in half a minute (though I have seen a fuming Merckx wait a full minute as his fumbling mechanic developed stage fright). With a little backing from his team-mates the rider should be able to regain his place in the bunch within a couple of miles. But there are periods in the race when help isn't at hand. Team cars cannot keep up with the riders on a long descent, nor, since there are only two cars to a team, can they support every one of their riders if the race fragments. At these times a puncture can be extremely costly. And so it can be if it happens on the run-in to the finish; half a minute then is lost for good. That is why you often see riders finish on flat tyres, sometimes even the rims, or carrying their bikes (this is allowed, although a competitor may not simply run across the line; he must have his bike with him).

The organisers cannot do anything about this kind of random chance, and they wouldn't wish to if they could. Luck is a necessary element; in what other sport will you find the equivalent of a daily award to the Most Unfortunate Rider? But quite apart from selecting the basic route, there are infinite adjustments that the organisers can make to the balance of advantage within the race. It's obvious, for instance, that if they choose a particularly mountainous route they will favour the better climbers. But to what degree it helps them will depend on whether they put the stage finish at the summit, which will effectively deliver the race into the climbers' hands; or in the valley on the other side, which will suit those climbers who are also fast descenders; or at some distance from the final ascent, which will allow some of the modest climbers to catch up with the race again. To help the sprinters they can introduce time bonuses on the flat stages so that the winner gets, say, twenty seconds deducted from his time, the second man fifteen seconds, and so on. Alternatively, when the route is flatter than usual, they can compensate the climbers by attaching bonuses to one or more of the mountain summits. They can intersperse the stages run as straightforward massed-start races with more and longer time trials. In fact the race is theirs and they can do anything they like with it — provided that they don't outrage the public notion of what is traditional (the search for novelty being part of the Tour tradition anyway). Each winter, usually before the New Year, the route and the new regulations are finally unveiled in their entirety, like a work of art to be criticised in its own right. And until that moment nobody would think of naming a favourite.

The year's route and regulations are critical because, although it isn't immediately obvious, the cyclists in a road race have skills as distinctively different as the leg-break bowler and pace bowler, opening batsman and number five in a cricket team. Which doesn't mean to say that there aren't all-rounders too. In the Tour the three basic categories are climber, sprinter and time-trialist.

The classic breed of climber is a small birdlike figure like the Spaniard, Julio Jiménez. As it happened, he was also balding, grey-faced and never looked particularly well, but on the first steep slope would prance away as though he had springs in his calves. Yet lightness isn't everything, nor is heredity, since tallish nordic riders like the Dutchman Joop Zoetemelk have made themselves successful climbers, and so have many riders from Belgium and Luxembourg. Some of these are even more adept at descending from the summit; they have the deftness and the nerve of alpine skiers.

Roadmen-sprinters, too, are often small men, but with big thighs not slender bird legs. If the climbers are everyone's heroes, the sprinters live more dangerously in the public affection. Nobody is likely to deny their courage as they emerge from the bumping and boring and jersey-pulling of a bunch finish to jump their front wheel first across the line. For them to crash at this point would be like falling in front of a threshing machine running out of control at thirty-five miles an hour. All the same they must be careful how they use their gifts. If they only come to the front in the final sprint there's a rich stock of titles waiting for them in the cycling Thesaurus: opportunist, limpet, wheel-sucker, parasite, jackal, to print only the printable.

Time-trialists are the intellectuals of the company since theirs is the most finely calculated effort of all. Riding alone over a set course they have to solve their own equation of speed and distance, measuring out their energy so that it all goes into the ride but doesn't run out before the finish. It's the one discipline of road racing that really deserves the name, but because the time trial lacks visual drama, it also does little, in itself, for the rider's popularity.

A fourth and vaguer category perhaps should be added, the *rouleur*. He is the man who can ride long stages over almost any country and still be among the leaders at the finish. He is the mixer, the escaper and pursuer, the strong man, adaptable and durable. But his are not so much the attributes of a specialist, but of any rider with serious expectations.

Easily the most important of the four categories in a stage race as long and spiky as the Tour de France is the climber. The best climber doesn't necessarily win. In his early Tours Federico Bahamontes, the Eagle of Toledo, used to make a point of bouncing away on the cols, stopping to chat with spectators and eat an icecream at the summit while he waited for the others to catch up. He didn't press his advantage and although he was five times King of the Mountains he only once finished in the leader's yellow jersey (which now hangs in the cathedral at Toledo). All the same it is the mountains that split the field, and any potential winner must at least be capable of limiting his losses in the climbs.

Time trialing ranks second, for here again the best performers can take minutes rather than seconds out of their rivals. Jacques Anquetil won five Tours on his ability to die against the clock, though even he could not afford to fail in the mountains. Sprinting is the least useful talent — except for earning money — since a man can win a sprint at the head of the bunch without gaining even one second's advantage in the race. In 1976 Freddy Maertens imposed himself on both the sprints and the time trials and altogether won eight stages, but because he was left behind in the Alps he finished only eighth in the Tour, more than sixteen minutes down.

The man most likely to succeed is the all-rounder, the *coureur complet,* as embodied by Eddy Merckx. But no man's armour is impenetrable, and by its nature the route of the 1975 Tour discovered his weaknesses. Admittedly there were other factors in his defeat.

He had recovered his health, but not his form, after an attack of tonsilitis. He also found himself losing weight in the excessive heat of southern France. Finally he had a bad crash (though only after he had effectively lost the race). He might still have got away with it, however, but for the fact that there were four summit finishes — and an opponent, Bernard Thévenet, who was better able to exploit them.

For a man of his sturdy, footballer's build, Merckx is a remarkable climber, rarely out of the first half dozen over the cols. But his main strength in the mountains is his skill as a descender, which he uses to attack and defend, and this wasn't of the slightest use to him when the stage came to an end at the top of a mountain. Thévenet, in contrast, is a clumsy downhill rider, but that summer at least he found the energy and resolution doggedly to pedal up the climbs ahead of a more generously gifted rider. Merckx didn't finish lower than fifth on any of the four summits, but three times Thévenet had got there between half a minute and two minutes before him. On this route and in this company it wasn't enough for Merckx to be the fastest time trialist, a talented sprinter, an implacable *rouleur* — and simply *one* of the best climbers.

Before returning to Saint-Jean-de-Monts and the 1976 Tour, a word (broadly speaking) on the various contests within the race, and the prizes they offer. Each daily stage, half-stage or one-third-stage is treated as an event in itself with its own separate prize list which runs down to thirtieth place. The winner gets £310 (these are the 1976 values converted at ten francs to the pound), the second rider £250, the third £210, down to £5.50 for the thirtieth man. The two short time trials are worth roughly half. Any rider who fails to finish within a time limit calculated on a sliding percentage of the stage winner's time is eliminated. At least in principle; passionate objections and good excuses sometimes win a reprieve.

Overall positions in the race are calculated by adding up the time each rider has taken to cover each stage so far (minus bonuses if they apply). These totals are tabulated on a General Classification list published daily. The first name on the list, the man with the shortest aggregate time, is race leader. He wears a yellow jersey to identify him on the next day's stage, and for as long as he keeps the lead; he also receives £120 a day up to the fourteenth stage, and £50 a day thereafter. The overall winner, the man who covers the total distance in the shortest time, gets £10,000, the runner-up £2,500, the third man £1,550. The thirty-fifth £65.

The next most valuable prize is to be won in the points competition. At every stage points are awarded to the riders who win the top placings at the finish — regardless of whether it was by inches or minutes. On a flat stage, for instance, twenty-five points go to the winner, twenty to the second man, sixteen to the third, and so on down to one point for the fifteenth man. Since the contest is designed to reward sprinters, fewer points are given out on mountain stages and in time trials. A running total is published daily for each rider who has qualified, and the current leader on points wears a green jersey; he also gets £100 a day and the runner-up £50. There are only two overall points prizes at the finish of the Tour: £1,200 and £600.

Almost as richly endowed is the climbers' prize, the Grand Prix de la Montagne. This is also based on points which are attributed to the leading riders at the crossing of certain summits. According to the severity of the climb the summits are placed in one of four categories. First-category climbs, the hardest, are worth twenty points to the first man, sixteen to the second, one point to the twelfth. Fourth-category hills offer only three, two and one point. The mountain leader wears a white jersey with red blobs, the *maillot à pois* (introduced in 1975, it is a bit of an embarrassment and will probably be changed). There is no daily allowance attached to this, however the best climbers are rewarded as they go along with £70 and £50 to the first men over a first-category climb, and smaller prizes on the others. At the finish of the Tour there are three overall prizes of £900, £600 and £300.

Two substantial team competitions are run, one on a time basis which shares out a total of £8,450, and another on points for stage places worth £4,000.

The most important of the prime sprints, contested in passing a particular point along the route, is the Hot Spot valued at £40, £20 and £10 to the first three every day, and £600, £400 and £200 to the first three overall. But on almost every stage you will also find that a town or village has made a collection to put up its own prime.

It will be worth £10 or £20 to the rider who spots the advance warning painted on the surface of the road and slips innocently to the front.

It's an unlucky rider who can't pick up something. There are prizes for riders who have recently turned professional; for those who show the most *combativité* (unhappily rendered as aggression in most English races) or who makes the longest escapes. If all else fails there are daily awards of £27.50 both for elegance and amiability which have gone to some pretty scruffy, disagreeable people.

3

– A Certain Panic –

It is four degrees warmer today, though not so still. A breeze coming in off the Atlantic will blow straight into the riders' faces when they begin the time trial early this afternoon and make things even hotter for them. Mid-morning. Already the eight kilometres route from the village of Merlin Plage II to the seafront at Saint Jean has grown a thick hedge of spectators. They spot the riders who swish past them in pairs and groups, clap them, shout their Christian names. The riders ignore them, both as a matter of form and because they are out on the course to discover its problems and work out the solutions: which side of the road offers more shelter, what line to take at the corners, where, if anywhere, to change gear. At the same time they're stretching their legs which — in the manner of West Indian cricketers bowling in sweaters at the height of an English heatwave — they keep covered in tracksuit trousers. The crowds expect no response and have their own devices to follow. Particularly thick on the sandy ground where the road drives through the dunes and pine trees, they have set up beach umbrellas, laid out table cloths and colonised every patch of shade.

In a time trial the riders set off at intervals of one minute — or two minutes over a longer course — and are timed in at the finish to the nearest tenth or hundredth of a second. It's a very precise business. The start is from a platform which has a white line marked across it and a ramp leading down to the road. In turn each rider is called up and positioned so that the leading edge of his front wheel is exactly over the line. Then, as the time-keeper counts down the seconds, another official, with his legs astride the rear wheel and his hands (or just two fingers) pressing upward beneath the saddle, supports the bicycle. This allows the rider to keep both feet strapped in the pedals ready to move. At *zéro* he slides away from his human bike-rest and launches himself down the ramp.

As he accelerates up the road his service car drops in behind him carrying a spare bike and spare wheels, and his name on a placard across the radiator. But this is the only aid he gets. He must cover the distance without any of the pacing assistance from friend and foe that he takes for granted in the close formation of a normal day's riding. For that reason the time trial is rather too often called 'the race of truth', but as in most other human activities the truth is not wholly indivisible. For instance, according to the regulations, if he overtakes the rider who started ahead of him — his 'minute man' — he must pass him with at least two metres' clearance. Similarly, if he is himself overtaken and passed, he must stay at least twenty-five metres behind the other man. In practice the overtaken rider is rarely willing to admit defeat, and it may take several minutes for the faster man to extricate himself. Which is simply to say that time trials aren't free of incident and accident. Even so, they remain the purest form of competition on the road.

This is one of several insufficient reasons why the Tour puts on a time trial Prologue. Another is that it allows an extra day's racing. Nowadays the Union Cycliste Internationale, the world governing body based in Geneva, restricts the Tour to twenty-two stages. But the Prologue doesn't count as a stage provided that it takes the form of a time trial, is no more than eight kilometres long and — a ruling conveniently forgotten here — is not held before four o'clock on the eve of the race.

The Prologue is also good theatre, a neat device for introducing the cast to the public one by one. 'I would prefer to use the word overture, as at the opera,' writes Antoine Blondin in *L'Équipe*. 'It brings together all the themes and motifs.' But on another page Jacques Goddet demolishes that argument with his usual benign authority: 'Larousse tells us that the Prologue can be a little opera which precedes and prepares the way for the grand opera. A definition perfectly suited to a situation which is created by a battle lasting just over eleven minutes.'

Finally the Prologue has the practical function of establishing a pecking order before the show gets on the road. On the kind of flat, 160–200 kilometre stage which is the normal daily ration in the opening week of the Tour, it is perfectly possible for the first hundred riders to finish together and be credited with precisely the same time. But in a time trial even as brief as today's, the winner can gain ten seconds or more on the runner-up, and a couple of minutes on the slowest rider. So by tomorrow, when the race leaves for Angers, one man will already have set himself up as a target for the rest.

All the chances are that the man will be Freddy Maertens, a prospect that Bernard Thévenet, for one, faces with no great enthusiasm. If Maertens leaves Saint Jean in the yellow jersey, then he will certainly be anxious to wear it into Belgium four days later. And this, as Thévenet reads the situation, will make problems for everyone. It's not as if Merckx were assuming control; then the others would watch and wait for him to falter. Maertens hasn't Merckx's authority, and the race isn't yet ready to accept him as more than a temporary leader. There will be schemes to depose him, and these in turn will bring a hasty reaction from the Flandria team. Instead of an orderly procession to the last thirty kilometres — where the sprinters can sort things out for themselves under the eyes of the favourites — there is likely to be a state of nervous unrest throughout the stage. Frequent attacks and counter-attack, escapes and pursuits across the plains. Not Thévenet's style of racing at all. He feels he can look after himself in the mountains, but that his team isn't strong enough to protect him through a hard campaign on the flat. What he dreads in the opening phase is 'a certain panic among the main teams, frightened of seeing their leaders trapped'. Though, of course, that might be nothing to the panic if Maertens were still struggling to win the yellow jersey from someone else.

For the moment this is all speculation, the Tour's favourite pastime. And before the time trial comes the activity that runs it a close second. The Merlins' *buffet campagnard* is a model for all those to come in the next three weeks. It is held in a sports hall which they have built at the edge of their holiday village and now decorated with flags and banners. Across the width of the basketball court they have set up trestle tables, and on these are arranged, like exhibits in a county show, pyramids of cold chicken, country and Paris hams, pâtés, terrines, sausages and cheeses, cherries, peaches and apricots flanked by barrels of wine. Reporters, members of the organisation, guests of honour from the town, we all stand around waiting for some sign. We move closer to the table and sidle along it as if looking to see who has won the chutney prize. Then someone takes a drumstick in his hand, and within an hour this elaborate delicatessen counter has been laid waste. As a final benefaction, the Merlins hand over the sports hall to the mayor so that the children of Saint Jean can use it throughout the year (as they already use the Merlins' swimming pool) and the philanthropic triumph is complete. We disperse, a little flushed, to watch the Prologue.

Although no rider is on the road for longer than thirteen minutes, the trial and prize-giving last well over two and a half hours, ticking away to their climax with no greater sense of urgency than a metronome. In later trials the riders will set off in reverse order to their position on general classification — red lantern first, race leader last. Today, with the hierarchy still to be settled, the managers work out their own rota from raw recruit to team captain. So it happens that the first man to turn his pedals in the Tour is Luciano Conati, a twenty-six-year-old *domestique* from the Valpolicella vineyards; he is in Baronchelli's service, and would have preferred not to draw attention to himself so early in his first Tour. And to bring up the rear is Thévenet, entitled to wear No. 1 in the race and his 1975 yellow jersey for at least another day.

At the finishing enclosure on the front, an airless, open-topped oven formed by the crowds and the equipment vans, the times of the early riders are meticulously set down in sign-writer's lettering on the blackboard (in fact, for television's sake, a greenboard). But they can all be discarded except for the 11–23.37 of Raleigh's slight, bespectacled Albert Pronk, which remains at the top of the leader board for nearly an hour. When it falls it is to another unexpectedly successful rider, the Spaniard, Jésus Manzanèque, who goes three seconds better. And from now on the results begin to have some significance.

It's interesting that the specialists are failing. A lot was expected from Roy Schuiten, the elegant Dutchman who fell out with Raleigh at the end of last season and is now with the French Lejeune team. He holds the world pursuit title and was winner of last year's Grand Prix des Nations, the only one of the classics to be run as a time trial; but he is fourteen seconds outside Manzanèque's time. The Norwegian, Knut Knudsen, as shaggy and unkempt as Schuiten is debonair, and the Dutchman's closest rival in the world championships, returns the same time. Ferdinand Bracke of Belgium, a grey fox of a man and another past pursuit champion, goes one second worse. You would think that men who are among the world's fastest over five kilometres on the track would give the rest a bit of trouble over eight kilometres of smooth road. But today their talents won't translate with any ease.

Maertens's gifts are more robust and adaptable. Riding in black, yellow and red stripes as the Belgian national champion — but with his jersey made of silk instead of wool to reduce its wind-resistance — he pounds over the course pushing a gear which carries him more than nine metres forward with every turn of the pedal. When his time is announced it is 11–03.29, more than thirteen seconds better than Manzanèque's. Yet he shows no sign of stress (others have been near collapse, their heads slumping over the handlebars, and the sweat pouring so heavily from their faces that it looks as if they're being sick). Maertens simply says that the course was very like the roads he trains on between Nieuport and Ostend. The only difference is that here the wind is blowing over the dunes from the Atlantic, not the North Sea.

Although Maertens refuses to accept that he has won until the last seven riders have finished, it's clear that nobody will match him. Thévenet, whose quality is endurance not speed, does well to limit his losses to twenty seconds; working furiously at a smaller gear, he pushes into third place between Manzanèque and Pronk. But none of the other potential leaders gets into the first six. Zoetemelk is at twenty-two seconds, Poulidor at twenty-seven, Ocana at twenty-eight, Van Impe at thirty-four (although more concerned at the fourteen seconds he has lost on Thévenet) and Kuiper at thirty-seven.

Maertens goes up to take the first yellow jersey of the sixty-third Tour. To be precise, it's not a real yellow jersey, but a yellow tunic, open at the back, which has been designed for quick-change appearances on the platform. But it's the symbol that matters to Maertens who remarks to a reporter: 'It would not displease me to return to Belgium wearing the jersey.' All Thévenet's misgivings appear to be confirmed.

So the first small snippet of racing, which will be multiplied by 500 before Paris is reached, has achieved its purpose. It has provided a hare for the hounds to chase. But in the newspapers there's a brief item which says that the col du Tourmalet, 'the Pyrenean giant' of stage 15, has just been reopened to traffic after the winter. And that comes over like a distant horn from another hunt altogether.

4

– 'The Tour is Finished' –

By the year 1903, when the Tour de France was founded, cycle racing had already taken a grip on Europe, and on France in particular. The first recorded race had been held thirty-five years before on the 31st May 1868, at the parc de Saint Cloud on the outskirts of Paris; it was 1,200 metres long and won by an Englishman, James Moore, who happened to be friendly with the Michaux family, coachbuilders and inventors of the pre-penny-farthing 'boneshaker'. Again Moore won the first inter-city race from Paris to Rouen eighteen months later. He covered the 134 kilometres in ten hours, twenty-five minutes to beat the next of the 325 starters, a Frenchman clattering along on iron rims, by three-quarters of an hour.

Yet oddly enough, although this was the period when the English were inventing, patenting and exporting healthy outdoor pastimes with all the zeal of a Birmingham foundry owner, they got the wrong end of cycling altogether. The inventiveness was there (see chapter 12), so was the enthusiasm; by 1896 there were 700 factories turning out machines for the daring young scorchers of the English middle class. Track meetings, especially when they included record attempts, drew big crowds and the bookies. But road racing was stifled by a legal speed limit of twelve mph, which brought hundreds of prosecutions for 'furious riding'. And after a woman had been killed in a fall when passing cyclists made her horse shy, racing on the public highways was prohibited. To get around the ban time trials were discreetly organised at dawn in lonely places, and they turned into a sport in their own right: the English vice in the eyes of French cyclists.

It was not until after World War II that massed-start racing was reintroduced in Britain with official approval, and faced the same kind of problem that soccer has done more recently in the United States. How to promote a sport with no indigenous tradition?

On the Continent road racing grew without being stunted by any such restrictions. Several of the classics — the Bordeaux–Paris,

61

Paris–Roubaix and Liège–Bastogne–Liège among them — had already been established as annual events before the turn of the century, and a number of magazines had sprung up to cater for the racing fans and Sunday cyclists, among them *Le Vélo, La Vie au Grand Air, Le Monde Sportif, La Revue Sportive.* It was out of the circulation battle between these little revues that the Tour de France emerged. Another of them was a daily paper, *L'Auto,* which did what it could to correct its misleadingly precise title with a line of type beneath the masthead. It read: Motoring, Cycling, Athletics, Yachting, Aero-navigation, Skating, Weight-lifting, Horse Racing, Alpinism. Cycling, as it happened, was the principal interest of its editor, Henri Desgrange, a one-time solicitor's clerk who had been told by his employers to choose between the law and his undignified hobby (a client complained that he had been seen riding in public with bare calves). Desgrange chose cycling, turned professional, and at Neuilly in 1893 set the first world unpaced hour record of 35 km 325 (previous records had been set behind tandems and various multiple bicycles up to fifteen-man quindicuplets). Having made his name he retired into journalism.

Desgrange ran *L'Auto* with a business partner, Victor Goddet (father of the present Tour director, Jacques Goddet) and backing from Count de Dion, a fiery nationalist. The count had previously financed *Le Vélo* until one day it imprudently criticised a political demonstration at Auteuil racecourse; de Dion had been one of the demonstrators. He cut off *Le Vélo* without a sou and set up *L'Auto* as its competitor, adding personal rancour to their natural rivalry. *Le Vélo* owed its large circulation to the fact that it was officially recognised by the cycle race organisers and so had a monopoly of certain information. To make any impression on its sales Desgrange had to come up with a sensational idea.

In fact it was the chief cycling reporter, Géo Lefèbvre, who suggested that *L'Auto* should organise a cycle race round the whole of France. As a publicity venture it was suitably grandiose; it would certainly get the paper talked about. The question was whether any riders would reach the finish. But the more Desgrange developed the idea, breaking down the race into stages with several rest days in between, and making the whole contest practicable, the more enthusiastic he became. Finally he felt confident enough to reveal his vision in florid sentences which helped to set the mandarin style of cycle reporting which has endured to this day. 'From Paris to the blue waves of the Mediterranean,' he wrote in *L'Auto,* 'from Marseille to Bordeaux, passing along the roseate and dreaming roads sleeping under the sun, across the calm of the fields of the Vendée, following the Loire which flows on still and silent, our men are going to race madly, unflaggingly.'

The 1903 Tour passed off with surprising smoothness. Sixty riders — some of them sponsored, notably by Peugeot, the rest classified as *touristes-routiers* or freelances, and nearly all of them wearing *Belle Époque* moustaches — turned up for the start at Villeneuve-Saint-Georges outside Paris where a large crowd waited to see them off. Lefèbvre was otherwise engaged as *commissaire-général,* a job he did by cycling along among the competitors, so the reports in *L'Auto* came from Olivier Margot. Catching the tone of his master he wrote: 'The men waved their hats, the ladies their umbrellas. You felt they would have liked to touch the steel muscles of the most courageous champions since Antiquity. Yes, the most courageous because — a revolution in our splendid sport of cycling — the race will be run without pacemakers except on the final stage. An end to the combines and the *apaches* of every stamp. Only muscles and energy will win glory and fortune. Who will carry off the first prize, entering the pantheon where only supermen may go? I do not hesitate to make Maurice Garin, 'the white bulldog', my favourite.'

The 2,428 kilometres were divided into six stages ending at Lyon, Marseille, Toulouse, Bordeaux, Nantes and Paris, and Garin led from the start. He reached Lyon, after covering nearly 500 kilometres, in eighteen hours, the first of only thirty-six surviving riders. Those who dropped out of one stage, however, were this year allowed to ride the next if they chose, although they lost their overall standing in the race. So it was that a rider called Aucouturier, who abandoned with stomach pains on the opening stage, lined up for the start of the second at Lyon at two in the morning. And at Marseille he won: 'Forgotten, the recalcitrant stomach! From the start his blue and red jersey illuminated the starry night.' Again he was first at Toulouse after 'a leaden sun had forced the riders beyond human limits'. But that was the last that was heard of him. Garin won the last two stages, and the Tour itself from Louis Pothier, a butcher's boy, by 2 hr 49 min. His prize was 6,125 gold francs.

If the first Tour was a qualified success, the second was an unqualified disaster. The same starting point, same route, same stage towns were used, and the same basic rules applied except that riders who quit the race could no longer rejoin it. What had changed, however, was people's attitude to the race. It was no longer a novelty; it was the second part of a serial story, and they had become deeply involved in the plot. Some of them, too, remembering from the previous year how unprotected the race had been as it travelled by night along lonely country roads, realised how easily they could influence it in favour of one rider rather than another. Life was pretty rough in rural France, and sportsmen didn't travel with the Thoughts of Baron de Coubertin in their pockets.

The first sign of trouble came on the second stage when, after Saint-Symphorien, an open sports car drew up alongside Garin and Pothier, still the leading contenders, crowding them for five or six kilometres while the passengers, their faces hidden behind goggles, threatened them and insisted that Faure must win the stage. Faure was a native of Saint-Etienne, which came up shortly along the route, and was followed by the col de la République. On the climb Faure took a short lead, and then in the grey light at three in the morning, the other riders saw that there were a hundred or so men armed with sticks and stones waiting near the summit. They let Faure through, shouting encouragement at him. Pothier managed to get through after him. But as the rest came up they were set on. Garin was hit with sticks and a stone struck his cheek; several others were similarly beaten; and an Italian, Gerbi, the main target for Faure's partisans, was brought down and overwhelmed. Gerbi was too badly injured to continue. The crowd dispersed only when Lefèbvre arrived in the official car firing pistol shots into the air. As it happened Faure wasn't even strong enough to take advantage of the diversion. He was caught soon afterwards and slunk to the back of the file without saying a word. The officials waited until the race reached Marseille and then disqualified him.

This was only the start of the crowd participation. On the next stage some fifty cyclists from Alès demonstrated in favour of their man, Payan, who had been dismissed earlier in the race. This time it was the police who drew their revolvers. And in spite of secret starts, altered routes and heavier police protection, the most dramatic sabotage came on the final stage into Paris with felled trees and farm carts blocking the way and nails strewn across the road. And even this was tolerable compared with the scandal that followed Garin's second win. There were rumours of 'irregularities' in the riding in the Tour and the Bordeaux–Paris before it (irregularities like competitors travelling by car when they should have been on their bikes), and hints of collusion between the wayside thugs and some of the riders. After four months' prevarication, with the full facts never publicly revealed, the first four finishers in the Tour were disqualified and forfeited their prizes. Desgrange was in despair. 'The Tour de France is finished,' he wrote in his editorial, 'and the second edition, I truly believe, will be the last. It has been killed by success, by the passions it has released, the injuries and filthy suspicions caused by the ignorant and the wicked.'

Just the opposite, of course. The Tour continued and so did the scandals. In 1913 a bed of nails caused twenty-nine riders to abandon the race. At various times a rider has collapsed after accepting a seemingly poisoned drink from a spectator, the whole Belgian team has withdrawn after pepper was thrown in their faces, and innumerable bikes have been tampered with. It became second nature for riders to lock themselves and their machines into their bedroom at night. And whatever damage this did to the spirit of sportsmanship, it did nothing to discourage public interest in the Tour. People followed it even more avidly wondering what would happen next.

Outside interference to affect the course of the race is scarcely a factor nowadays (though Merckx, after being struck on the Puy-de-Dôme, might argue differently). Riders are rarely out of sight of the police or the race officials for more than a few seconds at a time; and anyway the French have become a more comfortable people, devoted to sport provided someone else is playing, but not so easily tempted to intervene. The only people now who keep up the old traditions are the political demonstrators. They have the necessary organisation, the strength of numbers, the moral righteousness; and the presence of so many reporters and television cameras on the Tour makes for wide publicity. One of their most active years was 1974. There was an unpleasant little scene in Brittany where pigs had been driven onto the route in protest at meat prices. Some had been accidentally killed or injured by Press cars travelling ahead of the race, and their bodies left there to slow the rest of the convoy so that leaflets could be pushed through windows. Later a piglet hanging from a gibbet announced the start of another sombre demonstration. Then, once the Tour approached the Pyrenees, the Basque Nationalists became active. At Saint Lary three bombs set off in the middle of the night accounted for a Press car, a food supply lorry, an outrider's motorcycle, two reserve team cars and two private cars which happened to be close by. Again, one of the Tour's sponsors, *Le Parisien Libéré,* has had a two-year running battle with the union representing the printers; it puts in an appearance from time to time. In almost every case however the demonstrators have had the tact not to interfere with the racing; the Basques, who threatened the Spanish riders, were the exception. Otherwise they have only disturbed the passage of the convoy or the filming of the ceremonies. It is a small price to pay. The Tour goes out to the people, and must expect to take them as it finds them.

Desgrange's reaction to the debacle of 1904 may have been spontaneous, or may have been contrived, a warning to the public not to push him too far. But whatever else he was a showman, and having announced the end of the entertainment he was crouching in the wings waiting for the first cry of 'Encore!' Far from modifying the Tour in 1905 he increased its length by 500 kilometres; he just took the precaution of shortening the stages and multiplying them to cut out the dangerous overnight excursions. In 1906 he added yet another 1,600 kilometres and before World War I the Tour was annually running at over 5,000 kilometres. It was Desgrange who thought up the publicity caravan, experimented with trade teams and national teams, introduced the races within the race and in 1919, his master-stroke, put the race leader in a distinctive yellow jersey (yellow being the colour of the paper on which *L'Auto* was printed), a trick that almost every stage race in the world has copied.

Above all Desgrange turned his riders into champions and his champions into heroes, and by the simple expedient of setting them more and more inhuman tasks to perform. Road racing on the scale of the Tour de France was not an arena sport to be enjoyed for its skills and its shapely, obvious drama. It was a series of tales brought back from the mountains and related by the riders themselves, the newsmen and just a handful of impartial eyewitnesses. The tales were of disaster and deprivation, treachery and honest courage, extremes of heat and cold, and the triumph over man and nature. These were Giants of the Road, and their exploits required the truth of legends not of newsreels. The Tour de France had to have an epic quality.

If the early riders had been at war with some sections of the population, they now found themselves increasingly at odds with the Tour itself. It was a typical ploy by Desgrange to include the Pyrenees in the route for the first time in 1910 on the 'colossal stage' of nearly 330 kilometres from Luchon to Bayonne. The Pyrenees were then a wilderness populated only by shepherds and their flocks, and it was sincerely believed by some that the riders, on top of their other problems, were in danger of being attacked by bears. The cols were lower than in the Alps, but the ways up to them were little better than mule tracks. However the organisers had reconnoitred them and pronounced them passable. At the first crossing of the 5,610-foot Aubisque, Desgrange and the waiting officials began to fear that the long-overdue riders had either abandoned the struggle or fallen into a ravine. At last one dusty, exhausted figure came into sight, but neither could nor would speak. Then fifteen minutes later came Octave Lapize, one of the favourites, who was to go on and win the Tour. He was walking beside his bicycle; to ride was out of the question. He too was pressed for news of the others, but as he drew level he just spat out one word: 'Murderers!' Another man might have felt reproached. Not Desgrange. He revelled in the compliment, and from there on made the climb a regular feature of the Tour.

After the laxity of the early years, Desgrange tightened up the regulations, making, it seemed, impossible demands on riders who already had to cope with deficient machines and roads which tested their breaking strains to the limit. Eugène Christophe, the handsome, popular Cri-Cri, was the most celebrated victim of official rigidity. In 1913, while race leader, he broke the stem of his front fork descending from the

Tourmalet. No service was provided at that time, and there was nothing to do but pick up the bike, jog seven miles to the next village and find a blacksmith's shop (it bears the plaque to this day).

There Christophe began laboriously to shape a piece of metal which he could weld onto the broken stem. This he managed by himself but now, with both hands occupied, he let a small boy work the bellows on the forge. He completed the job and, true to the spirit of the Tour, remounted and rode on. He had lost two hours, and with it the overall lead, but he wasn't giving up that easily. One for the Golden Book of the Tour all right, but what really endeared Christophe to the public was the inflexible rectitude of the officials who had watched the whole incident. Under the rules no rider was permitted to accept any outside aid. For employing the boy on the bellows our hero was penalised an extra three minutes.

To describe 'the glory and the servitude' of the Tour, the writers have inherited the elevated style of Desgrange. Its most distinguished exponent today is Jacques Goddet, a patrician figure who can still be seen from time to time in the Press Room (normally *L'Équipe* has its own office) battering out his editorials. If the mountains bring out the best in him, he is not short of fine words to depict a fairly routine stage under the grey skies of the north: 'A battlefield in the old tradition, designed for trench warfare, the road narrow, often enclosed like a ditch between high banks, strewn with cobbled stretches of evil intent, cut across by endless changes of direction, encouraging attack. A hard, hard day this 30th of June (to the urns, citizens . . .).'

What more can Goddet, and his co-director Félix Lévitan, do for the Tour in the way of aggrandisement? Lévitan would like to see it lengthened; Goddet has spoken longingly of a Tour de France which would become a Tour of Europe (the organisers in fact own that title). 'It appears difficult,' says Lévitan mildly, 'to include the United States in the construction of the Tour.' But with the help of a military airlift, an American start for the race would not be impossible. It is certainly the kind of idea that would have appealed to Desgrange.

5

– Freddy-la-Dynamite! –

Angers, 25 June

Shortly before noon the people of Saint Jean are drawn to the north end of the promenade where the teams are gathering in the curve of the Arc-en-Ciel, a raised apartment block with flying balconies like a great white chest of drawers. As they arrive the riders sign their names at the open window of a La Bohême caravan, then drift over to the canopied table set out by the TUC biscuit company. TUC will provide *all* the food — not just the biscuits — which they eat between their hotel meals. Similarly Contrexeville will supply their non-gassy mineral water during the stage, and Perrier their sparkling mineral water at the stage finish. As it happens most of the riders at the moment are taking their water in the form of cordial or cold tea, topping up their *bidons* (furnished by Specialités T.A., but decorated by Contrexeville) with squeezed lemon juice and lumps of sugar. Last year tea was dispensed by two ladies dressed in saris to remind onlookers where it came from; that concession seems to have lapsed, but the publicity battle rages on. Nobody on the Tour ever asks for bread and is given a stone. On the other hand he must expect the bread to have the maker's name boldly printed on the wrapper.

Having collected their rations, the riders take them across in the TUC plastic carriers to the benches in the deep shadow beneath the Arc-en-Ciel. There they transfer the food to the pouch pockets of their racing jerseys or, as often as not, to their mouths. Before any race cyclists eat like rescued castaways.

It's a good chance to look at the phenomenal Freddy Maertens, already seated and holding court since his fetching and carrying have been done for him. He rummages in his carrier, pulls out a piece of jam tart, looks at it with more curiosity than it seems to deserve, gobbles it up and goes on talking with his mouth full to everyone around. You couldn't call him relaxed, exactly; he has too much wiry energy for that. But he looks untroubled, cheerful, one of the boys, and would not stand out from the rest of them except for his yellow jersey. He is under medium height, not stocky but with strong arms and shoulders. Below the fair hair his most noticeable features are blue eyes, set a little close together, and a pointed chin. But really there is nothing that the cartoonists can make much of, and they have yet to produce an instant likeness of him. It is only when he is riding a bike in a test of pure speed — a time trial or a finishing sprint — that Maertens becomes at all remarkable. Then he becomes remarkable indeed.

Born at Lombardsijde, a small town three kilometres outside Nieuport on the Belgian coast, Maertens is the first of four sons of a cycle dealer and the most persuasive advertisement for his business. As a boy Freddy did all the traditional things that make up the professional's potted biography: delivered papers on his bike, began racing locally at thirteen, and became a fan of Jean-Pierre Monseré, a rider from the area who won the world road race championships at Leicester in 1970. A year later Monseré was killed in a race when he collided with a car; Maertens is now married to Monseré's niece, Carine.

A responsible boy, said to be careful with his money, Maertens stayed on at school to study economics until he was eighteen. But he could not deny a talent which, six years later, has proved as singular as Merckx's, if more specialised. Last season he won three of the one-day classics. This spring, in three successive salvoes, he has done even greater damage. It's worth naming names and giving dates since they convey, if nothing else, the great distances he has had to travel on and between his races, and his unusual powers of recuperation from one race, and often one day, to the next.

In mid-March he won the prologue and five of the nine stages and half-stages in the Paris–Nice. Between 27 March and 6 April he won the 230 kilometres Amstel Gold in the Netherlands, the opening stage of the Tour of Belgium and the 262 kilometres Ghent–Wevelgem. In his third burst of fire during the first nine days of May he picked off the 228 kilometres Henninger Turm at Frankfort, the

254 kilometres Championship of Zurich and the Dunkirk Four-Day stage race. All of which left the Belgian fans curiously unimpressed. In an impartial moment they would have to admit that Maertens conducts himself well, even if they didn't go as far as his team-manager, Guillaume Driessens, who says: 'Freddy has only one fault, only one. He is too polite. He has a heart of gold.' They must accept him, too, as a conscientious professional. He trains harder than most, and this winter, for instance, he has been working at his French — Flemish is his first language — in order to give a better account of himself to the reporters. Yet for all his great deeds and good intentions, the response to Maertens at home has been decidedly chilly.

He suffers under two disabilities. The first is that he is a sprinter, and while sprinters win classic races and a good deal of money, it is climbers who win big tours and public affection. Sprinters are always under the suspicion that they snatch the prize after others have done the work, and there's something in that. Maertens's other disadvantage is simply that he isn't Eddy Merckx. 'It's true that I'm not very popular because of Merckx,' he said with surprising candour earlier this year. 'Those who like him, and they're numerous, can't like anybody else. It's normal — he's a great champion. But what a pity that there's six years' difference between us. Still, I'm not too bothered. I'm used to it now.'

In fact Maertens's behaviour completely contradicts this. Increasingly he acts as though he is trying to force some acknowledgement from his grudging countrymen. In the Amstel Gold, for instance, instead of keeping his effort for the final sprint he deliberately did things the hard way, striking out thirty kilometres from home and winning alone by nearly four and a half minutes. Last weekend he took the Belgian national championship in the same manner, attacking with thirty-five kilometres to go and crossing the line thirty-nine seconds clear. According to Driessens this approach has begun to convince the Belgians that 'Freddy is neither a wheel-sucker nor a profiteer, but a generous rider in the style of Rik Van Looy'.

This is a big, but also slightly ambiguous, claim. Van Looy, known as The Emperor, was twice world champion in the early sixties and the only man to win all the road race classics of his day. But his generosity was to his own riders, the members of his Red Guard who worked to get him into position for the final sprint. He rewarded them lavishly, not only with money but with any racing victories that he could set up for them and didn't need for himself. He was not so celebrated, particularly outside Belgium, for generosity of effort. Like all the great sprinters he was criticised for relying too heavily on his ability to win a 200 kilometres race in the final 200 metres. These undercurrents of resentment towards the successful sprinter are only too well known to Maertens, and his reaction to them only too predictable to the rest of the riders in the Tour. Maertens has said repeatedly that his immediate ambition is limited to winning stages and the points leader's green jersey. But since, as a consequence, he has brought the yellow jersey down upon his shoulders, he is sure to try and prove that he is not just a jumped up sprinter. He can wear the yellow jersey with the best, and for many days to come.

Still, for the moment he doesn't seem to be looking for any trouble, and the 173 kilometres of the opening stage are fairly uneventful. They begin with a minute's silence for Juan Manuel Santisteban, the Spanish rider who was killed in the opening stage of the Tour of Italy. Racing accidents are a daily, even hourly, occurrence; fatal ones in major races are extremely rare since the roads are closed to all other traffic. What happened to Santisteban might happen to any other cyclist in a hurry. After dropping behind with mechanical trouble, he was racing to catch up with the field when he lost control as he tried to get by some roadworks. He ran into a guardrail at the edge of the road, his skull was fractured, and he died before reaching the hospital.

Santisteban had been competing in the major road races for five years, so he was well known to nearly all the riders on the start-line, not just his team-mates in the Kas group. But a month has passed since his death and it isn't grief or shock which explains the *peloton's* slow progress early in the stage. It is what Jacques Goddet fulsomely describes as 'the heat which beats down on our countryside, which dries it up, which sterilises the surface of the earth as well as human energies'. The *domestiques* keep dropping back into the convoy to fetch fresh *bidons* from their team cars — as they can comfortably do when the speed is reduced to thirty-six kph — and there's no panic until, at seventy-four

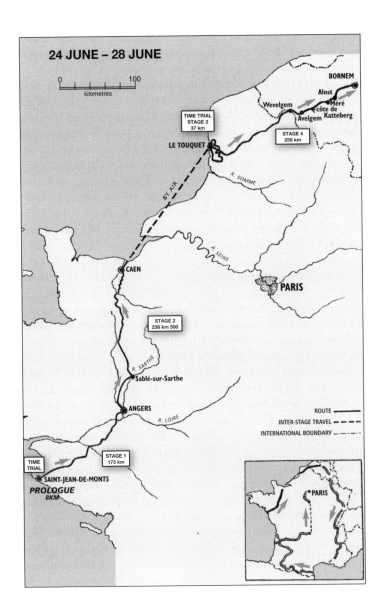

24 JUNE – 28 JUNE

0   100
kilometres

TIME TRIAL
STAGE 3
37 km

LE TOUQUET

BY AIR

R. SOMME

R. SEINE

CAEN

PARIS

BORNEM

Alost
Wevelgem   Meré
côte de
Avelgem   Katteberg

STAGE 4
258 km

STAGE 2
236 km 500

R. SARTHE

Sablé-sur-Sarthe

ANGERS

R. LOIRE

TIME
TRIAL

STAGE 1
173 km

SAINT-JEAN-DE-MONTS

PROLOGUE
8KM

ROUTE
INTER-STAGE TRAVEL
INTERNATIONAL BOUNDARY

PARIS

kilometres, a minor figure, Joel Hauvieux, attacks. At once the pace picks up at the front, and at the rear several of the water-carriers find themselves stranded among the accelerating cars.

The Tour is still at the point when the margins of difference between the riders can be counted in seconds, and almost anyone with cheek and persistence could conceivably take the lead. Hauvieux, who will be passing close to his home tomorrow, sees the splendid prospect of doing so in the yellow jersey. And knowing that Maertens will have nobody but his own Flandria team to help him in the chase, he pushes his luck to the limit. With his energies far from sterilised, he reaches a lead of seventy-one seconds, and since he was only seventy seconds slower than Maertens in the Prologue, this makes him the new race leader 'on the road'. It's an honour he enjoys for only fifteen minutes. Flandria gather at the front of the *peloton* as loco-motives to the train, and it begins to gain inexorably on the Frenchman.

Then just before Hauvieux is caught, the pursuit gets out of hand. Twelve men split away from the front, potentially a far greater danger than Hauvieux on his own, and this time it isn't left to Flandria to retrieve them. It is Poulidor who brings up the bunch to close the gap. In the absence of a captain with Merckx's general command over ally and foe, Poulidor is dutifully playing the role of the senior profession-al, keeping the unrulier members in check.

In Maertens's position, Merckx might have put one of his own lieutenants into the attack, partly to give the opposition someone else to think about, and perhaps to relieve him of the yellow jersey for a few days. But it's a risky business and Maertens hasn't enough confi-dence in his team or in himself to try it. He continues to play the stage defensively, using his riders to limit a short foray by the Italian, Arnaldo Caverzasi, and a more threatening escape, only twelve kilometres from home, by Poulidor's man, Jean-Pierre Genet. What Maertens asks of Flandria is simply to act as sheepdogs, keeping the flock together so that he can play the slaughterer at the finish.

Flandria do their job well. As the race wiggles through the back streets of Angers, its passage mapped out by bales of hay at all the cor-ners,there are only ten men missing from the compact field, and these are all stragglers behind the race. The remaining 120 sweep across the finishing line beside the River Maine, then on for a final four-kilometre circuit near the city centre before reappearing. Maertens remains in total control, and at the second approach to the line he leads the cavalry charge contentedly looking back over his shoulder.

Second is Regis Delépine, who managed to bring his front wheel level with Maertens's saddle, but got no further. He screws up his face to wring back the tears; Angers is his own city, and he desperately wanted to win here. Third, Ercole Gualazzini is noisily furious at what he claims to be Maertens's rough riding in the splendid prospect of doing so in the yellow jersey. And the sprint. Tears and recriminations: everything, as the French would say, is normal. Even for Maertens it has been a modified triumph; apart from the £130 in cash, he has gained little more than a moral victory. Since 120 riders are credited with the same time, his hold on the yellow jersey is no more secure than before. But at least he can wear it another day and, after two successive wins, with a little extra jauntiness.

That evening we go round to the Hotel de la Gare where Peter Post and the Raleigh riders are staying. We find them outside on a grass-covered traffic island opposite the station. Kuiper is being interviewed by two Belgian reporters, so we sit down beside Post and his assistant, Peter Bonhuis. An elderly tramp perches nearby, cocking his head in bird-like curiosity first at the Flemish speakers, then at the group speaking English.

Post is well known in England; he rode, and generally won, the London six-day races when they restarted in 1967, and is now their race director. A long, slim, elegant man in pink-and-white striped shirt, white trousers, sandals, with a silver scarab hanging from a thong round his neck and small, blue scars, like a miner's on his forehead, he sprawls comfortably on the grass, breaking off the conversation to shout messages in Dutch up to the hotel windows. He is happy with the way things have gone so far. Today he had three men — Karstens and the two Van Katwijk brothers — in the first eight, and so took the team points prize. Pronk is still fourth overall and leader of the TUC biscuit competition for young riders. All good for Raleigh cycles, and Post is a man who knows exactly where his sponsorship comes from. More important, Kuiper is going well, and with Pronk to support him in the mountains, could finish in the first ten, a fair return for the company's £15,000 investment in the Tour.

We turn, naturally, to Maertens. Post thinks he will win six or seven stages in the next three weeks. Could he also win the Tour? 'No, not possible. But he is a very good rider for publicity.' Coming from Post this is no back-handed compliment.

Caen, 26 June

No change in the weather, little in the racing. It weighs heavily on the riders' minds that this evening they will have to fly on to Le Touquet for tomorrow's thirty-seven kilometre time trial, a terrible stage if you're not just in it for the ride, one that's bound to reshuffle the picture cards. So this is no day to waste on reckless attack and hot pursuit.

Setting out from Angers before nine in the morning to cover 237 kilometres through the heat of the day, the riders adopt an even slower pace than the day before, only just over thirty-five kph. First Ocana, who quickly gets bored, then Tierlinck, Van Impe's junior partner, prod the *peloton* to see if it's really asleep. At once it growls and snaps to discourage any more teasing, and settles back into its slumber until it reaches Sablé-sur-Sarthe. There, with forty-nine kilometres covered, Maertens gets up out of his saddle to win the Hot Spot prime, just as he did yesterday, and hoard another three points towards his green jersey (it's the first time the Hot Spot has counted in the points competition). At the moment he's behaving like a shopper saving trading stamps. So far, except for the little molehill mountain primes which rise up from time to time in the riders' path, he has snapped up every prize on offer, which isn't thought becoming in a race leader.

Afterwards there is a brief attack by half a dozen riders, the most ardent of them Alain Meslet, who wants to get far enough ahead to stop and greet his family; they are waiting at his home town, Evron. But once these diversions are over, there follows almost three hours when the pedals turn in unison, carrying the race on from Anjou into the gentle corrugations of Normandy. Just to hear its own voice, Radio Tour gives out the kind of announcements you would normally find on a company notice board: 'Would team-managers please ensure that their riders return their empty *bidons* for cleaning and re-use instead of discarding them at the roadside.' It lists the distinguished visitors, managing directors of the sponsoring firms, politicians, government officials, who are following today's stage in the convoy. It announces the daily awards to deserving riders. For Amiability, the local rider, Meslet, gets £27.50 from the National Bank of Paris. For Elegance, an expanding watchstrap from Fixo-Flex goes to Baronchelli. Meanwhile the riders plod on in close formation and are grateful to the man in vest and dungarees who stands outside a garage and plays a waterhose on them as they pass. When next the radio has anything important to say, it is at 185 kilometres where Bernard Thévenet touches wheels and falls — the kind of accident most likely to happen when the field is travelling slowly — and brings half a dozen riders down with him.

Although he hurts his right shoulder as he hits the ground, Thévenet remounts and regains the bunch for the last forty kilometres, when even the dullest stage begins to look lively. Again Flandria appear to have all of Maertens's enemies under surveillance until, four kilometres from the finish, they take their eyes off Giovanni Battaglin. The twenty-four-year-old Italian starlet slips away to win at Caen by ten seconds. Jan Raas of Raleigh goes after him, shadowed by Battaglin's teammate, Pierino Gavazzi who, quite properly, doesn't help the chase but helps himself to second place by beating Raas at the line. And all that is left for Maertens to do is lead in the bunch to take fourth place. He isn't put out about it, nor should he be. The loss of ten seconds to Battaglin is trifling; Maertens could have spared him almost a minute. He has increased his lead in the green jersey competition to twenty-two points. And nobody has even challenged him for the yellow jersey which, after tomorrow's time trial, should fit even more comfortably on his shoulders.

Altogether the stage has been pretty unadventurous. Even so it has taken something out of the riders simply to pedal at their own pace for nearly 150 miles in heat like this. No need for a thermometer, you can read the temperature from the Decisions of the Commissaires listed in the official bulletins. Three men are fined twenty francs for carrying glass 'recipients' in the *peloton;* these must be bottles of water handed up by spectators. Another twelve are fined fifty francs each for using *bidons* not issued by the organisation: in other words, falling back on their normal team *bidons* when they had used up the special supply from Contrexeville.

The heat wave, which shows no sign of letting up, is becoming a serious worry. Poulidor, an old sweat in these *legionnaire* matters, is careful to ration himself to two litres of water on a stage. Others are less prudent. Although it is part of the collective wisdom of the *peloton* that too much water leads to depression and fatigue, a sort of teetotal boozer's gloom, some of the less experienced riders are drinking much too heavily. Older race followers recall the summer of 1951 when, suffering from the Languedoc sun, Fausto Coppi lost thirty-three minutes on the stage to Montpellier. More recently, and nearer home, there was the dog-day Tour of 1957 when the burning roads of Normandy did the damage which eventually forced sixty-four of the 120 to retire. So far none of this year's 130 starters has dropped out, but if the heat continues it could have a delayed effect and bring mass defections in the mountains.

Le Touquet, 27 June

It was the British who invented Le Touquet as a seaside resort, built the first summer homes behind its beaches in the 1880s and formed the Le Touquet Syndicate to develop the town. Not that you'd guess this today. Paris-Plage, where the time trial starts and ends, is a typically French high-production tannery with its changing cubicles, family plots marked out by canvas screens, and huge concrete car-parks on the esplanade above. The villa area, through which the riders will wind their way towards Stella-Plage and Merlimont-Plage and back, has admittedly a more relaxed, colonial air; but on the lawns and terraces nowadays you are more likely to hear German than English spoken.

In the morning Freddy Maertens, and his closest friend in the Flandria team, Michel Pollentier, ride round the course twice behind their service car, and Maertens finds it good. With its twenty or so corners and its short, abrupt changes of gradient, it is agreeably hard. And since it suits a strong rider with dexterity, it suits Maertens's purpose very well.

From the Boulevard de la Mer the course heads south through the dunes, across the golf links and into the first of three distinct suburbs — this one with large, white houses set in well-kept lawns, Weybridge-style, and given boastfully romantic names like Fleur-des-Dunes and La-Belle-en-Bois. Then sharp right and straight towards the sea, turning back in the nick of time at the brink of Stella-Plage, climbing a short, steep hill to the Camping de la Forêt, and entering the second area of smaller, homelier villas which, like boats, are named after the owners' wives and girlfriends: Jacky, Natalie, LuLu, Myriam. Out into the country, another stiff little climb, and back towards Paris-Plage through the third villa district where, hidden in the pine trees, the big summer houses are much too grand to introduce themselves by name.

Setting out before the start, we don't drive right round the circuit but wait for the humbler riders to go through at the approach to Stella-Plage where there are shops and cafés on either side of the road. At Au Lillois four Belgian fans are already boisterously drunk. One of them, in a faded Eddy Merckx racing cap, which looks as though it has kept the sun off at a few world championships, is shouting 'Coucou!' at every passing rider. His big moment comes when Romero goes by: 'Ey, Romero. Coucou! Ey, Romero . . . Romero et Juliette.' They all fall about the tables laughing.

We decide to follow Herman Van Springel, at thirty-three the oldest member of Maertens's team, a man with a long, melancholy face and dismal memories of the time trial that concluded the 1968 Tour. At lunchtime on that final day he was race leader by sixteen seconds, having worn the yellow jersey for three days. Within a few hours he had lost the fifty-five kilometres time trial from Melun to the 'Cipale track at Vincennes, and with it the Tour. The man who overtook him was the Dutchman, Jan Janssen, who had never had his nose in front at any time in the Tour. Nowadays Van Springel has more limited ambitions, but much the same vulnerability in the time trial. We see him caught from behind, snatch a few moments' rest in the slipstream of his opponent's service car, then accept defeat. We drive on to the finishing area.

There the event, spun out like a budget speech for over four hours, suddenly spills all its secrets in the last twelve minutes. Pollentier, Maertens's team-mate, riding fifth from last, goes to the top of the leader board with a time of 48–45. Then the Raleigh rider, Pronk, does 49–34, a pretty good time which will keep him among the first half-dozen overall. And that just leaves, in order of start, Thévenet, Manzanèque and Maertens out on the road. For the three of them it is like a handicap race with Manzanèque gaining on Thévenet while, at the same time, the ineluctable Maertens gains on them both. Glowing like a lantern in his yellow silk jersey, Maertens wipes out the two minutes' difference on Manzanèque, catches him and drops him. Ahead Thévenet, with only half a minute left of his four minutes' lead, is labouring to hold off the Belgian; he is still feeling the effects of yesterday's crash and a sleepless night. From the announcer's commentary it seems that Maertens will catch him too before the line, but Thévenet, fighting with his bike all the way and finding little rhythm, gets across still twenty-eight seconds clear. Now Maertens arrives, perfectly composed as though he has just been on an errand. And twelve seconds later, Manzanèque.

So Maertens has won again, and by a massive 1–37, stretching his overall lead from seventeen seconds to 1–58. And even that is deceiving. Pollentier, the runner-up, is no rival. Next comes Manzanèque and a group of time trial specialists who have done much better over thirty-seven kilometres than in the elongated sprint of the Prologue. They are Schuiten, Pronk and Bracke. Schuiten — who rode the event with a wedge rather like a boxer's gum shield between his teeth to let more oxygen reach his lungs — is probably the most talented of the three, but no serious threat over three weeks' racing. In fact it's not until you get down to seventh place on the general classification that you find a recognised contender, the exemplary Poulidor, at 3–25. The other favourites are strung out at intervals with Kuiper at 3–34, Baronchelli at 3–45, Van Impe at 3–48, Thévenet at 3–52, Zoetemelk at 3–59, and so on down to Ocana at 4–25.

Just as at Saint-Jean-de-Monts — is it genuine insight or complacency? — none of these men views Maertens's performance as anything more than a brilliant sideshow. Thévenet, apart from concern at his own lack of punch, expresses most regret that Van Impe has gained eighteen seconds on him. If there is any other rider whose display has been a revelation to him it is Pollentier, for this man can also climb. Maertens can't, and Thévenet feels that it will be enough to keep an eye on him over the next few days. He does have the grace to admit that this may not be so easy. Tomorrow the Tour enters Belgium and, as he says with that capacity which Continental cyclists have for talking like a book, the change of scene will provide enough motivation 'to imprint an infernal rhythm on the race'. All the same he would rather have Maertens than Van Impe or Zoetemelk leading the dance.

As for Maertens, he has done everything in his power to ensure a triumphant return to Belgium. He has controlled the race, won three stages out of four, and at Le Touquet, surely, he has laid the ghost of a more cautious past. Riding to his limits he covered thirty-seven kilometres at a speed of 47.10 kph — 47 min 8.1 sec of chilling concentration on the treadmill. Maertens won, but more to his satisfaction he won 'with panache'.

Bornem, 28 June

The fourth stage is 258 kilometres long, which even Goddet admits is 'a journey to the edge of boredom'. Apart from carrying the Tour across the Pas-de-Calais from Le Touquet to the Belgian border, the opening 139 kilometres bring nothing but the first retirement. Eulalio Garcia goes into a ditch, and still unnerved, he says, by the memory of Santisteban's death, cannot bring himself to continue. For the rest it's a route march which the Belgians hope to convert into a victory procession. Grouped near the front of the file they cross the frontier near Wevelgem, the finishing point of one of their spring classics, the Ghent–Wevelgem, and immediately plunge into the terrain of another, the Tour of Flanders. We are now in the heartland of Belgian cycle racing.

It's a distinctive region. Just outside the factory walls stand the gingerbread houses, all sliced up in different shapes, decorated on the outside with coloured bricks, fancy tiles and impractical balconies, and on the inside with window-ledged plants and patterned net curtains. But if the first impression is Dutch, second thoughts lead on (or in my own case back) to South Wales. A similar mixture of industrial grime and domestic spit and polish, the same buttoned-down romanticism.

To crank the analogy on a little further, in both these subnations a people who feel themselves, at least to some degree, exploited and out-smarted have come to use sport as a means of demanding recognition of their worth and separate identity. And their success in this has been remarkable. South Wales has used rugby football in this way, and cast an influence on the game out of all proportion to the size of its population. Flanders has chosen to express itself through cycle racing, and with just as great an impact on the sport. Of the eighteen Belgians in the Tour, seventeen are Flemish and only one a Walloon from the French-speaking areas. This is Ferdinand Bracke, the honourable exception, who occu-pies much the same place in Belgian cycling as the occasional North Walian like Dewi Bebb does in Welsh rugby.

As chauvinists the French yield to few, yet you feel that their loyalty — at least in an individual sport like cycle racing — is mainly excited by their heroes' personality. They are not strictly home-town supporters; Poulidor, for instance, is as much loved in Alsace as in his native Limousin. But in Flanders, as in Wales, though personal style is much admired, local patriotism is the dominant passion. The rage for success breeds strong attachments and in turn deep jealousies. More often than not to love the Llanelli rugby team is to loathe Cardiff, to respect Merckx is to despise Maertens. Every man who fights his way to the top is avidly searched for the flaw in his character.

All this becomes pretty obvious over the next section of the stage. Several of the Belgian riders live along the route, which contributes almost as much sourness as sweetness to the spectators' welcome and the riders' response. At Avelgem the whole town has taken an unof-ficial holiday to single out Marc Demeyer, the local boy who won this year's Paris–Roubaix. He goes ahead, with no hindrance from the rest, to accept the applause. Shortly before the côte de Katteberg it is Jean-Pierre Baert who nips off to greet his family who have travelled down from Wetteren to see him. And then at Méré comes the big-gest popular demonstration of all in favour of Van Impe, but in the Flemish manner, the encouragement to him is double-edged.

The most innocent banners carry the message, 'Lucien take your time — you will wear the yellow jersey in Paris', which is perhaps no worse than a tactless remark in the presence of the Belgian who is actually wearing the jersey. Another banner, however, repeated with variations, reads: 'Van Impe, show you are the fastest on the cols, and don't just bring the mountain jersey to Paris.' The tone of reproach is unmistakable. Van Impe may be Méré's favourite son, but he must try harder.

Unluckily for Maertens his own birthplace of Lombardsijde is too far away to produce a counter-demonstration. All the same he is Flemish; this is as close to home as the Tour will go; and he is the race leader by virtue of two prodigious rides and five days' vigilance. So the constant assumption of his people that he is only there as Van Impe's stand-in must be miserably discouraging. There is a sprinkling of placards in his name, some polite applause for his yellow jersey, but considering all he has done for Flemish cycling, he gets an ungenerous reception.

It isn't only for Maertens that the home-coming falls flat. Distracted by the public clamour and torn by their private rivalries, the Belgians lose their grip on the racing. Flandria take charge at Alost to enable Pollentier to win the Hot Spot sprint, but only after allowing the Dutchman, Kuiper, to steal the Katteberg hill prime from under their noses. This was a typical little Flanders climb over heavily cambered *pavé* — brick-sized paving stones roughened with wear and intended for cart wheels not bicycle tyres — and rightfully should have gone to Van Impe. It is Kuiper, too, who makes the running over the last seventeen kilometres, stretching the *peloton* out like elastic until finally it snaps. Flandria send a policeman to keep him under observation, but ironically even then it isn't a Belgian; the job happens to fall to Eric Loder, one of the two Swiss riders in the team.

Ten kilometres from the line the pair have thirty-five seconds lead and, faithful to Maertens's interests, Loder is doing nothing to help Kuiper. He is simply riding tandem at his rear wheel. But this puts Maertens in a dilemma. The expectation is that if Kuiper is doing all the work, Loder will beat him at the finish; the parasite generally kills its victim. So Maertens must not be seen to urge the bunch along in case he thwarts his team-mate.

Coming in to the dusty finishing circuit at Bornem, the great Belgian cross-roads to the north of Brussels, the two men find their lead diminishing but still intact. Here virtue triumphs or, if not virtue, a rugged will to survive. Kuiper, veering from his line in the sprint, almost carries Loder into the crowd barrier and, having discouraged the Swiss from trying to pass, beats him by a length. Behind them, five riders have filtered away from the *peloton* and are led in by the Italian, Gavazzi, at nine seconds. And at fourteen seconds Maertens takes the bunch sprint, the first Belgian, but no better than eighth man on the stage.

It's no real skin off Maertens's nose, but it is a wound to his pride, the final anticlimax to a day which has treated him roughly. He is not very talkative at the finish. In *Les Sports*, the Belgian equivalent of *L'Équipe*, Joël Godaert heavily reproaches the spectators along the route and at the finish: 'He [Maertens] was disappointed at coming only eighth, but above all at having been faced with a public that has still not accepted him . . . Bornem was a blow to his morale, and we expect the people of Verviers and the whole of Wallonia to make amends. Fanaticism, whether it's of language of nationality, is certainly a very bad judge and makes mockery of sport.'

6

– Arrival of the Cannibal –

Eddy Merckx has never gone out of his way to make himself loved. He has simply forced admiration out of everyone, giving his fellow riders and the public no excuse to deny his exceptional qualities. Women, in particular Frenchwomen with their surprisingly decided views on cyclists and cycle racing, find him cold and austere; they complain that, unlike the bashful, gentle Poulidor, who looks as though he needs mothering, Merckx is too much in control of himself. His manners are impeccable, but he lacks grace. Well, maybe. Just over six foot tall, with more the build of a soccer full-back than the usual light-boned frame of a champion cyclist, Merckx is undeniably a good-looking man, but he has the high-cheeked, graven features of a totem pole, and they break into laughter just about as often. So much so that it has become a kind of game with the Press to record instances of him smiling, as though they had caught the late Jack Benny absent-mindedly pressing dollars on a beggar.

All the same how could you fault a man who conducted himself as Merckx did in the final week of the 1975 Tour? He was still wearing the yellow jersey, but for fifteen days Thévenet had been shadowing him, just waiting for the right moment to spring an ambush. Between Nice and the alpine ski resort of Pra-Loup Merckx determined to get his blow in first. It was the ideal route for his purpose with two mountains of over 7,000 feet within sixty kilometres of the finish. Here he could surely dislodge an opponent with no taste or talent for the long, fast drop to the valleys. They were atrocious descents. The one from the col des Champs was rutted with broad gullies to take the water gradually thawing from pockets of ice. From the Col d'Allos the winding road had crumbling edges and prospects of nothing but doom. As it happened Merckx was first to the top of both, and increased his distance on the headlong rush downhill, but it was only after the Allos that he persisted with his attack, and twenty kilometres from

Pra-Loup appeared to have the stage and the race in his complete possession. Then the action slowed like a film winding down as Merckx's power deserted him, leaving behind only a floundering will to survive. Gimondi found him in a pitiful state and, as probably Merckx's only close friend among the leading riders, tried to rally him and lead him; but Merckx hadn't the strength to accept the offer of pace at his rear wheel. And next to arrive was the dogged Thévenet. No Samaritan — why should he be? — Thévenet passed him on the other side, but too embarrassed to look at his distress. When Merckx, who had been leading the Tour by fifty-eight seconds, trailed in fifth at Pra-Loup, he found that Thévenet was now ahead by precisely the same margin.

On the following day Merckx was dropped by Thévenet on the Izoard, which put an end to his ambitions but not to his troubles. Next morning, during the neutralised section at the start of the stage, he and the Dane, Olé Ritter, collided and Merckx hit the ground hard. The doctors advised him to retire, since he was sick and dazed, but he declined. Their urging became even stronger when an X-ray in the evening revealed that he had broken his cheekbone. He had practically no sensation in his jaw, which made it impossible for him to take any solid foods; and when, compounding the injury, he refused to be treated with antibiotics for fear they would weaken him, the doctors said that if he rode on it would be against their advice and entirely at his own risk. Almost any other beaten rider would have accepted this abundant excuse and abandoned the Tour. Merckx not only continued to Paris, subsisting on liquids, but went on contesting the race, in fact he regained some seconds on Thévenet in a mountain time trial and on the last of the summit stage finishes. He had never known as much sympathy in France as when, beaten for the first time in the Tour, he completed the final laps on the Champs-Élysées.

Much was made of Merckx's courage, but what this episode illustrated even more forcefully was his generosity and his professional conscience. By carrying on — and especially by doing so as an active combatant, making light of his injuries — he granted Thévenet a total triumph. Had he retired, that victory would have been questionable, as was his own over Ocana in 1971. Merckx's behaviour in defeat made an even greater impression than his seemingly endless succession of victories. The Italians, for instance, have always regarded Coppi as the *nonpariel* of the sport. Yet in June 1976, a public poll conducted by the *Stadio* newspaper revealed that 21 million Italians were followers of cycle racing, and that of their sample 31.5 per cent (32.8 of the women, 30.2 of the men) now regarded Merckx as the greatest champion of all times. Coppi scored 24.9 per cent and Gimondi 17.8.

The riders tend to share this slightly grudging admiration for Merckx, referring to him as 'the cannibal', since he devours everyone. He is a detached figure, not unsociable but more inclined to mix with the management and play poker with the doctors than to spend much time with the riders outside his team. They, in turn, regard him with more respect than warmth, deeply regretting the accident of birth that made him their contemporary. Not so the members of his own team, which found new sponsors, Fiat, at the end of the 1976 season. Merckx's men are devoutly loyal to him, for though they are not employed to show initiative, devotion to duty is rewarded by high wages, a liberal share of prize money, the occasional gift of a stage win or even a short lease on the yellow jersey, and the advantage of Merckx's influence in gaining contracts to ride in minor races. They rarely make their name, but they do make a pretty steady living.

In fact the most serious accusation made against Merckx is that he has developed the role of team racing to the point where it stifles competition. Not only does every member of his team put Merckx's interests first, but collectively they dictate the rules to everyone else in the race. Merckx didn't invent team racing in the Tour. It was a product of better roads, more reliable bikes, more efficient methods of servicing them, and the use of guile and experience in the refinement of tactics. The early Tours were contested by free agents who rode their own race and treated it virtually as a time trial, pacing themselves and separating as quickly as possible from the others. But gradually conditions made it possible for the riders to move along in a compact group, the *peloton*, which became a kind of mobile base of operations from which sporadic sorties were made and posses set out in pursuit. Even a great individualist like Coppi, celebrated for his long, lone attacks, depended on the support of his team until the moment came for him to break loose. What Merckx has done is to build around him a team of even more gifted riders, and persuaded them that it's in their interest to work for a common cause — himself.

Clearly once a team decides to act in concert instead of as a random collection of individuals one of its main problems is communication — between the managers and the riders and between the riders themselves. The manager has much the same strategic role as in a professional football team, but no bench on the touchline from which he can shout at the players. When things are slack and the *domestiques* are dropping back to the team car for fresh *bidons,* the manager can pass messages up to the front. He is also entitled to drive forward alongside his riders to give them advice and orders — provided that he doesn't abuse the privilege and also give them pace and shelter. But on narrow roads and in the mountains this often becomes impracticable, and he must leave the riders to their own tactical devices.

Frequently, too, a team will appoint a captain, as distinct from the leader, to set the *domestiques* their tasks, watch for any gleam in the eye of the opposition, assess the importance of hostile acts and organise attacks and pursuits. But although there is continuous chatter in the *peloton,* passing the word along its entire length is like playing the children's party game of Rumours. Especially on a winding road riders can attack and escape out of sight before their principal rivals even learn of it.

If communication in the bunch is difficult enough, once the field fragments it becomes impossible. At that point riders must rely on their instincts and a couple of visual aids. One is a strip of surgical tape, stuck to their wrist or the crossbar, on which they have written down the kilometrage of certain landmarks along the route. The other is the blackboard carried by a motorcycle marshal on which is chalked the time-gaps between the different groups along the road. All the same, much of any busy stage is passed in blissful or anxious ignorance.

Nearly all the tactics of cycle racing are based on a simple mechanical principle: that all else being equal, two men who take it in turn to pace each other will travel further and faster than a man riding on his own. Of the two men one will ride in front to give the other a comfortable passage in his slipstream; then the second man will go ahead to return this aid. In the same way, three men relaying each other will go faster than two, and four men faster than three just because the stint at the front will come round less often. And so on up to, say, ten or a dozen men when the law of diminishing returns begins to apply. It will no longer be practicable for the lead to rotate fairly, and by then the group is sure to have picked up some passengers who are just there for the ride. Even so it is the collective pacing within the *peloton* (you can feel the displacement of air when it goes by) that enables it to keep up twenty-five mph or more for hours on end when there are riders with a sense of urgency at the front.

Pacing is the basic service that the rank and file rider provides for his leader. It takes various forms. If the leader punctures and drops behind the *peloton,* one or two of his riders will stay with him; the rest will wait at intervals up the road ready to form a flying column to carry him back. If the leader attacks, then as many of his team as are capable of it will go with him to bear the brunt of the effort. If an opponent attacks, a team rider will give chase in the hope of stringing out the *peloton* and, in effect, pacing it up to recapture him. If he fails he will stick with the opponent, but refuse to relay him; then at least he will have an easy ride and perhaps stay fresh enough to beat him at the finish. Meanwhile, of course, the other members of his team will be trying to pace the leader, or the whole *peloton,* in pursuit. Again, if the leader is contesting the final sprint, the fastest member of his team will lead him out to give him a flying start.

In general pacing is not effective on the climbs, because the riders go so slowly, but Merckx has made good use of his lieutenants, Bruyère and De Schoenmaecker, to guide him up the foothills, and also to catch up with him on the other side and protect him on the trek to the next ascent. Without this kind of help a rider may win a stage, but he cannot hope to impose himself on the racing day after day.

This is not all the team rider does for his leader. He gives up his wheel — or his bike if it's the right size — when his leader punctures and there's no team car right behind to provide service (this kind of exchange, forbidden in the early days of the Tour, is now permitted, but only among members of the same team). He gives up his food and drink if need be (and as a *domestique* does strictly domestic tasks like stopping at a fountain or dropping back to the convoy to replenish his leader's water bottles). But what he principally gives up is any immediate prospect of personal success. I've simplified a little. Often there is more than one protected rider in a team. And a *domestique* who is also a good sprinter will get the occasional crack at a stage finish or a Hot Spot prime — provided that it doesn't cut across his leader's plans. But the more highly developed the team system, the sharper the distinctions within the team, and the more dependent the leader becomes on the support of a helot class. In any team game, of course, sacrifices have to be made and the attackers can expect to get more glory than the defenders. But it's an odd team game in which only those who score the goals get the major prizes.

Some riders accept this as the way of the world. They know that they will get a share of the prizes that their leaders win, and accept that they haven't the ability to lead themselves. But there is a good deal of grumbling in the ranks. One French rider, on the point of packing up the game after two years as a professional, complained that cyclists were being indoctrinated as children. Even for a local one-day race, amateur clubs would appoint a *chef de file* and assign the rest of the team the task of *domestique*. So what chance was there for a young professional to beat the system? He watched the attempt of Johan De Muynck to do so in the summer of 1976 with some envy but with even more scepticism.

De Muynck was a fairly mature Belgian professional of twenty-eight who had spent the last three years as a competent *domestique*. Under contract to Brooklyn he had no fewer than three bosses to satisfy — Roger De Vlaeminck, a highly successful classics rider, Patrick Sercu, the one-time world champion track sprinter who won the points prize in the 1974 Tour de France, and Ronald De Witte, the slightly less distinguished number three — but De Muynck had never quite become reconciled to his subservient position. The chance to reveal himself came by accident during the Tour de Romandie in May. De Vlaeminck and Merckx were deadlocked; neither could move without the other following, and it looked as if the Italian, Battaglin, might slip through and take the lead. So, to create a diversion, De Vlaeminck sent De Muynck ahead on the second stage. He was amused to find that De Muynck not only won the stage but took the leader's jersey. He was less diverted to discover that De Muynck had no intention of giving it up.

Two days later De Muynck won another stage at the top of a six-kilometre climb leaving De Vlaeminck in second place and Merckx in especially bad shape. 'He is not,' said Merckx wrily, 'the type of man you lead to the bottom of a mountain.' Enjoying De Vlaeminck's embarrassment, the other riders wittily referred to the upstart as Johan de Vlaemuynck. But the hierarchy reacted sharply, not just De Vlaeminck but Merckx himself as the elder statesman. The final day had a split stage, and in the morning's race the two of them repeatedly attacked in the hope of wearing out De Muynck before the afternoon's time trial. Instead they exhausted themselves. De Muynck won the trial, and with it the Tour, leaving his ostensible leader nearly three minutes behind. An obscure *domestique* only a week before, he had beaten half a dozen of the best riders of his day, and seemed neither contrite nor surprised.

Shortly afterwards Brooklyn entered the Tour of Italy and 'took advantage of the opportunity' to announce that both De Vlaeminck and De Muynck had signed another year's contract with the team — 'which tends to prove that things aren't too bad between them'. They could certainly have been better. De Muynck felt he had won the right to exploit his own chances, but when he attacked on the fourth stage, De Vlaeminck immediately countered to foil him and took the leader's pink jersey himself. 'He has crossed me once,' said De Muynck, 'but one day he will forget to watch me and I will slip through his fingers.' That day came on stage six when, a little too early in the race for prudence, he took the overall lead by five seconds. He held it for only one stage and was succeeded first by Moser, then Gimondi, from whom he regained it on stage 19. It was at this point that the disenchanted French professional who had been following his progress remarked that the 'occult mafia' of older riders would get him. They were simply waiting for 'a propitious moment when they can put the outsider in his place — that is the fate to which De Muynck is condemned'. And so it happened. On stage 21, though quite by accident, De Muynck crashed and badly cut his face and hands. The next morning, still in pain, he lost the final time trial and the Tour to Gimondi. The Brooklyn team car wasn't there to support him on the course; it was left to a Belgian television commentator to follow him with his spare wheels. A bitter six weeks ended even more spitefully, but at least De Muynck had proved that the system could be beaten.

7

– Now it's a Spaniard –

Louvain, 29 JUNE: *morning*

This morning's team time trial at the Brasseries Artois — 'the breweries that made Louvain the capital of Belgian beer' — belong to the history of public relations rather than sport. The stand at the start and finish line is reserved for company guests. The Press Room and buffet have been set up in compounds built out of beer crates. No photographers can lift a camera without the words Stella-Artois appearing in the view-finder. It seems a very private fête.

The course is only 4.3 kilometres long, and the riders have already pedalled ten times as far from their hotels to reach Louvain. So to encourage them to take the event seriously, a system of bonuses and penalties has been introduced of such hair-splitting complexity that only a particular kind of French legal mind could have devised it.

Let's take it slowly. Most team time trials held on the Tour are perfectly simple to follow. The teams set off at intervals of two minutes, and the time of, say, the fifth member to cross the line counts for the team as a whole. But not in this case. The team's time is the sum of the times of the first five members to finish, so some very large and puzzling figures appear on the board.

Bonuses are given to members of the three fastest teams, but only if they finish with the leading man in their team. Similarly penalties are imposed on the laggards. These are calculated by taking his team's aggregate time, dividing by five, and adding twenty per cent. This figure is then subtracted from the slow rider's time, and what's left is the penalty. However . . . but you wouldn't thank me for going into any more detail.

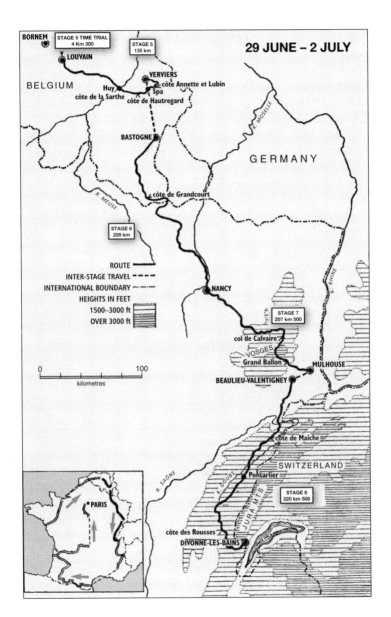

The upshot is that Raleigh, who come in like a flight of ducks with only three stragglers left behind, win at an average speed of over forty-eight kph. So seven of their men, including Kuiper and Pronk, collect bonuses of ten seconds. Flandria come second, but only Maertens and Van Springel get six seconds bonus. Third are Peugeot, with four seconds gained by Thévenet, Danguillaume and Ovion.

Another figure to conjure with is a fifty French francs penalty on Maertens, but that's another matter. Last night, without leave from the organisation, he left the Holiday Inn at Brussels Airport to visit his sick mother. At least nobody except an official is going to hold that against him, but altogether it has been a morning for the time-keepers and the book-keepers. The Tour will not be sorry to get back on the open road.

Verviers, 29 June: afternoon

The stage that follows moves on 144 kilometres, leaving Flanders for the Ardennes and the close-grained hills and valleys over which another of the Belgian classics, the Flêche Wallonne, is run. Most of the riders know the course from past experience, and as they emerge from Louvain across a quilted eiderdown of cornfields, they are in no hurry to anticipate the battle. But when it comes at sixty-two kilometres on the côte de la Sarthe — a sharp hill after the feeding station at Huy — it is with a calculated suddenness and produces the first real divisions in the race.

The field splits into four parts, the first two reuniting at eighty-four kilometres, with three middle-rankers in the lead: Talbourdet, Conati and Perret. Looking back from the top of a rise we see the trio dancing up behind us while the three chasing groups form echelons across the road, sheltering each other from a wind which only they can detect and which is doing little to cool the afternoon. The gaps between are short but unbridgeable, and while all the favourites are at the head of the race, several of the riders who owe their leading positions to successes at Saint-Jean and Le Touquet have let themselves be trapped at the rear. A genuine 'selection' is in progress.

On the côte de Hautregard, the only classified climb of the day, the pace becomes too hot for Talbourdet and Conati, and they drop back. Perret persists, crossing the summit with twenty seconds lead on Pedro Torres, King of the Mountains in the Tour three years ago, and half a minute on the *peloton*. Needing help, Perret waits for Torres on the plateau, and the two form a partnership which keeps its distance through Spa and to the foot of the last hill, the côte Annette et Lubin.

With only twenty kilometres to go they must have some expectation of fighting out the stage between them, but whereas Maertens and Pollentier, with diminishing help from a tired Flandria team, have been leading the chase so far, on the hill it is Van Impe who takes over, lightly climbing away to test the others. Maertens responds, the group accelerates, rounding up Perret and Torres in the process, and the Belgians return to their customary business of denying each other what they cannot win for themselves. At eight kilometres from Verviers, Guy Sibille — champion of France but for the duration of the Tour another work-horse in Thévenet's stable — attacks with Miguel Lasa at his wheel. It is Lasa who takes the one remaining Belgian stage, leaving Maertens to his inevitable sprint win from the chasing group. 'Now it's a Spaniard!' complains *Les Sports* with disgust in its headline.

Although the Belgians have ridden as if they were bound by a suicide pact, it has been the most significant stage so far. Maertens has protected his yellow jersey, and indeed improved his race lead by the six seconds he won (and Pollentier didn't) as a bonus this morning. But the time trial specialists like Manzanèque, Schuiten, Pronk and Bracke have begun to drop away, and are being replaced by harder, more versatile men.

Although Pronk missed the break, Belgium has been good to the Dutchman of the Raleigh team, and the rider who now lies third overall behind Maertens and Pollentier is Hennie Kuiper. His race number is 51, and it hasn't escaped the notice of the reporters, who are great searchers after coincidence, that 51 was the number worn by three recent winners: Merckx in 1969, Ocana in 1974 and Thévenet last year. This morning *Les Sports* talked of Kuiper's 'legendary timidity', but there's not been much sign of that since he won the world championship, also in Belgium, late last summer.

Nancy, 30 June

The Tour has moved on nearly 100 kilometres from yesterday's finish. Today we start from the Place MacAuliffe, dedicated to the Battered Bastards of Bastogne, the Americans who held that city during the winter of 1944–45. It is a neat square, shaded with awnings and trees, but not cool enough for Gualazzini who drops lumps of ice in his racing cap before he puts it on, and then turns it back to front so that the peak shades his neck. There's no let up in the heat, and with 209 kilometres to cover through the hilly Belgian province (not the Duchy) of Luxemburg, and along the banks of the Moselle and Meuse, it looks as if Maertens and the Flandria team will face another exhausting stage on constant patrol. Instead the heat is taken out of the day by a tall, gaunt-faced Italian of twenty-five, Aldo Parecchini, who hasn't figured at all in the race so far.

There are several teasing attacks by minor riders in the opening kilometres — quickly dealt with by the leaders in the interest of a quiet life — and then at thirteen kilometres a more puzzling breakaway by Ocana himself. It's not clear what he is up to. He is not in form and has complained of sciatica and trouble with an old saddle sore, so nobody regards him as a current threat to the favourites' peace of mind. On the other hand he is Ocana, a rider of distinction, a past winner of the Tour, and it's unthinkable that Maertens, Thévenet and Van Impe should allow him too much rope. He must know this as well as anyone, so perhaps he doesn't have anything serious in mind; his attack is just a diversion to relieve the tedium of the stage. At any rate the *peloton* doesn't over-react. It allows Ocana to gain a minute, no more, and leaves him out there to stew.

Ronald De Witte, leader of the Brooklyn team, however, is sufficiently intrigued to send his man Parecchini ahead to keep an eye on Ocana. At thirty kilometres Parecchini joins the Spaniard, and the following little pantomime takes place. Ocana, delighted to have a companion, waves him through to take a turn at the front. Parecchini declines, since it is not his job to help one of De Witte's rivals. Ocana therefore sits up and says he'll wait for the *peloton* to catch them both, at which Parecchini sprints ahead and leaves him. This is too much for

Ocana who starts pedalling again and catches up with Parecchini, at which it is the Italian's turn to sit up and refuse to work. At last Ocana tires of the game. He admits that if Parecchini feels strong enough to attack, he has a much better chance of success by going on alone. ('Ocana isn't just a great champion,' Parecchini says afterwards. 'He is a man with heart.') For the final time Ocana slows down to wait for the field, and Parecchini is left with the freedom of an open road which stretches away for 170 kilometres.

If Ocana's move was doomed from the start, you might expect Parecchini's to be equally short-lived. But he knows himself that his own humble position in the race is his best protection. At the start of the stage he stood fifty-sixth overall, 8–56 behind Maertens, and nothing suspicious is known against him. Ever since he turned professional in 1973 he has ridden as a *domestique,* first to Merckx in the Molteni team, then to Roger De Vlaeminck, Patrick Sercu and De Witte with Brooklyn. In all this time he has never won a stage in a big tour, or made a name for himself as a sprinter or a climber, or been particularly envious of those who did. His father was a thwarted cyclist who had to work as a bricklayer to support the family; Parecchini is simply grateful for the chance to earn his living on a bicycle.

So this early flight suits practically everyone. Maertens's enemies can be pretty sure that Parecchini hasn't suddenly developed ideas above his station; he wants to win the stage, not the Tour. He might briefly take the yellow jersey, but that would only be Maertens's loss. If Maertens wants to prevent this he must lead the chase himself. Maertens, on the other hand, can also relax a little since the others are showing no initiative. If Parecchini's effort doesn't burn itself out, there will be plenty of time to set up a counter-attack.

So Parecchini prospers while behind him the leaders bluff it out, and he has ridden too long in their company not to sense that this is the chance of his career. Lifting out of the saddle on the hills, settling back on the flat, he keeps the rhythm going without any strain. For once he has the undivided attention of his team-car. Every quarter of an hour it draws alongside to take back his empty *bidon* and replace it with a full one. And from the roadside an almost continuous fountain of hoses plays over him. (In the *peloton* the only rider who gets this individual treatment is Van Impe, and he is brought down by a specta-tor who hits him with the bucket as well as the water.) At seventy-three kilometres Parecchini's lead is given as 10–5, which makes him the yellow jersey on the road. And at the top of the fourth-category côte de Grand-court, a tree-covered hill which takes the Tour back across the frontier into France, it has reached almost quarter of an hour.

On this hill Kuiper and a small group of climbers try to break away, but Maertens personally retrieves them, and once more the *peloton* settles back while Parecchini forges on. At 102 kilometres he wins the Hot Spot sprint by the ridiculous margin of 15–40, and at 116 kilometres he achieves his maximum lead: seventeen minutes.

The most perilous section of his journey is still to come. His team car has to go ahead to the feeding station, leaving him with a folded tubular which he stuffs in his jersey pocket. If he punctures, instead of getting a new wheel in a matter of seconds, he will have to take out the wheel, strip off the old tyre, put on the new and pump it up himself, which will cost him several minutes. Fortunately he doesn't have to face this problem, but by the time the team car rejoins him he is having to cope with another: the leaders have begun to pick up the threads of the race. Parecchini is riding as strongly as ever: no dullness in the eyes, no nodding of the head, no rubberiness in the legs. But with every kilometre he is losing ground as the *peloton* accelerates. It's not only Maertens, now, who is anxious to limit the Italian's gains; even Van Impe, Poulidor and Thévenet feel that things have gone far enough.

At just over twenty kilometres from Nancy, Maertens regains his title to the yellow jersey, but with no hope of winning the stage. Parecchini comes through, his arms raised even before he has crossed the line, still with 4–29 in hand on Paolini and six other chasers, and 4–41 on Maertens and the bunch. So, after all, it was simply a diver-sion, leaving Parecchini £430 richer, and giving Maertens an anxious but not particularly arduous ride.

Mulhouse, 1 July

It was only a minor mountain stage that ran for 207 kilometres from Nancy to Mulhouse, and therefore only a minor irony that the sprinter,

Maertens, won it. The greater irony is that this victory, his fourth in eight days, came so promptly after he had left Belgium. The disappointment of his return home seems to have lifted now, the buoyancy returned. Having brought the yellow jersey to Belgium, his first aim, and then carried it back into France, Maertens is now certain of wearing it at least to the foot of the Alps.

Today's was a really imperious win imposed on a peer group of forty-four riders which included two of the fastest finishers — Esclassan of France and the Italian, Gavazzi — and nearly all the men of any consequence. This group was over two minutes clear as it came up to the final 900 metre circuit formed by the roads on either side of a canal and two bridges which crossed it. Trying to anticipate the sprint, Périn, Martos and Danguillaume detached themselves and led by six seconds at the entry to the circuit. But Maertens had taken a bead on them across the angle of the canal and let them spend themselves on the first dummy run to the finishing line. It was not until the second lap that he began moving up the column, and at the final bend he opened out. Only Esclassan could draw level with him, at which Maertens produced a second, demolishing burst of pace, crossing the line with his head characteristically twisted to one side. In that sprint, beside raw power there was nerve, concentration and grace.

Otherwise the beauty of the stage was mostly in the eye of the reporters who had time to look around them. It moved into the foothills of the Vosges and then upward along the route des Crêtes — the ridge road — through a rounder, more sumptuous version of mid-Wales. And even the riders seemed to be enjoying it as a club-run. The forecast had offered 'very sunny weather, with temperatures of 30–35° and wind from the north-east, light', and except that the wind was stronger on the summits, there was little to amend. It was a good day for riding, a bad one for racing and nobody made a serious move until the halfway mark was passed.

Even then on the col du Calvaire, the first third-category prime of the Tour, the gradients weren't fierce enough to force a split. The climbers edged ahead, then soon settled back after sharing the points, deferring their next struggle until the Grand Ballon. This took the Tour to 4,670 feet, its highest point so far, with vast aerial views towards Germany and across the gold and brown Plain of Alsace. But the climb was less divisive than the descent. There Kuiper, who had come second on both hill primes and taken the lead in the Mountain Grand Prix, sped away downhill drawing thirteen men in pursuit. They are worth listing since they were Van Impe, Zoetemelk, Poulidor, Pollentier, Panizza, Martos, Thévenet, Battaglin, Maertens, Riccomi, Perret, Lopez-Carril and Sibille — in fact everyone who is anyone with the exception of the Italians Baronchelli and Bertoglio, Ocana, De Witte and Schuiten.

Yet the strength of the group was also its weakness, for a forty kilometre slog seemed hardly worth the candle when it would leave the main leaders in just the same relative positions. It would have been another matter if Thévenet or Van Impe or Maertens had been dropped. As matters stood it seemed as well to let the closest of the chasers catch up, and, sharing the work among forty-four riders, proceed in a brisk but orderly manner to the finish.

Afterwards Maertens said he was surprised that the favourites hadn't shown a little more initiative and exploited their chance of shedding three or four rivals. Merckx would certainly have done so. Still, who was Maertens to complain?

The Decisions of the Commissaires listed on Communique No. 14 tonight are an unusually mixed bag. The entire Peugeot team have been fined for not signing on at the start. So have two men for using a glass water bottle, one for taking shelter behind a car on the race, one for jersey-pulling in the sprint, and another for what is vaguely described *mauvaise tenue en course.* This covers various forms of misbehaviour but in particular the one which the British also disguise with a euphemism — committing a nuisance. It's obvious that the riders can't afford to stop and urinate behind a tree while the race is on. They have to acquire the knack of doing it on the move. This is understood, and offends no one; although there is a time and place, which is not in the middle of a village where the crowds are lining the pavement. But what if — as often happens — an empty road makes a sudden twist into a high street. Well, that's not just bad luck, it's *mauvaise tenue* and costs a one pound fine.

Incidentally, Manzanèque, who was second in the Prologue and has remained buoyantly fourth overall until today, has lost seven and a half minutes and dropped to fifty-third. Parecchini, yesterday's man, has also moved back to the accustomed obscurity of sixtieth place. And by a happy chance the rider who is currently carrying the *lanterne rouge* as last man overall is called Fin.

Divonne-les-Bains, 2 JULY

The last stage before the first rest day on the borders of Switzerland. The last that Maertens can count on finishing with the race still under his control; at any rate, that is the majority opinion although Anquetil is quoted as saying that Maertens has been under-rated. The last, too, of the prolonged heat-wave; by mid-afternoon the sky has turned from deep blue to smokey grey, and at the summit of the côte des Rousses, to the crackle of thunder, large blobs of water begin to spatter down. As *La Dernière Heure* reports, it is the first rain to have fallen on a cycle race since 25 May, when the first stage of the Dauphiné Libéré was 'copiously watered'. As a dramatic effect the change of weather has arrived almost suspiciously on cue.

Otherwise the transition is gradual. After thirty-five of its 220 kilometres the route winds up into the Jura mountains, tracing the Doubs back towards its source, but not putting any fearsome obstacles in the riders' way. The first and last climbs of the day are third-category, but in between there is only one fourth, and the terrain looks more hostile than it really is. The riders move along stern rock-faced valleys (you wonder how the Doubs, trickling along in the drought, was capable of all this wear and tear) and take their feed at Pontarlier, the Home of Mountain Gruyère, but for most of the way they are on a fairly level trek at 2,500 feet. It's mountaineering without tears, and they are not disposed to create any pain by their own efforts.

The thought that tomorrow's a day of rest and Sunday a day of stone-breaking labour is in everybody's mind. Before the stage sets out from the Peugeot cycle factory at Beaulieu-Valentigney, the management lays on a *buffet campagnard* beside the start line and several of the riders drop in as though the holiday has already begun.

The abstemious Poulidor seems more interested in the soft drinks, but Cigana tops up his *bidon* from one of the wine barrels. The atmosphere is relaxed and only the organisers are at all put out when the start is interrupted by a workers' demonstration.

It's the second day running that this has happened. Yesterday at Nancy about fifty members of the print union which, since a year last March, has been in dispute with *Le Parisien Libéré*, dumped old newspapers on the road to a depth of four inches; the riders had to get off and push their bikes over this drift of fallen leaves. There was a rough passage between the printers and a unit of the CRS — Compagnie Républicaine de Sécurité — which had been following the convoy. Today it is the cycle workers who hold up the race. In their leaflets — 'Yes! To the Tour de France . . . No! to the Peugeot profits race' — they say that, except for certain busy workshops the factory has been closed for the visit of the Tour, and the workers laid off. Peugeot has a team in the race, and is paying at least half the cost of today's stage. 'We are all for the sporting contest, but it is not up to the workers to finance it.' Needless to say, nothing of this comes over Radio Tour or appears in the next day's *L'Équipe*.

The only persistent attack in the early part of the stage is by the Portuguese, José Martins, who takes the initial step into the Juras, the côte de Maiche, by forty-eight seconds, and his lead to 1–45. But since there's no sign of reinforcements, he slackens off and waits to be caught. Next to make a move is Patrick Perret, born in La Rochelle but a 'regional' by adoption, who builds two minutes' lead. But he too desists after failing to find his family at the roadside (at times it's hard to know whether riders have appointments with destiny or their mothers). And so it goes on, one optimist after another losing the battle with himself or with more powerful opponents until the last climb on the côte des Rousses. This is not as severe today as when it is crossed from the other direction and becomes the more familiar col de la Faucille. But it's hard enough to stagger the field a little, and its opportunities aren't to be ignored. From the summit there remains only forty kilometres to the finish, and they're downhill nearly all the way.

Firxt across is the Italian, Giancarlo Bellini, who takes over from Kuiper as leader in the Mountain Grand Prix, and then on the gentle rise that comes before the final swoop, the *peloton* splits in three. Fortunately for the riders in the second group, they come under the direction of Maertens who has dropped back after a puncture. He draws them up to the leaders by his own efforts, at which point Bernard Labourdette, a member of the undistinguished Jobo-Wolber team, attacks.

The move is nicely timed, for the leaders are engrossed in each others' progress, and after a brave career downhill he has a lead of forty-five seconds only thirteen kilometres from the line. But then Labourdette becomes yet another name in the long list of riders who fall victim to sudden, arbitrary bad luck. With only ten kilometres to cover, he hits a stone and buckles his rear wheel. He has to ride on his brakes, and on this fast descent his team car can't get by to change his machine. Eight kilometres from home he is caught and seventy-two riders arrive together at the entrance to the Divonne hippodrome, a hard, gritty trotting track, 1,750 metres long. Flandria are guarding the front of the *peloton* and Maertens's fifth win seems to be a formality. But coming round the circuit for the second time, he gets himself momentarily boxed in, and at 250 metres from the line he has left himself too much to do. He loses by a wheel to Jacques Esclassan, Thévenet's representative in the sprint, the man he had beaten yesterday, and the first Frenchman to win a stage so far in the Tour.

So the first phase of the race is at an end. Here the riders will spend their Saturday relaxing, most of them in the four-star Hotel du Golf et du Parc built in the style of an opulent country club. Esclassan, in fact, is entitled, as part of his prize, to stay on in Divonne for eight days and take a cure at the Thermal Centre. Instead on Sunday he and the other 119 remaining riders (there was just one abandonment today; Parecchini, still exhausted from Wednesday's win, finished the stage asleep in the broom wagon) will be setting out again on the next brutally short section. Three days in the Alps with four first-category climbs — two of them summit finishes — one second-category and three third, which will take the Tour to its half-way point and second rest day.

In nine days' racing Maertens has scarcely made a defensive error. The only rider of any importance to beat him to the finish was

Kuiper at Bornem, and then by only fourteen seconds. As a result he still leads his friend, Pollentier, by 2–4, and his foes, beginning with Kuiper, by 3–16 or more. (To bring you up to date, the others within four minutes are, in order, Danguillaume, Poulidor, Pronk, De Witte, Bellini, Baronchelli, Van Impe and Thévenet, with Zoetemelk and Bertoglio at 4–5.) It's as much insurance as he could hope to carry, though whether it's sufficient cover for his modest talents as a climber is a question best answered by hindsight on Sunday evening.

Of course if Maertens does fail, and loses not only his yellow jersey but his place among the leaders, then it will be hard to appreciate Thévenet's early worries about him. Far from stirring up the race, Maertens and the Flandria team have smothered it. Their ideal has been an uneventful stage and a mass sprint finish — led in by Maertens, like lightning outrunning a storm. All but Kuiper have gone along with this. Well, maybe Van Impe and Poulidor have occasionally demurred, but never with enough force to compromise themselves. And there hasn't been a peep out of Thévenet or Zoetemelk. The favourites have risked nothing, extending themselves only in the time trials, and by and large they are still separated only by the seconds won and lost at Saint Jean and Le Touquet. Take away the lead of Maertens and Pollentier, as the mountains may well do, and you are left with a group from third to thirteenth overall who are all within forty-nine seconds of each other. It says more for their cunning and prudence than their sense of adventure.

A last, disquieting footnote. The commissaires announce that a dope test taken at Le Touquet has proved positive for Jésus Manzanèque. He has been fined £230, penalised ten minutes and will be suspended from racing for a month if he repeats the offence. It's a familiar story, and a light enough sentence to ensure that we'll hear it again.

8

– Illicit Substances –

It can't be said that the Manzanèque affair caused any great stir; newspapers gave the text of the commissaires' decision down the page and under a neutral heading. Nor was there any obvious reaction from Manzanèque's fellow tourists. They didn't treat him like a man who had been caught cheating at cards, but more like a motorist who had committed some minor traffic offence and then failed the breath test. Cycling under the influence wasn't something to be encouraged, of course, but it might well happen to anyone. Which of us could put our hand on our heart, etcetera!

Cycle racing has lived with the drug problem for several decades, and until the mid-sixties few people outside the medical profession — and not everyone within it — regarded the 'sensible' use of stimulants as any problem at all. It was well known to exist, but seldom mentioned in print. In 1966 Jack Olsen, writing about the Tour in the American magazine *Sports Illustrated*, brought up 'the touchy subject of goofballs', and in a flippantly sour portrait of the typical *lanterne rouge* wrote that he 'may have lost his toenails from the constant forward pressure in his cycling shoes, his backside may be pocked by suppurating ulcers and his mind so addled by amphetamine that he is not sure of his name, but he is a hero, a major athletic figure, a finisher in the Tour de France, the most trying sports event in the world'. But that wasn't, either in style or content, the kind of description the French went in for.

Then from the mid-sixties official bodies, encouraged by the State, began to speak out strongly against the use of drugs — despite opposition from the riders themselves who condemned dope tests as an interference with the freedom and dignity of their profession. Today that argument has been resolved, at least to the extent that in public nobody has a good word to say for doping. In private, though, the practice continues at a disconcerting level. While the Manzanèque incident was irrelevant to the race, it couldn't easily be shrugged off as a trivial side-issue by anyone who knew the extent of doping in the sport, or whose memory stretched back to the death of Tom Simpson in the 1967 Tour.

That year the riders were competing in national teams instead of trade teams, and Simpson was the British captain. Three of the men who supported him lived and rode on the Continent — Van Denson, Barry Hoban and Michael Wright, the last of whom was Hertfordshire-born and held a British passport but, having been brought up in Belgium, spoke very little English. The rest belonged to the small class of shoestring professionals who do most of their racing in England. In effect, though, Simpson was riding his own race independently of the others, as might have been expected from a man of his talents; there was little the others could do for him, or he for them. It was eight years since he had first come to Europe, alighting in Brittany, moving to Paris, then settling in Ghent, and in that period he had been more successful than any British rider before him. He was the first to wear the yellow jersey in the Tour; he won four classics including the longest of all, the Bordeaux–Paris; and in 1965 he took the world title. Impetuously ambitious, he was, as one French newspaper put it, driven by 'the need for money which attacks immigrants, the fear of having to take the boat back one day with empty pockets, the obsession with the future'. In this race, for reasons that we'll come to, he was more anxious than ever to do conspicuously well.

This seemed likely. After a good ride on the Ballon d'Alsace he had risen to seventh overall, and this was still his position on the morning of July 13 when the Tour set out on the thirteenth stage from Marseille to Carpentras. He had been sick on one heavy ride through the Alps, but now he seemed well again. We happened to meet him the evening before outside his team hotel on the quai des Belges in the Old Port of Marseille, and though he seemed nervously excited he was cheerful enough. An Algerian pedlar tried to interest him in some carved wooden figures, and Simpson spun out the bargaining to amuse himself and the others.

Stage 13 reached Carpentras after 136 kilometres. It then made a seventy-five kilometre loop to cross the 6,200 foot summit of Mont Ventoux before curving back for the finish. The mountain was the day's chosen battle theatre. It was desperately hot and heavy — a thermometer outside a restaurant on Ventoux showed 55°C (131°F) — and this is a bare, bleached mountain with no trees for shade on its 1–10 gradients and the sun glaring off its broken limestone surface.

Poulidor and Jiménez began the action. Two small groups went in pursuit of them, and Simpson was in the next wave of chasers. At the bottom of the hill there had been a raid on a cafe-bar (a custom tolerated at that time, but now heavily punished) in which mineral water, pastis and cognac were taken and passed around the riders. According to a race official, Simpson drank a little of the cognac (ironically, only a short while before, he had warned one of the younger British riders against eating an ice cream).

Simpson was not going well, and several people ran out from the crowd to push him up the slope. But he was past that kind of help. Three kilometres from the summit he fell and was still in a confused state as he was helped back onto his bike. A further kilometre on he collapsed a second time, unconscious now, and a spectator was sufficiently alarmed by his condition to attempt the kiss of life. Dr. Pierre Dumas, the Tour doctor, coming quickly on the scene, radioed for one of the police helicopters. He continued the attempt at resuscitation until it arrived and Simpson, accompanied by another doctor and a nurse, was put aboard and flown to Avignon general hospital. At 5.40 he was pronounced dead.

These bleak facts were announced at the Press Centre, a school classroom in Carpentras, and the last sentence of the announcement ran: 'The doctors concerned have decided to refuse permission for interment.' Dr. Dumas, a stubby, bearded, hearty man who had a great affection for Simpson and was very evidently shaken by his death, said that he would not prejudge the case; he simply considered it abnormal that a young and physically well-prepared athlete should die in the course of a competition. We were left to draw our own conclusions, which were soon reinforced by the facts which were gradually brought into the open.

Two medical containers had been found in the pockets of Simpson's jersey, one empty and labelled Tonedrin, the other half full of anonymous tablets about half the size of aspirin. (This report was later amended to three containers, two of them empty.) Coincidentally that morning at Marseille the first drug tests — or at any rate the first to be acknowledged — had been carried out on half a dozen French and Italian riders. The job was done by four doctors and they were escorted by police because since June 14 of the previous year, under Law 65412, it had become a criminal offence to consume, prescribe or offer certain listed drugs which artificially improved an athlete's performance. The maximum penalties for the guilty were a fine of roughly £400 and one year's imprisonment. The British team had not been involved in this particular check, but next day their two cars, their van and personal belongings were searched. The team-manager, Alec Taylor, and the two *soigneurs*, Auguste Naessens (Belgian) and Rudy Van der Weide (Dutch) also left their hotel with the police and were rigorously questioned into the night. They were released only when the police were satisfied that none of them knew that Simpson had been using stimulants. There could no longer be any reasonable doubt that he had been. In the baggage van there was a box belonging to Simpson which contained various tablets and medicines, among them tubes of Tonedrin and Stenamina, both drugs in the methylamphetamine group.

Alec Taylor sensibly persuaded the four remaining members of the team to continue in the race. It was better for them to occupy themselves and share their misery than to separate and go home. The following morning they filed through the back of the square at Carpentras, each wearing a black band on the sleeve of his white jersey with its Union Jack epaulettes. Denson, who had been close to Simpson for fourteen years, was in tears; so was Hoban, another member of the small, expatriate group which had made its home in Ghent. Colin Lewis and Arthur Metcalfe, two British-based riders, walked stiffly behind them. They were immediately recognised and greeted with applause, which only made matters worse. Before the start there was a short oration, then a moment's silence, and when the *peloton* moved off on the flat road towards Sète, Denson was invited to ride ahead and take the stage as a tribute to Simpson. He declined, but Hoban, who was glad to be alone, accepted.

Denson left the race shortly afterwards while the other three continued to Paris, but it was not until early August that the official medical report on Simpson's death was released by the Avignon public prosecutor. Simpson had died of heart failure due to exhaustion. The report continued: 'The unfavourable atmospheric conditions, intense over-exertion and the use of dangerous medicines could have contributed to the exhaustion syndrome. Toxological experts confirm that a certain quantity of amphetamine and methylamphetamine, substances making up in part the pharmaceutical products found in Simpson's clothing, have been discovered in his blood, urine, stomach-content and intestines.' These same experts confirm that the dose of amphetamine taken by Simpson would not have been enough, by itself, to kill him but would have permitted him to pass the limit of his endurance and thus allow him to fall victim to excessive exhaustion.

This was much as we had supposed. In normal circumstances an athlete's muscles will cease to respond long before his heart fails, but drugs impair the natural fail-safe mechanism. Simpson's death made tragic nonsense of the received idea in cycle racing at the time that the use of stimulants under medical supervision was not simply harmless but positively beneficial, enabling a rider to get through the arduous tasks his profession set him. The specious argument was used that if a reporter had to work when he was tired wouldn't he drink a cup of coffee before he sat down at the typewriter? And wasn't caffeine a stimulant? I remember, too after an exceptionally long split-stage across northern France, a French cycling correspondent surveying the imposing litter left on the dinner table, the crab and oyster shells, the empty wine bottles, the full ashtrays, and declaring that if we had needed refuelling on that scale after travelling by car, weren't the riders entitled to something which would help them cycle all that distance? But the drugs available to the cyclists were a good deal more lethal in the short run than coffee and Muscadet. There was no 'sensible' use of them in the breathless, oven temperatures of the Ventoux. And there was no protection against their abuse under the stress of ambition.

On the night of Simpson's death Jacques Goddet described him as '*un chic garçon* who was probably afraid of defeat'. Both observations were precisely accurate. Simpson was a man with considerable style, sharp and cynical with a birdlike alertness, a snappy dresser who, for the sake of publicity, used to dress up as Major Thompson in a stockbroker's suit with bowler and rolled umbrella; the outfit looked well on his thin frame. But as a rider he probably had more talent and courage than a meagre physique could sustain. He had never been physically strong enough to keep in command of a race as prolonged as the Tour de France, which worried him. And in 1967 he felt it was particularly urgent that he should prove himself as a *touriste* and not just a man of the one-day classics. He had explained why this was when I went to see him a week before his death in his room at the Hotel Central in Metz.

He was stretched out on a double bed in the grand, shabby room he shared with Bill Lawrie, the Australian in the British team, who had been left with the single divan. The place was littered with clothes, ointments, bits of equipment, but neither would make a move to clear those up until the morning. It was the dead spot of the evening. Dinner had been taken by inflexible custom at seven-thirty. Now in the hour before Simpson settled to sleep (an insomniac like most riders when under pressure, he had been sleeping briefly but well this year) he could relax and explain himself without that defensive facetiousness that often made him difficult to question.

So far he had been reasonably satisfied, riding well within his limits and moving only when the favourites moved. 'I'm doing no work at all. I'd be telling lies if I said that my legs didn't ache in the evenings. But I'm not finishing the day in the same state of fatigue as other years. And I think this will pay off later in the Tour.' He was also riding more prudently because he didn't have to impose himself on the British team; it accepted him unquestioningly as leader. Often in the past, riding for his trade team, he had felt he had to act like the boss of a chapter of gangsters, getting a vicious blow in first just to show them who was master.

This brought him round to his decision to break with his old sponsors, Peugeot-BP, and his particular anxiety to make an impression in this year's Tour. He had not joined Peugeot from choice in the first place. His contract was simply sold to them by his Paris club, Rapha/VC-12, in 1963; like the other riders, he had no say in the deal. He had been unhappy with the team from the start, and only one thing had prevented him moving on. Unless he agreed to renew his contract for the following season they would not find a place for him in their Tour de France team. The Tour was the one race he could not afford to miss.

What had broken the deadlock was the Tour's sudden switch from trade teams to national teams. With or without Peugeot's blessing, Simpson could be sure of a ride for Great Britain in 1967. He was free, and had already been offered contracts as good as Peugeot's; but this time he wanted something better. 'I can only get that if I prove I can be a danger in the Tour. Last year I nearly went through without an off day, but then I fell and that was that. I've got no more excuses. At my age [he was twenty-nine] I can't say next year I'll be better. The only person I'd be kidding is myself.'

He didn't hope to win the Tour. 'Supposing I took the yellow jersey, would the team be strong enough to protect me? I don't see how they could.' The only hope, he suggested with a touch of his old sarcasm, was if he took the jersey at Versailles on the final morning, and then protected it himself on the time trial into Paris. But he could still ride a good Tour within his own terms, and these were quite specific in his mind. He must either finish in the first three overall; or win a couple of important (which to him meant mountainous) stages and finish in the first ten; or take the yellow jersey and hold it for five or six days. Nothing less would really do. He hoped to ride another four Tours, and extend his career a few years longer than that as a Six Day rider on the winter tracks. He had already bought a place with citrus trees in Corsica, and had laid the first stone of his new house a few months before. 'If I can put away another £50,000 I'm finished.' It was that future he was pursuing eight days later on Mont Ventoux.

Simpson's death made a deeper impression than the nature of the immediate reaction suggested. At the time he was mourned as a lost hero, a lively, engaging young man (*'Un britannique qui n'était pas flegmatique'*) who had fallen bravely in a pitiless event. It was only gradually that he came to be accepted as a victim of official leniency towards drug offenders. In fact three days later Jacques Anquetil, writing in *France Dimanche*, went so far as to blame his death on the new anti-doping measures. To climb the Ventoux in that heat 'it was absolutely necessary to take something simply to breathe. Some solu-camphre, for example. But with this idiotic prohibition of all injections, it is possible that Tommy, that day, used a product less proven, less understood and perhaps more dangerous than solucamphre.'

Anquetil was not alone in his attitude. Although resort to stimulants had been made illegal a year before, there was constant opposition by the riders to any form of regular testing; and since none of them raised the point that doping gave one rider an unfair advantage over the others, the supposition must be that the practice was fairly widespread. The riders' non-cooperation, and even sabotage, was in turn sufficient to deter the pussy-footing authorities. At Bordeaux during the 1966 Tour two doctors and a policeman had visited Poulidor during the evening at his hotel and requested a urine sample for laboratory analysis. It was the first attempt to enforce the new law. Under protest Poulidor complied. But the following day on the road to Bayonne the riders first reduced their pace to ten miles an hour and then to walking pace. They dismounted, pushed their bikes along and, in the cause of professional dignity, chanted *Merde*! with every step they took. After three minutes or so they got back on and resumed the race. The implied threat wasn't difficult to interpret. No more testing or no more Tour. The samples taken from Poulidor's room were never mentioned again.

The biggest strike against tests came in the world championship road race at the Nurburgring later in the season. The winner, Rudi Altig of West Germany, and the next five finishers, Anquetil, Poulidor, Motta, Stablinski and Zilioli, all refused to go to the control. Yet Altig kept his title, and all the others were reinstated after a brief suspension. None was prosecuted.

Anquetil remained the most vehement and articulate opponent of tests, keeping up his campaign against them right to the end of the 1967 season. Late that September he went to the Vigorelli track in Milan to make an attempt on the world hour record set by Roger Rivière nine years before — and also, it seemed, to challenge the authorities to another bout of litigious arm wrestling. Before considering any world record for ratification, the UCI now required that the rider should submit himself for a dope test within five hours of

Geoffrey Nicholson, celebrated sports journalist, author and the *Observer*'s
'resident cyclopath' *photo: courtesy Mavis Nicholson*

Freddy Maertens on the way to his Prologue individual time-trial victory

Lucien Van Impe relaxes with his team ahead of stage 1 in Saint-Jean-de-Monts

Diversion on the long, hot road to Bornem, which even Jacques Goddet called a 'journey to the edge of boredom'

The riders wheel their bikes over protest newspapers that have been thrown into the road on stage 7 to Mulhouse

Joop Zoetemelk crosses the finish line to win on L'Alpe d'Huez

Bernard Thévenet, Raymond Poulidor and Raymond Martin focus
on the climb ahead

Jose Luis Viejo, hero of the long escape on stage 11, makes his successful break from the peloton

A timing board shows Viejo's considerable escape time on the 224km road to Manosque

Lucien Van Impe catches Luis Ocana in the Pyrenees on stage 14 to Saint-Lary-Soulan

Van Impe climbs on his way to claiming the yellow jersey in the closing kilometres of stage 14

One lap to go on the Pau motor circuit: the peloton in fairly cool pursuit of Panizza

The essential struggle of 1976: Van Impe (left) and Zoetemelk shoulder
to shoulder closing on the summit of the Puy-de-Dôme

Aad Van den Hoek rides at the back of the peloton holding the *lanterne rouge* on stage 21 to Versailles

Maertens (extreme left) takes the sprint in the slippery, sodden finish at Versailles

For the second year running the Champs-Elysées is turned into a criterium track for the final stage of the 1976 Tour

Flanked by his family in Paris, Van Impe lifts his cup and the key to his newly-won apartment

All photographs courtesy Offside/L'Équipe unless stated.

the attempt. Anquetil rode, covered 47 km 493.66 in the hour, beating Rivière's distance by almost 347 metres — and then missed his rendezvous with the doctor appointed by the Italian federation to supervise the dope test. Instead he returned home and only after reflection visited a doctor in Rouen and provided a specimen for analysis; this was forty-eight hours after the record attempt. The official doctor of the French federation described this gesture as valueless, for after that lapse of time no trace of stimulants would have been detectable. At once the two sides took up their battle lines. For Anquetil it was argued that his record was valid since it had been set in the same permissive conditions that Rivière and all the other holders had enjoyed. Against him Jean Bobet, younger brother of the triple Tour winner, Louison Bobet, wrote in *Le Monde*: 'Jacques has committed a capital error in sport: that of not abiding by the rules of the game. Either one plays or one doesn't play.'

The director of a Paris cycle club suggested a compromise: records in future should have the letters SC or AC printed after them: *sans contrôle* or *avec contrôle*. AC records might be less impressive for some time, but at least they would represent the honest efforts of 'a new, better educated generation'. Instead the UCI simply refused to ratify Anquetil's record — which anyway was beaten by Ferdinand Bracke (AC) in Rome a month later. For once public sympathy was with the authorities, not with the rider, and professional cycling took the hint.

The Tour of 1968, starting from the sedate little spa of Vittel, was billed as the Tour of Health. From now on six to eight riders had to pass through the control every evening. 'Doping,' wrote Jacques Goddet in his editorial on the eve of the start, 'is no longer a mysterious sickness, hidden, uncontrollable, uncontrolled. For it really seems that there is a common determination among the riders to be rid of this scourge. Dear Tom Simpson, you will not have fallen in vain on the stony desert of the Ventoux.' This was over-optimistic. Two riders — the oldest and the youngest, as it happened — were dismissed from the race after positive dope tests. Unfortunately, too, the Tour was uncommonly dull. In order to make it less strenuous — and so give the riders less excuse for resorting to drugs — the organisers postponed any contact with the mountains until the twelfth stage. There were to be no monstrous stages, no great set-piece ascents like the Ventoux on which the giants would win or lose the Tour. Instead there would be more small climbs, more cobbles, more intermediate prizes which would give the young, athletic rider an incentive for attack. This plan did not work out. The first half of the race produced an unadventurous sequence of close sprint finishes and a list of nonentities at the head of the race. Reporters yearned for the old reverberating clash of big personalities and complained about this Tour of (albeit healthy) pygmies. In response Félix Lévitan went on television and said that younger journalists were needed to interpret the racing. Reporters of the old guard, looking at the Tour 'with worn eyes' (the phrase that particularly rankled) couldn't be expected to appreciate the vigour of a young field of largely unknown riders who were constantly making and checking attacks. That did it.

Now the Press went on strike, leaving the start of the Bordeaux–Bayonne stage and driving forty-five miles up the road to Labouheyre to wait in a car park for the race to arrive. As a piece of industrial action it passed quite pleasantly. We sunbathed and ate our sandwiches and the more gifted wrote out slogans: 'Field glasses for Félix' and 'Riders — Worn Eyes are Watching You.' While the gendarmes held up the publicity caravan, some tried to tie a banner — 'Liberate Goddet' — across the road, but in the way of these amateur efforts, the string snapped. At last Lévitan's car was sighted, and as the car horns were blown in protest, he drove past blandly smiling. Then the main bunch of riders, who clearly didn't understand what the fuss was about, were waved to a stop (Poulidor, not to be a spoil-sport, gave a Communist salute). Finally Dr. Dumas arrived in the medical car: '*Ah, la Sorbonne des vélos,*' he said. The race resumed and that was an end of it.

As an advertisement for the merits of drug-free racing, the Tour of 1968 had not been a great success. Still, it established certain principles. If a rider took dope he might well be caught. If he was caught he would be punished. And if he was punished he could expect no intervention from his fellow professionals. The days of organised boycotts and mass protests were over. Unfortunately the days of doping were not. There were still riders who gambled on the long odds against being picked out for the tests, or who cheated the controls, or put their faith in so far undetectable drugs. Some controls were administered with greater laxity than others. And penalties became less severe. Whereas in 1968 offenders were dismissed the Tour, later a fine and a suspended sentence of disqualification were introduced.

In 1974 Professor De Backere of Ghent University, previously an expert on horse doping, developed a new method of analysing urine samples. To the eight (out of thirteen) amphetamine-based drugs which were detectable, he could now add a ninth, called Ritalin. It was intended for sufferers from nervous depression but was often employed by professional riders who were convinced it couldn't be traced. But that still left a number of 'safe' alternatives. It also said a lot both for the naivety and the drug-dependence of many riders that they not only risked using traceable products, but then went on to win — so facing the inevitable consequence of a dope test. Every year race results had to be revised after samples had been analysed.

Obedient to UCI regulations, the medical control unit tested five or six riders almost every day through the 1976 Tour. The five were the winner and runner-up on the stage, the man who had begun the day in the yellow jersey, and two riders picked at random (two more were kept in reserve in case of duplication). In split stages the selection was slightly different but the numbers stayed the same. After the two long time trials just the first four were tested. So in all 108 tests were made, and of these only three proved positive.

Dr. Dumas thought that these results showed some progress; he felt he could say with certainty that the majority of riders were not using products on the official proscribed list. Summing up the situation, he argued that more must be done to improve the techniques of analysis and bring other drugs into the net, and also to define explicitly the difference between stimulants taken to enhance performance, and preparations used for valid medical treatment. He was most saddened, though, by the failure of mounting propaganda against the danger of drugs. 'What I do say, with regret, is that in this area any attempts at education are less successful than systematic repression.'

All Dumas's fears were realised by a sordid little incident at the end of the season. After the final stage of the Étoile des Espoirs, two riders of the Peugeot-Esso team, Rachel Dard and Bernard Bourreau, were caught trying to cheat the dope control by substituting someone else's urine for their own. While pretending to give a sample, they were filling the flask from a *topette*, a rubber bulb concealed in their racing shorts. Strictly according to the regulations, they should have undressed completely to give the sample, but for reasons of modesty riders are often allowed to stay clothed, and such frauds are not that uncommon. They have provided a familiar story to the folklore of cycle racing, that of the rider who was told that his test was negative, but warned that he was pregnant.

It was the sequel to the fraud that made the greater scandal. The young doctor in charge of the control obliged the two riders to give correct samples. Each was divided into two flasks, the first to be analysed immediately it reached the toxological laboratory in Paris, the second kept in case the rider exercised his right to a second opinion. After the riders had tried to persuade him not to reveal their crime, and a third, unidentified man had threatened to intercept the flasks, the doctor decided that it would be best to take them himself by train from Dax to Paris. But early next morning he reached the gare Austerlitz to find Dard and an accomplice, who had travelled north by car, waiting for him. This time the doctor weakened under their pressure and after an argument agreed to destroy the flasks. More than a week passed before his conscience persuaded him to disclose their guilt and his own weakness.

As a result of these disclosures, Dard and Bourreau were fined 5,000 Swiss francs (roughly £1,200); Dard was disqualified from racing for six months, while Bourreau received a suspended sentence of three months. At the same time there were revelations of interference in the controls at other races — doctors physically attacked and samples stolen before they could reach the laboratory. The French federation announced that of 1,049 tests it had made during the season, only twenty-four had been positive and two fraudulent. It could be, and was, argued that over four years only two per cent of those tested had proved to be using stimulants. But in November Dard blew the gaff on that. Acknowledging that the doctor's account of the events following the Étoile des Espoirs had been true in every detail he provided *L'Équipe* with a horrifying dossier on the widespread use of undetectable drugs which included painkillers, often taken with strychnine, to relieve their depressing effect; hormone treatment with cortisone; the misapplication of cardiac and cardio-respiratory aids. He implicated doctors, organisers and team officials in the scandal; it was, from Dard's experience, the innocent who formed the slim minority.

9

– Roads of the Cross –

Alpe d'Huez, 4 July

In the biblical metaphors of French reporting, where a rider's saddle sore becomes his cavalry, and the word 'agony' is charged with New Testament overtones, the ninth stage of the Tour is, in several estimations, a road of the cross. It is also, quite simply, a cross-roads. Starting from Divonne it runs through the Haute-Savoie and Savoie towards two looming summits in the Isère: the col du Luitel at 208 kilometres and the Alpe d'Huez, where it drags upwards to its close after 258 kilometres. The riders approach it with apprehension, the followers with greedy curiosity. Even the most fearful mountain stage can be inconclusive if the climbers fail, or don't choose, to press home their advantage to the finish. But a stage which ends on the top of a mountain cannot really fail to scatter the field. If we don't have a new leader by the end of the day, we shall certainly have a new chain of command.

Setting off at eight in the morning, the riders briefly show the flag in Switzerland where, by the vagaries of Continental time this summer, it is an hour earlier. It is also Sunday morning, when even the Swiss relax a little, and understandably there are few people on the streets. Those who come to the gates and balconies in their dressing gowns are visibly unexcited, and the riders are doing little to stir their interest. The speed is down to a steady thirty kph — under nineteen mph — a pace they could maintain for twenty-four hours if need be, and there is a tacit truce in force. It is as if opposing forces had decided to cut costs and take the same excursion coach to the battlefield.

Back in France and back on schedule, they now begin ploughing over a hill which, on a lowlier stage, would have been worth at least

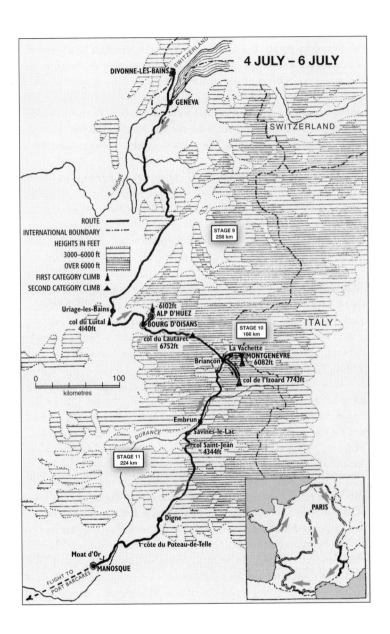

4 JULY – 6 JULY

DIVONNE-LES-BAINS

SWITZERLAND

GENEVA

SWITZERLAND

R. RHÔNE

ROUTE
INTERNATIONAL BOUNDARY
HEIGHTS IN FEET
3000–6000 ft
OVER 6000 ft
FIRST CATEGORY CLIMB
SECOND CATEGORY CLIMB

STAGE 9
258 km

ITALY

Uriage-les-Bains
col du Luital
4140ft

6102ft
ALP D'HUEZ
BOURG D'OISANS
col du Lautaret
6752ft

STAGE 10
166 km

La Vachette
MONTGENÈVRE
6082ft
Briançon
col de l'Izoard 7743ft

0   100
kilometres

Embrun
Savines-le-Lac
col Saint-Jean
4344ft

STAGE 11
224 km

R. DURANCE

Digne
côte du Poteau-de-Telle

Moat d'Or
MANOSQUE

FLIGHT TO PORT BARCARÈS

PARIS

third-category points. But now crossing the summit must be its own reward, and at the same loping pace they spend four hours winding through the passes and valleys of the alpine foothills, here with open views of crags and mountains, there along a narrow corridor of rock, and nearly everywhere with a ribbon of spectators on either side. The sultriness has been washed from the air, but once the sun breaks clear the riders are not disposed to raise a sweat. The Alps are bridges to be crossed when they are reached.

The action begins at the small valley town of Uriage-les-Bains, where just beyond the banner for the Hot Spot sprint — taken by Friday's stage winner, Esclassan — stands the placard announcing the start of the twelve kilometres ascent of the col du Luitel. For a first-category prime it is something of a disappointment, though obviously not to Maertens. It rises for 900 feet to an altitude of 1,300 feet, but over well-made roads with long, gradual transitions at the hairpins. There are no abrupt changes of rhythm. The next half-hour sets off the classic process of selection from the rear as the weaker climbers drop away, but with no corresponding pressures at the front. First to the top is not one of the overall favourites, but Bellini, who is simply after the mountain prize, and Maertens is able to keep in step with the forty leaders. So far, no cause for concern.

If anything, the descent is more worrying. It is a narrow lane overhung by trees and with continual erratic twists and curves. On the way down the front group parts leaving Maertens back with the chasers, and they get back in touch only just in time for the final manoeuvres. These take place over twenty kilometres of *faux plat*, a road that looks flat but is imperceptibly rising towards the base of Alpe d'Huez.

Spurting away from the front in pairs and groups of up to five, hoping to get a footing on the mountain before the others, go most of the Italians and Spaniards, occasionally joined by Zoetemelk, Van Impe, Danguillaume and Poulidor. But each time they are hauled back to be succeeded by another little band of restless spirits. The role of Maertens in all this coming and going is to join the chase — he has no need to lead it — and with the pursuers riding more doggedly than the pursued, the struggle plays itself out. This allows a second group of riders to catch the first, and at Bourg d'Oisans, a little tall-roofed, heavy-eaved town at the foot of Alpe d'Huez, some fifty riders come together to scale the final fourteen kilometres.

For sheer insistent demand on calf muscles and forearms, this is probably the severest climb on the Tour, lifting 1,270 feet in a series of steep ramps to the thin keen air at over 2,050 feet. Each bend has a signpost, counting down from *virage* 20 at the bottom, which tells you the altitude and helpfully points the way to the nearest telephone; each, that is, except *virage* 10, where disturbingly a car-sized section of the parapet is also missing. It is on these slopes that the climbers will set the pace, challenging Maertens to match it, and for most of the non-climbers increasing the pain beyond tolerable limits. The ability to ride quickly uphill is variously explained in terms of build, lightness, lung-capacity, moral fibre, posture on the bike and early environment. In other words there is no acceptable explanation. It's an advantage, of course, to have been brought up among, say, the mountains of northern Spain. But even that glimpse of the obvious becomes obscured when you remember the number of notable climbers that Benelux has produced. All you can say is that the gift for climbing is as distinct as an aptitude for sprinting, and a good deal more durable. If Poulidor were a sprinter he would now be a passenger in the Tour.

The difference tells almost at once. On the first bends Delisle edges away, marked in turn by Van Impe and Pollentier with Zoetemelk and Thévenet following closely behind. But within two kilometres the pattern has been rearranged: Van Impe and Zoetemelk are alone in the lead; Pollentier is at sixteen seconds; and a group formed around Thévenet at half a minute. A slow dissolve to the end of the next kilometre, and we find Pollentier has disappeared from view. The two leaders now have fifty-five seconds on the Thévenet group of thirteen men, which includes Poulidor, Romero (in spite of his surname a Frenchman from the Landes), Galdós, captain of the Kas team, and the two Italians, Bertoglio and Baronchelli. But no sign of Maertens. We have to pan some way downhill to discover him plodding on, losing ground with every turn of the pedals, in company with two equally disappointed men, Pollentier, who has dropped right back after his early effort, and Kuiper who has never managed to get on terms with the leaders or the first group of chasers.

Over the last eleven kilometres the intervals stretch still further. Van Impe continues to set a steady rhythm, stepping lightly on the pedals, while Zoetemelk, sometimes coming up to ride shoulder-to-shoulder with him but often giving way, makes hard work of the climb and has to overcome obvious spells of discomfort. At last they reach the outlying chalets, a row of giant beehives against the sky-line, and with a final wrench they turn into the flat centre of the ski station surrounded by its cafes, boutiques and hotels. Despite his erratic form on the climb, it is Zoetemelk who is able to react with a sudden change of pace at the finish. Accelerating through he makes for the line as if it was the last seat in the lifeboat, and reaches it three seconds ahead of Van Impe. But though he loses the stage, Van Impe still keeps eight seconds clear of Zoetemelk overall, and when 3 min 54 sec have passed, and Maertens is still out of sight, he is brought up to the platform as the new race leader. Only 5 ft 6 in and under nine stone in weight, he steps out from the shadow of the officials, grinning like a boy who has scored the winning goal.

Next to arrive, after breaking away from the chasing group, is Galdós at fifty-eight seconds, then Romero at 1–38 followed by a ragged file of riders stretching back for half an hour. Maertens comes in twenty-second at 4–51, still with Pollentier and Kuiper, to find that Van Impe is already wearing the yellow jersey. In the new order Maertens lies third overall, behind Van Impe and Zoetemelk, and there are five others also placed within two minutes of the leader: Poulidor, Baronchelli, Thévenet, Bertoglio and Galdós. They're all mountain men, though not one of them so far has a stage win to his credit.

Whatever hopes we had for Maertens, commonsense had forewarned us of his defeat, and now we accept that it's irreversible. But even Maertens himself — despite his habit of promising less than he tries to deliver — had expected to postpone it for another day. Last December he and Pollentier came on holiday to Alpe d'Huez, and by the time they had climbed the mountain a score of times, Maertens had conquered his fear of it. But making the ascent after nine days' defence of his yellow jersey, and with Van Impe not Pollentier setting the pace, was a totally different matter. He did not collapse, as some people had predicted he would; in fact he climbed much better than

Van Impe can sprint. But that's irrelevant. In a sprint you don't lose 4–51, even if you come last.

Montgenèvre, 5 July

The Galibier is free of snow, but not of the engineering works which put the pass back into repair for the summer months, so with only a week's warning the Tour has had to find a new route for stage 10. It has done the job well, and pitilessly. The loss of the Galibier means the loss of one of the classic cols together with its familiar stepping stone, the Télégraphe, and the col du Glandon. But the Hautes Alpes has been the Tour's adventure playground since 1905, and between the scheduled start at the village of Bourg d'Oisans below Alpe d'Huez, and the scheduled finish at Montgenèvre there are plenty more familiar grey areas on the map. The main road to Briançon will take the riders over the second-category col du Lautaret after thirty-eight kilometres. Then by making a loop beyond that city, and extending the route from 158 kilometres to 166 kilometres, the stage can replace the Galibier with the equally famous and ferocious col de l'Izoard, a first-category climb introduced in 1922. This is only thirty-four kilometres — via Briançon once more — from the finish which, as yesterday is a ski resort at the top of another first-category ascent.

After some melodramatic rainstorms, the temperature has dropped a good deal, and the early action of the stage is a good deal brisker than we are used to. Each year a special mountain prime, the Souvenir Henri Desgrange, is awarded in honour of the founder of the Tour, and this will now be judged at the summit of the Lautaret. It's worth £250 to the first man across, £150 to the second, and except from tactical necessity, it's not considered good form for the race leaders to compete for it. So, after two kilometres, a Spaniard, Anastasio Graziano, and an Italian, Luciano Conati, draw away on a long, narrow shelf which slopes upward beside a gloomy, dessicated canyon. Graziano drops away, but others come up singly and in pairs until at twenty-four kilometres there is a determined little band of eight men with 2–25 on the *peloton*. There are three team-leaders among them: Kuiper, De Witte and the young French discovery, Michel Laurent,

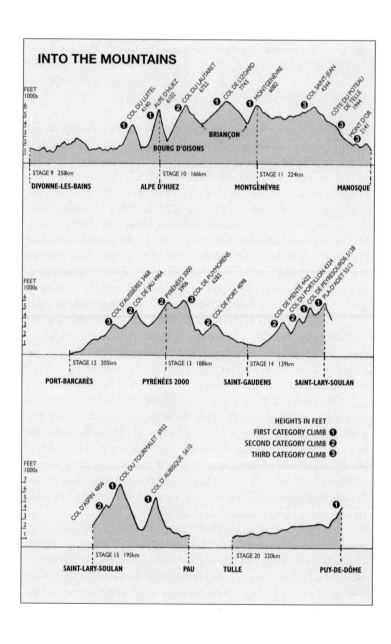

INTO THE MOUNTAINS

FEET
1000s

Col du Luitel 4140
Alpe d'Huez 6102
Col du Lautaret 6752
Col de L'Izoard 7743
Montgenèvre 6082
Col Saint-Jean 4344
Côte du Poteau de Telle 1944
Mont d'Or 2141

BRIANÇON

BOURG D'OISONS

STAGE 9 258km

DIVONNE-LES-BAINS

STAGE 10 166km

ALPE D'HUEZ

STAGE 11 224km

MONTGENÈVRE

MANOSQUE

FEET
1000s

Col d'Aussières 3468
Col de Jau 4964
Pyrénées 2000 5906
Col de Puymorens 6282
Col de Port 4098
Col de Mente 4422
Col du Portillon 4324
Col de Peyresourde 5128
Pla d'Adet 5312

STAGE 12 205km

PORT-BARCARÈS

STAGE 13 188km

PYRÉNÉES 2000

STAGE 14 139km

SAINT-GAUDENS

SAINT-LARY-SOULAN

HEIGHTS IN FEET
FIRST CATEGORY CLIMB ❶
SECOND CATEGORY CLIMB ❷
THIRD CATEGORY CLIMB ❸

FEET
1000s

Col d'Aspin 4856
Col du Tourmalet 6932
Col d'Aubisque 5610

STAGE 15 195km

SAINT-LARY-SOULAN

PAU

TULLE

STAGE 20 220km

PUY-DE-DÔME

whose fanfared victory in the Paris–Nice has been followed by four months of failure for which a neglected attack of hepatitis is now held to blame; he is taking a risk to be riding at all. There is also the Portuguese, José Martins, who lies twelfth overall. The other four are Conati and Grande, both Baronchelli's men, Bourreau, who rides for Thévenet, and Menéndez representing Galdós and the Kas team. It's by no means a negligible attack.

Rising through a Gothic landscape of waterfalls and mountain torrents, black rock and deep shadow where patches of dirty snow still cling, they gain ground and lose only the physically-weakened Laurent. With some justice, since he was in at the start of the break, Conati, a small, long-nosed, solemn man known as Il Pritino, the little priest, wins the Desgrange prime at the summit from Menéndez.

The group now has a 4–20 lead which makes Martins the actual race leader. So the question is whether they should try to press on to the Izoard, ninety-five kilometres ahead, and, if they do, how much rope the others will give them. Their indecision costs Martins his imaginary yellow jersey on the descent, but the *peloton's* faint-heartedness in pursuit returns it to him on the flat. On the first passage through Briançon the seven still have 3–37 in hand, and they extend this to 4–40 before Van Impe decides that enough is enough and begins to stir up the chase. At 115 kilometres they are caught, and fifty riders set out together to scale the Izoard.

If Alpe d'Huez was a rigorous climb, with its mathematical progression of tight corners and steep inclines, the Izoard is far more awesome, a rocky wilderness at 7,741 feet which needs only a few bleached skulls at the roadside to complete its scene of desolation. It begins complacently enough. A hairpin bend takes the riders along the slope of one narrow, V-shaped valley, to be succeeded by another which broadens out on either side of tinroofed Brunissard ski resort, a place which can only look its best under several feet of snow. Then a steep ladder of hairpins rises to the most imposing sight of all, the Casse déserte, a ledge of road cut across a vast incline of small rocks like an arrested landslide. From this rubble jagged pinnacles of brown rock protrude, and on the side of one of these is a plaque to the memory of Fausto Coppi. Subscribed by readers of *L'Équipe*, it bears a bronze relief of the Campionissimo's head looking back along the route of his great solo ride in 1951. Another right-hand bend, a final rack of zig-zag climbs, and the col itself.

The setting calls for the kind of heroic action which most notably Coppi, and most recently Thévenet, provided. Only last year Thévenet, wearing his yellow jersey for the first time on a blazing Bastille Day, crossed the Izoard alone to beat Merckx by over two minutes at Serre-Chevalier. But today the grand gesture is not made on, but after the climb. Five kilometres from the summit there are still twenty-two riders — all the leaders save Maertens — in a compact leading group. On the Casse déserte this splits in two, but at the summit Van Impe is only just ahead of Zoetemelk and ten others.

At this worst imaginable moment, just as they begin the hairy descent, the rain begins to pour down. And only Gian-Battista Baronchelli — the man whom Merckx tipped at the start of the Tour as the greatest threat to Thévenet — takes any pleasure in it. He breaks away leaving his more prudent rivals to navigate the slippery bends at a crawl. Thévenet, who has no haste for this kind of slalom over rough, metalled roads, skids at a corner, falls and injures his right elbow and knee; he regains the others, but on a bike with a bent pedal crank and damaged handlebars. Behind him Bourreau, Romero and Perret also come off.

Baronchelli rushes on, chancing everything on this escape. A tall, silent, unsmiling young man who will not be twenty-three until September, he reveals himself as one of the great Italian downhill riders, for these moments at least, as flamboyant and daring as that elegant absentee, Moser. Coming back into Briançon he has 1–50 in hand on Van Impe's party, and is therefore the day's second and far more credible race leader on the road. By now this farmer's son from the Bergamo district, who dutifully sends home his winnings to be invested in the land, seems certain to have an even bigger contribution to make by the end of the day. At the Hot Spot in La Vachette, with only nine kilometres left to cover, he leads by 1–58, and is still edging away when suddenly, on the last climb to Montgenèvre, the strength drains out of him. It's something that occurs so often after a reckless descent — it did to Merckx last year — that you wonder if it isn't delayed shock.

Baronchelli rides on, but his rhythm has gone and his discomfort is completed by the steady acceleration of Van Impe behind him. At five kilometres from the line he still has fifty-one seconds lead, at four kilometres, thirty-five seconds, but at three kilometres he is caught and at once discarded by his pursuers.

The finish is a near-repeat of yesterday's; the only difference is that when Zoetemelk makes the winning sprint, Thévenet jumps ahead of Van Impe and Galdós. Next come Bertoglio and Poulidor at thirteen seconds, and then only Kuiper and Delisle within the minute. In the space of three kilometres the unfortunate Baronchelli has lost 3–51 on Van Impe, slumping to twelfth overall at five-and-a-half minutes. He has wagered and lost the lot, and the £50 Total petrol prize for combativity is no consolation at all. Yet Maertens, now wearing the green jersey of points leader, loses even more; five minutes down on the day he drops to fourteenth overall at 5–56. He was right after all to fear today's stage more than yesterday's. It has brought the heaviest casualties of all. Seven men, including Schuiten and Manzanèque, arrive in the broom wagon. Seven more are eliminated for finishing outside the time limit. Only 106 riders will set out on tomorrow's flatter stage to Manosque.

In the new line-up, Van Impe leads Zoetemelk by seven seconds; Poulidor is at 1–36, Thévenet at 1–48, Galdós at 2–4, Bertoglio at 2–5 — then a big jump to Pollentier in seventh place at 4–2. So apart from Baronchelli's self-destruction, the Alps have settled nothing but Maertens's hash. The favourites are still tied together by invisible threads. Zoetemelk's challenge has been confined to the last 100 metres, confirming a submissive nature easily satisfied with small success. Thévenet hasn't yet shown he can throw off Poulidor, let alone Van Impe. And Van Impe himself is cautiously saving everything for the final climbs. When you think what happened to Baronchelli, maybe he's wise. But when you judge it against the feats of the past, you must admit that the racing in the Alps has not been equal to the grandeur of its background.

Manosque, 6 July

José-Luis Viejo is not a name that anyone has bothered to conjure with so far in the Tour. He was seventh at Nancy, and has figured in one or two minor breaks, but the proper function of this long-faced, twenty-six-year-old Castillian has been to cater for the needs of the two Super Ser Stars, Ocana and Pedro Torres, and for a time Manzanèque. Not a particularly thankful job when the stars themselves are waning. Viejo might have hoped for better. As an amateur he won the Tour of Poland, came third in the world championship at Mendrisio, and sixth in the Olympic road race in Munich. He is a proficient climber, sprinter and time trialist — a *coureur complet*, if not of the highest rank. But ever since he turned professional in 1973 he has earned his living as a *domestique*, and might well have continued his career being seen but not heard of. Instead this evening at Manosque we are checking through the records to see when a rider last won a stage by as great a margin as Viejo's — 22–50.

The stage began where it ended on the mountain top at Montgenèvre, and stretched away south for 224 kilometres through the departments of the Hautes Alpes and Alpes de Haute Provence. But these names are misleading. There was nothing more to stir the ambition of the climbers than three third-category primes, and it's the climbers who are now in charge of the race. We anticipated little but a steady excursion to the finish at Manosque and the second rest day at Port-Barcarès.

We retraced the end of yesterday's route — with Laurent, a sick man, losing contact even on the drop from Montgenèvre — and travelled through an oppressive landscape of rocks striped like cross-sections in a geology textbook. Pipes the size of brickyard stacks ran down the mountain-sides with no attempt at concealment; red and white pylons marched brazenly down the valley; the Durance was flowing like lava. Since Radio Tour said nothing to take our minds from the scene, the thought of coffee at Embrun, the Nice of the Alps, became irresistible.

All we missed was the start of a puzzling sequence of events. First came a thwarted attack by José Casas of Super Ser, then another by eight men including the unknown warrior, Viejo. At Embrun everything had been tidied up for the Hot Spot sprint, but shortly afterwards the seemingly feckless action started up again. Casas made a second attempt to escape, and although it was quashed within three kilometres, he tried again at sixty-four kilometres, just after the first feed had been picked up at Savines-le-Lac. This time Viejo joined him, but more peculiar still, as soon as the two were clear, Casas dropped back, leaving his team-mate to face 160 kilometres on his own. A pure suicide mission.

It was only afterwards that we found the explanation. So far the Tour had been a disaster for the sponsors of Super Ser. Only Manzanèque had brought them any useful publicity, and even that turned sour when the dope test went against him. Now they had delivered an ultimatum; unless the team put on a show before Manosque it would be withdrawn. Therefore knowing that Ocana and Torres could expect no indulgence from their opponents, Gabriel Saura, the team-manager, detailed Casas and Viejo to do or die this day. The rest was diplomacy. As the bunch rolled along, Ocana explained the team's predicament to Van Impe and the other leaders; and though he may no longer be a contender, he remains a person of influence among them. Casas they would not accept; although 29–32 down overall he could still cause some upset if his escape got out of hand. But they could see no possible harm in Viejo, seventy-seventh overall and 40–28 from the top. If he went off alone they agreed not to make things too difficult for him.

So Viejo was given his freedom, but no more, it seemed, than the freedom of a condemned man to choose his last breakfast. Even if the bunch agreed to slacken its pace, Viejo was still faced, in effect, with a 100-mile time trial. And after getting permission for the attempt, it would be humiliating to crack before the finish. As it proved, there was no risk of that. Viejo is a more accomplished rider than his status in the team suggests. Bounding away, perfectly composed and physically at ease, he steadily increased his distance.

The whole atmosphere of the stage became more relaxed. Beside the lake created by damming the Durance, reporters stopped to photograph each other with the Demoiselles Coiffées, some curiously weathered stacks of earth crowned with boulders. On the col Saint-Jean, at ninety-seven kilometres, a police outrider drew alongside a Press car in which a man was standing with his head through the sun roof; gravely the two of them shook hands as they moved along. And after the col, which Viejo crossed with 12–10 to spare, even the countryside became gentler, more appealing. The race was quietly getting on with its own business and making no demands on anyone but the Spaniard moving along in a world of his own.

From here to Digne and the second feed it was an easy downhill run, and from the lack of radio contact with the bunch it was clear that Viejo was still forging on. Just after the town Félix Lévitan in the lead car tried to set up a running time check with Jacques Goddet who was back with the bunch. Viejo, he announced, was at a poster advertising the Lavender Fair . . . Now! The message seemed to disappear in the air. For an age there was no response. Finally it came. Viejo's lead had stretched to twenty-seven minutes.

Even now he showed no sign of flagging. He climbed the second prime, the côte du Poteau-de-Telle, dancing round the corners among the stunted oaks and pines and the herbal scents of the Provençal countryside. Then at the summit he emerged into fields of lavender, striped in every shade from pale mauve to deep purple, which greeted him like a fanfare. He punctured, which cost him precisely twenty-two seconds as the mechanic from the Super Ser car team changed his front wheel. There was also a little agitation at the rear to sharpen the pursuit. But by this time there was no catching Viejo.

After the first passage through Manosque, the route took in a last third-category climb, the Mont d'Or, on a six kilometre loop back to the finish. Yet by the time Viejo had completed this lap, and crossed the line a second time with his arms lifted in the air, the bunch was still six kilometres from the town. He could stand on the platform and watch them pass through like any other spectator. Karstens was the first man back, after breaking away on the hill. Then shortly after came a sixteen-man sprint in which yesterday's down-and-outs were suddenly found to be up and flourishing again. Maertens won it, and only two places behind him was the man whose larger ambitions had been wrecked in sight of Montgenèvre, Gian-Battista Baronchelli. All the leaders, too, were in that group, protecting their positions in the race. And there matters will rest — as will the riders — until Thursday. A plane to Perpignan, a day by the Mediterranean, and then the Pyrenees. Only one man will miss the trip. Michel Laurent, struggling on alone behind the bunch, had finished over three minutes outside the limit. In tribute to his gallantry, the organisers hadn't eliminated him; they had simply 'invited him to retire'.

10

– Travelling Salesmen –

Out of 440 professional cyclists in full employment on the Continent during the summer of 1976, only 130 took part in the Tour de France. And of thirty-two trade teams in business, only thirteen. Some riders were injured, exhausted or simply fed up. Some failed to make the team; Gan-Mercier, for instance, had to select their ten men from the eighteen they had under contract. Others didn't ride because their leaders wouldn't or couldn't; the withdrawal of the whole Molteni squad with Merckx attracted most comment, but equally without Gimondi there was no Bianchi team, without Moser, no Sanson. The rest of the absentees belonged to teams too poor, too inexperienced or just numerically too small to consider riding the Tour. All of which was perfectly normal. Probably there are fewer than 200 genuine international riders who circulate around the six Western countries that support professional road racing — Holland, Belgium, France, Switzerland, Italy and Spain — and make up the field for the major tours and the classics. They are the hard core, the dozen or so Great Men, and the riders who live for them and off them. But they can't all compete in the same race, so they pick and choose and, when all else is equal, tend to favour their own national events. This is largely for commercial reasons, although sentiment plays a part; to an Italian the prospect of racing on the Belgian cobbles in early April appears as cosy as a wet shirt. Yet for all of them the Tour de France, whether or not they happen to ride it, is the centre and turning point of their season.

Within a week or so of the Tour of Lombardy — the Race of the Falling Leaves — in early October, their season dwindles to a close. During the next four months a few of the riders transfer to the indoor track and perform in the lucrative Six Day races. But most of them sit at home and ignore their bikes (or say they do, like schoolboys swearing that they haven't swotted for an exam) until, around Christmas, comes the time for the almost mandatory winter sports holiday, the so-called *cure d'oxygénation* which tones up the muscles, clears the lungs and, in laxer days, was privately held to get the final dregs of last summer's dope out of the system. Freedom ends in mid-February when, just as the mimosa is beginning to break out, the riders rejoin their teams at training camps along the French and Italian Riviera. For the next five months the team has first call on their services.

Together they build up the road-work, putting, in the invariable jargon, the kilometres into their legs, and getting used once more to the monotonous rhythms of their trade. By the end of the month they are ready for a work-out in the circuit races which are put on by the resorts — Cannes, Monaco, Saint Tropez, Nice — which are thankful of any custom at this time of year. After which the season begins in earnest as they drive north and then cycle back to the Mediterranean in the first major stage race. This is the Paris–Nice, the Race to the Sun (and very often through the snow). It leaves them conveniently placed for the opening classic, the Milan–San Remo.

Their next trip north is more prolonged. It takes in the series of harsh, grey Dutch and Belgian classics — and in France the equally gritty Hell of the North, the Paris–Roubaix — and carries them through to the second half of April and the first of the big national tours. Although it gets a good deal of patriotic support, the Tour of Spain, the Vuelta, is the least attractive to outsiders. Spaniards apart, it's generally the second-grade teams that ride it, although even the Great Men feel they must put in an appearance once or twice in their careers.

The Giro d'Italia, which follows, carries far greater prestige; it is, after all, the theatre in which Fausto Coppi gave many of his best-remembered performances. But because it is as long as the Tour de France, in time and distance, many riders feel that to compete in both will ruin their chances in either. They opt for the shorter Tour of Switzerland, or else for one or both of the important stage races promoted in late May and early June by two French newspapers, *Le Dauphiné Libéré* and *Midi Libre.*

For almost every professional with large ambitions, however, the Tour de France is essential riding. Someone like Merckx, who has proved himself in it, can afford to take the odd sabbatical.

The Italians, too, will sometimes content themselves with a brave showing in their own Tour. But they are the exceptions. The majority see the Tour de France as the ultimate test of their professional abilities. More than pride is involved, of course. A rider's earnings are closely linked to his success in the Tour. And this is not just a matter of his winnings during the race, but in the weeks that follow.

From the moment the Tour ends the riders are released — or at least paroled — by their trade teams. From now until the end of the season, unless they are briefly recalled to take part in the autumn classics, they are free to make an independent living on their bikes. The important men in their lives are no longer the sponsor and the team-manager but the riders' agent and the criterium promoter.

For almost three months, from the end of July to early October, village and small town races — generally criteriums ridden round small road circuits — and roadmen's track meetings are held all over France and the Low Countries. And although they are simply local events, often connected with fêtes and patron saint's days, what the public expect to see at them are the names from the midsummer headlines. A world champion is an attraction, so is the winner of a classic; when Walter Godefroot took the Bordeaux–Paris in May 1976, the two principal agents, Daniel Dousset and Roger Piel, and the general secretary of the Association of Criterium Organisers, were all present at the finish to offer him twenty-five contracts on the spot. But freshest in people's memory, and most in demand, are the heroes of the Tour. Not simply the men who wore the jerseys, but minor stage winners, the Hot Spot sprinters, the climbers and, for sentimental reasons, the *lanterne rouge*.

To the Merckxes and the Poulidors, appearance money at these races can be worth £1,000 a day, even more. In fact post-Tour contracts make such a large contribution to the winner's income that since the war it has become the custom for him to renounce his Tour prize money altogether; he simply distributes it among the members of his team. In this way he can acknowledge their help and bind them closer to his service — knowing that his contracts will more than compensate for his generosity. For lesser riders the contract pickings are a good deal smaller — maybe £100 an appearance — but there are also primes to be won, and a *domestique* can't afford to turn up his nose at any crumbs that fall from the table.

It's hard to know whether the Tour de France is more important as a shop window for the rider's talents or as an endless commercial for his sponsors' products. Television coverage goes out to an estimated 150 million viewers spreading far beyond the French borders. Some newspapers with a puritanical distaste for free advertising refuse to mention the titles of the trade teams, instead referring to them by the surnames of their managers — *l'équipe* Guimard, *l'équipe* Caput and so on. And a student cartoon guyed the whole business with a radio reporter excitedly mouthing: 'Fixo-Flex watch straps have opened up the sprint shoulder to shoulder with Michelin tyres. Already Poulain chocolate and Miko icecreams, feeling the heat, have dropped behind. But now Gitane cigarettes have gone for the line. Will they make it?' But the sponsors must have blushed all the way to the bank. No TV or newspaper camera in 1976 could have photographed Van Impe, for instance, without recording the fact that his bicycle frames (not, in fact, his cigarettes) were made by Gitane and his gears supplied by Campagnolo. The brand names were printed on his chest and back, and embroidered on his shorts. Even the President of the Senate unconsciously added his own endorsement of the products when he helped Van Impe into the final yellow jersey.

This advertising isn't given away. It is often alleged that certain teams with stars who are important to the Tour are given a free ride. But in 1976 it was generally understood that every team had paid a flat entrance fee of £9,000. This covered the hotel expenses for eighteen people: ten riders, three *soigneurs*, two mechanics, one baggage man/driver, the manager and his assistant. It also provided petrol for three team cars, but not the fourth car which most teams found it useful to have with them. Peter Post reckoned that the Raleigh team would spend another £6,000 on petrol, supplementary food, medical and massage supplies, travel to the start and home from the finish. In all about £15,000, a price which only looks good if you think of the Tour as an advertising medium.

Not everyone finds this thought appealing. The commercialism of the Tour has always been a sore point. There's not much objection to the publicity caravan; that's a separate carnival. But people find it undignified that the racing itself should be stamped with trade marks. To meet this criticism national teams were introduced in 1930 and persisted until 1962. But since then the national formula has been used only twice, in 1967 and 1968, and was found to be impractical, open to abuse and highly unpopular with the sponsors.

In the first place there were only nine countries which made the grade, and four of these — West Germany, Switzerland, Luxembourg and Britain — were significantly weaker than the others. The Netherlands could muster one squad of some potential (indeed it provided the winner in 1968), but simply to make up the numbers Italy, Belgium and Spain had to be permitted two teams, and France three. This simply tilted the balance of power still further.

Another embarrassment was the clear evidence of divided loyalties. No rivalries have a sharper edge than those between fellow countrymen. Belgium in particular finds it difficult enough to get a national team together, just once a year, for the national championships; every prima donna wants to pick the members of the chorus. But if patriotism runs pretty thin in professional cycling, the blood brotherhood of the trade team cannot be so easily dissolved overnight by an edict from the Tour de France. If, say, a young Italian was normally employed as *domestique* to one of the leading Belgians he would have to be unusually brave or foolish to cross his master just because the two of them found themselves wearing different jerseys for a month. There is always the suspicion of secret pacts in the Tour, but when there are national teams the unspoken agreements become almost deafening.

Still, the argument that really carried the day, since it had the force of money behind it, came from the trade team sponsors. They protested that as they paid the riders' way through the rest of the season, it was grossly unjust to exclude them from the most highly publicised race of all. The controversy in part reflected the changing nature of the sponsors who had become involved in cycle racing. Before and immediately after World War II it was the cycle industry that supported racing, a sensible investment since the sport dramatised and glamourised its wares. But in the fifties the industry went into a recession (from which it has made a lively recovery in the seventies) and could no longer afford to maintain the professionals in their accustomed style and numbers. They might have lost their livelihood altogether but for an idea usually credited to the Italian, Fiorenzo Magni, a triple winner of the Giro. He suggested that the sport should invite firms outside the cycling trade to use the riders as pedalling sandwich-board-men. A burly, tough, balding man, Magni gave an extra zest to the idea by riding with the word Nivea across his chest. Makers of cars, coffee machines, soft drinks (although hard drinks and cigarettes were banned, at least in France), icecreams and ballpoint pens saw the advertising possibilities, and as *extra-sportif* sponsors they saved the day. But naturally they were particularly jealous of their place in the Tour de France. The cycle industry still got some return from a race between national teams since the riders were pedalling certain makes of bikes and pushing certain brands of gear. But without the trade names splashed across their jerseys there was nothing to connect the riders with BIC pens or Pepsi-Cola. The sponsors won their point.

Not all the *extra-sportif* backers are industrial giants. One of the most enthusiastic is Jean de Gribaldy, an ex-pro rider and self-made businessman who owns a prosperous furniture and domestic appliance store at Besançon. He has two co-sponsors, Miko icecreams and Superia cycles, but he is his own team-manager, and specialises in bringing on his own young discoveries like Michel Laurent and Patrick Perret. Of an annual turnover of £500,000–£600,000 from his business, he spends about a tenth on the running costs of the team, which he treats as a hobby but insists is a valuable asset in promoting his store.

De Gribaldy has twenty-one riders and the remarkable policy of removing any cause for jealousy by paying them all the same basic retainer: £200 a month. This in a sport where the rewards tend to be savagely graded, where the top half dozen are in much the same money bracket as leading jockeys (or racing drivers or tournament golfers) while the bottom two hundred belong with the stable lads. De Gribaldy's payments are not lavish, but they are respectable, especially when you consider that while the riders are with the team they have their hotels and travel expenses met, their equipment and clothing provided. If they make their name they can multiply their earnings many times in the local criteriums at the end of the season.

There is little point in speculating what riders like Merckx and Poulidor earn; nowadays probably more from their investments than their riding. Merckx is on good terms with the Belgian royal family, has a chic wife, the kind of home that's photographed for colour magazines. Poulidor, away from the sweat of racing, leads the life of a prosperous bourgeois. The terms of their contracts are not public property. Those of Joop Zoetemelk, Roy Schuiten and Marc Demeyer are, and provide some point of reference. Zoetemelk, co-leader with Poulidor of the Mercier team, but nominally his lieutenant, has been getting £80,000 a year under his contract, and probably more than doubling that with prizes and moonlighting. Schuiten, when he signed for Lejeune in the autumn of 1975, after winning the Grand Prix des Nations and the world pursuit title but making little impact on professional road racing, accepted £20,000. A little further down the scale, Demeyer is a well-respected professional, a sprinter of some talent, winner of the 1976 Paris–Roubaix; but until Maertens insisted after that victory that Demeyer's salary should be doubled, he was getting only £4,200. (On the riches to riches principle, that was almost precisely the sum that Maertens himself received from a single award at the end of his phenomenal season, the Prestige Pernod, a riders' championship based on the season's results.) At the bottom, where the basic wage comes to less than £2,000 a year, the hopeful summer still tends to be followed by a meagre winter back on the farm.

11

– A Sort of Little God –

Port-Barcarès, 7 July

On the fourteenth day the riders — 106 remain — are resting yet again. Last night they flew by Mercury from Salon-de-Provence to Perpignan, in effect from the Alps to the Pyrenees, and now they are staying in or around Port-Barcarès at the south-western end of the French Mediterranean coast. It is a slightly mysterious place, a younger sister to La Grande Motte. In other words another of those instant fishing villages built for the kind of seaman who buys his jerseys from a boutique in Paris and whose traditional terraced cottage has a patio where he can drink his Suze and Campari-soda before dinner.

I said instant, but that's relative. The resort isn't due to be completed until the year 2000, and its rawness, with undeveloped tracts between the three-star Hotel Lydia-Playa and the rows of cottages at the harbour side, contributes to the feeling that you are nowhere in particular. The Press centre is in a one-storey honeycomb of buildings which house the Centre Nautique Méditerranéen, and it comes as no surprise that the special telephone exchange, despite a lot of expostulation and irritable cranking of handles, can't yet raise Paris. What is Port-Barcarès to Paris, and Paris to them?

Then there's the setting, a level area of shallow lagoons as odd in its way as the Fens or Romney Marsh with Port-Barcarès rising on a tongue of land between the sea and the inland water. To the west the Pyrenees stand out like painted scenery. And blowing across it all is a rough, unsettling wind. The sky is clear again at last, but the *tramontagne* which curses this part of the coast at certain spells is whipping up the surface of the water and making the rigging of the moored dinghies vibrate against their alloy masts with a constant, high-pitched whine.

There are lots of unruly kids around, coming in from their sailing lessons to change in the cubicles alongside the area set aside for al fresco typing. They bang the doors, slap each other with wet towels and look over your shoulder to see what language you're typing in. Eengleesh! But although they fill the place with chatter they don't dispel the impression that Port-Barcarès is, and for some time will remain, out of season.

All of which is no concern of the riders. They poodle around the paths and through the flower beds like schoolboys on their first bicycles. It strikes you that whatever discomfort and disappointment they suffer during the stage is generally forgotten by the following morning. They really love their bicycles and are unhappy, even ungainly, off them. Especially so when they are wearing racing shoes, which have a metal ridge in the sole to slot into the pedal. These shoes are awkward to walk in and force the riders to take mincing, pigeon-toed steps.

Few of the team-leaders, of course, join the promenade around the town. After a steady training ride of forty kilometres to stop their muscles seizing up they rest on their beds, receiving their visitors like pashas, and on demand slip on sandals to go downstairs and hold an informal Press conference in the lounge. A headline in *L'Indépendant* reads portentously, 'At the foot of the Pyrenees four men face their destiny and their future', and none of them will quarrel seriously with that. They simply reshuffle the order according to their view of the next four stages and add one or two potential trouble-makers to the list.

Just as the weather has been paradoxical — blazingly hot in the north and chilly in the south — so has the influence of moving on from plain to mountain. Or rather, the lack of influence. In dramatic terms the Alps were as flat as a *crêpe*. All they did was remove the yellow jersey from Maertens and replace it with the green, which most would regard as his true colour. This has left Van Impe leading the chase from Zoetemelk, but by only seven seconds. And although he has shown willing at last to accept the role, he has done little to protect it. He is under-insured against sudden ambush in the next range of mountains or steady attrition in the forty-eight kilometre time trial on stage 17. The only reason he has got away with it so far is that

Zoetemelk isn't riding forcefully either. It is as if two stage wins and a place at Van Impe's shoulder marks the heights of his expectations.

Poulidor and Thévenet are also within two minutes. Serene and indefatigable, Poulidor, who is nominally Zoetemelk's team-leader, lies third overall at 1–36. Whereas at Nancy he was saying that he would be content to finish in the first ten, now he has revised that to the first five. At a meeting with a group of reporters he is asked pointedly whether he would be willing to sacrifice his own ambitions for Zoetemelk's sake. (A situation in which he faced this decision might arise at any time in the next four days. For instance, Zoetemelk attacks; Van Impe gives chase; and Poulidor finds himself left behind in company with Thévenet. How will Poulidor react? Will he work with Thévenet and risk foiling Zoetemelk's escape, or will he sit back and, to his own cost, let Van Impe get away? Or again, if Zoetemelk has a bad day in the mountains will Poulidor stay back to support him or will he insist on keeping up with the leaders?) Poulidor will not be drawn. He points out that the gap between the two of them is still very small, and for the moment the team is that much stronger for having two leaders. 'It would be a blunder,' he says, 'to save one drowning man by throwing another into the water.'

Fourth at 1–48, Thévenet remains an ambiguous figure in the race. The French reporters, who like him for all that's likeable about him, are finding it difficult to hide their disappointment and impatience with his riding so far. All he can say to them is that he feels his form is gradually improving, and with it his morale. But that doesn't fill many column inches.

Two outsiders are also worth considering. At 2–04 is the Spaniard, Francisco Galdós, a serious man who was intending to enter the Church until he found, as *L'Indépendant* delicately puts it, 'that a certain problem of abstinence was insupportable to him, and that he expressed himself better in cycle races'. The French, accustomed to Spaniards as voluble and opinionated as Ocana, can't quite make him out — 'he is as phlegmatic as the British' — but Poulidor himself thinks he is a man to watch in the Pyrenees. He climbs well. He will be cheered on by the Spanish fans who swarm across the frontier.

And he is still relatively fresh; after an attack of jaundice he had used the Tour of Italy just to ride himself in.

And at 2–05 is an Italian of some substance, Fausto Bertoglio, winner of the 1975 Tour of Italy (when Galdós came second), and third this year behind Gimondi and De Muynck. A record to take seriously, but with a pinch of salt. Bertoglio has the common failing that he submits to events instead of shaping them. And already we have enough leaders facing 'their destiny and their future' with every sign of deep reluctance.

Font-Romeu, 8 July

There was a late change in the Tour programme, overlooked by the travel agents and ourselves, which explains why we were booked last night into Font-Romeu, where today's stage ends, instead of Port-Barcarès, where it starts. We decide not to quarrel with arrangements that have given us an extra morning off, and to wait for the Tour to come to us.

Font-Romeu is an agreeable place to kill time, at first sight a quiet, one-street village, 5,900 feet up, with extravagantly splendid views across the Pyrenees to Spain and a healthy population of Pyrenean mountain dogs as big as Shetland ponies; they obstruct pavements and doorways, though whether from stupidity or dumb insolence is hard to say. But these aren't what the place is famous for. On the outskirts is the pre-Olympic centre where athletes come to finish their altitude training before the summer as well as the winter Games (much good it's done them, but that's beside the point). And on the slopes below is the world's largest experimental solar energy unit — at any rate the largest when the postcards were printed — a kind of Hollywood Bowl constructed out of mirrors. Even in the wilderness you don't get far away from the new toys of French planning and technology.

The finish of the stage is a few miles away: Pyrénées 2000, at the foot of the ski slopes but also, as far as the Tour is concerned, at the head of a second-category mountain climb. Also on the 205 kilometre stage, which rises in a series of jagged terraces from sea level, is the equally stiff col de Jau, preceded by the third-category col d'Aussières.

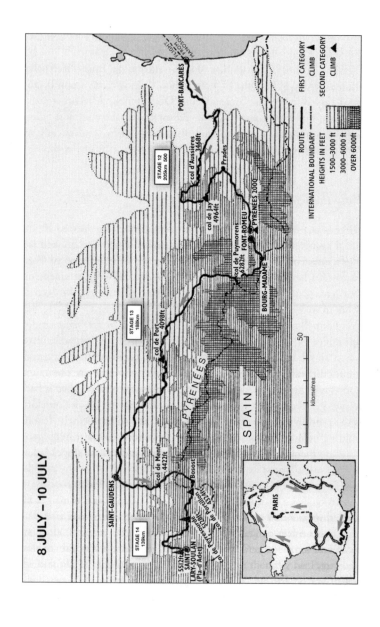

8 JULY – 10 JULY

FLIGHT FROM HANGOULÈME

PORT-BARCARÈS

STAGE 12
205km 900
col d'Aussières 3468ft
Prades

col de Jay 4964ft
PYRENEES 2000
col de Puymorens 6281ft FONT-ROMEU
BOURG-MADAME

STAGE 13
188km
col de Port 4098ft

PYRENEES

SPAIN

SAINT-GAUDENS

col de Menté 4427ft
Bosost

STAGE 14
139km

551?ft
SAINT LARY-SOULAN (Pla-d'Adet)
col de Peyresourde 5128ft
col de Portillon 4446ft

kilometres
0   50

PARIS

ROUTE
INTERNATIONAL BOUNDARY
HEIGHTS IN FEET

FIRST CATEGORY
CLIMB
SECOND CATEGORY
CLIMB

1500–3000 ft
3000–6000 ft
OVER 6000ft

Not a ride of overpowering difficulty, but a proper setting, you'd think, for some sharp guerrilla action. Instead it becomes the scene for something very like farce — a term from which only the winner, Raymond Delisle, is exempted.

In all yesterday's busy bookmaking, nobody had thought to offer odds on Delisle, the man in eighth place overall, 4-17 behind Van Impe. He is one of Thévenet's lieutenants and, at thirty-three, an experienced senior professional, but with no pretensions to be a leader. Yet at the end of a stage which he has won on his own by nearly five minutes, it is Delisle who leads the race by 2-41 from Van Impe and the rest of yesterday's men.

Word of Delisle's getaway has already reached the Press Room — today a row of army marquees — when, for once there is time to walk back down the hill and find out what the spectators see of the Tour; perhaps, too, what they see *in* it. The last 300 metres of the run-in to the finish are bounded by metal barriers leading up to the temporary stands for those who have paid for a view of the line or been invited as guests of honour. But 350 metres back everything is free and unconfined. Conveniently there is a steep earth bank beside the road topped with tussocky grass, scrub and stunted pines. It has attracted several thousand people, but there's still room to move about, even to sit if you avoid the ant-hills.

From the bank you can look across to the mountains, but nobody at present sees further than the stretch of road leading down to a sharp bend. Above it is a banner which says in white letters on red, 500 METRES AU GRAND PRIX DE LA MONTAGNE CHOCOLAT POULAIN (coinciding today with the finish). We're a mixed bunch, but not what you could call a cross-section. Older people, the local working class, in vests and heavy shoes, floral dresses and headscarves. The younger summer visitors, unclassifiable in shorts and tee-shirts and bikini tops. Serious race followers who have cycled here, newspapers folded to the list of riders and their numbers, transistors plugged into their ears. Occasionally they feed out a scrap of laconic information: '*Toujours Delisle*' . . . '*deux minutes vingt-cinq*'. It's like a party — although the main publicity caravan hasn't yet arrived, people are already wearing paper forage caps distributed by *L' Indépendent* —

143

with everyone talkative, good-humoured, determined to be pleased with everything that's offered in the way of entertainment. It is three forty-five. The stage is due to finish just after five. These are notes I made of what happened in the next hour or so:

Two vans from rival publications draw up. Loudspeakers shout in each other's ears. First offers today's *L' Équipe*, gifts, stickers and *casquettes des champions* (racing caps). All for five francs. Second varies this with copy of *Elle* for madame and coloured poster of Raymond Poulidor. Same price. Roadway briefly becomes a Petticoat Lane with vans flogging back numbers of cycling, home-making, fashion and photography magazines (with *casquettes* and *cadeaux*). Always five francs the lot. British Press would be solvent if it could sell its waste paper like this.

Now two motorcyclists of the republican guard on either side of the road cropping back the crowd like hedge-cutters. And the main caravan led by a fleet of yellow Pégasus buses used for transporting the riders on long hops. Beach buggy carrying giant packet of Boule d'Or, '*les cigarettes du Tour de France*'. Eight sexy Boule d'Or girls standing up in the saddle of even sexier white motorbikes. Tee-shirts of the Tour de France. Silly Putty with a lump of mock Silly Putty on the roof. La Mode Chic de Paris — an open limousine decked out with white ribbons like a wedding car with a bride who makes it look as though it's been quite a reception.

Nearly all the vehicles send amplified slogans and music into the air, drowning each other out. Even the Post and Telephone van whose driver croons the jingle, '*O PTT, quotidiennement vôtre*'. (Imagine translating that into English. The little red van. The singing postman. 'O Post Office, yours every day.')

Pelforth beer lorry with a giant bottle on the back. TUC biscuits — another beach buggy with a giant tin biscuit. Why do these people assume that big is beautiful or surprising? TUC biscuits, individually wrapped in cellophane, land among the crowd. Sunaire lunettes — and a shower of special offer leaflets. Idiocy! A child is nearly pushed into the road as the spectators scramble.

This is better. A cottage on wheels from Balamundi wall and floor coverings. You won't see that every day. Best of all the Michelin cavalcade. Bibendum, the tyre-man in racing goggles, riding a motorbike, in the back seat of a vintage open-top, on the back of an old fire engine. In each sweltering fancy dress a thin man seems to be waving for help.

At 4 hr 15 min 40 sec the Longines car with its digital clock. All around people check and adjust their watches, CATCH! insecticide sprays with a giant dead fly on the roof, its legs sticking rigidly upwards. (Giant flies, of course, are another matter.) Perrier, 'the water preferred by *sportifs*'.

The rest is traffic for a while. Cars of TV and radio commentators hurrying to their posts at the finish. Ordinary Press cars. Then a flash from the radio car of ITT-Océanic ('*information dynamique!*'). Delisle has a lead of four minutes and is the actual *maillot jaune*. It must mean that Van Impe is not among the first group of chasers.

4.45. A lull. Business picks up at the icecream van which had drawn up in the crowd.

4.55. Things begin stirring. Motorcycle photographers come through. The helicopter which takes aerial photographs for television over the last thirty kilometres can be heard, but not seen, as it hovers over the lower slopes. More police outriders. As they pass the crowd spills back on the road leaving only a narrow passage.

At last Delisle in sight at the bend, agonising his way uphill, head nodding over the handlebars. People press closer but have the good sense not to push him. Cheering travels forward like a rainstorm across a crowded beach.

Five minutes pass. Radio confirms that Delisle is certain of the yellow jersey. The first Frenchman to wear it in the Tour.

Now Menéndez. And in ones and twos over the next couple of minutes, Panizza, Pronk and Pollentier, Conati. And a straggle of riders. The handsome, unmistakable profile of Ocana near the front. All the leaders following in close formation.

And suddenly, fortuitously, an interruption in the laborious passage upward. The television cameras miss it. So do the paying spectators further on. But right in front of us we see Poulidor put out a hand to ward off De Witte who has strayed too close. De Witte loses momentum. So do those behind. And in slow motion Maertens and Thévenet topple to the ground. Nothing serious since they are grinding uphill. But both have punctured and it takes nearly half a minute for their team cars to reach them.

What we have witnessed, in fact, is the beginning of Thévenet's decline. In any other road race, if a rider crashes in the last kilometre, then provided that he gets up and crosses the line, he is credited with the time of the last man in the group he was with. The Tour is exceptional (even perverse) in not applying this rule on summit finishes. As a result of this trivial delay, which could easily have been retrieved further back along the road with the help of his team, Thévenet has lost another twenty-four seconds on Van Impe — and at a time when, for his own confidence, he needed to be closing the gap, however slightly.

But for that mischance, the manoeuvre by the Peugeot team could be counted a triumph. They now have Delisle in the lead and Thévenet in sixth place to balance Gan-Mercier's double-billing of Zoetemelk (third) and Poulidor (fourth). Each can be used as a decoy for the other, while Van Impe's closest team-mate is Meslet in eighteenth place. And the reason the manoeuvre worked, making temporary nonsense of yesterday's logical predictions, is that the riders subscribe to the same fortune-tellers as the rest of us. When Delisle first got away on the climb of the col de Jau, the men on the accepted list of contenders were more concerned to keep the magic circle intact than to chase the man who was usurping them. Which was exactly what Maurice de Muer, the Peugeot team-manager, had anticipated when he planned Delisle's escape.

It was not a clean break. After taking the lead Delisle was caught by the Spaniard, Menéndez, one of Galdós's troops, before Prades and the start of the final climb. Then the two of them were overtaken by Legeay. His visit was brief, but it was only in the last dozen kilometres that Delisle was able to shake off Menéndez, who was clinging to his rear wheel. (Menéndez had the excuse of loyalty to Galdós for refusing to do any work.) But though Delisle might be having his personal battles he was still gaining time on the rest. And as his lead went beyond two minutes even Zoetemelk was sufficiently concerned to ride up alongside Van Impe and suggest that they should join in a counter-attack.

Van Impe would have none of it. If Zoetemelk and Poulidor were worried then they must lead their own chase. For his part he had a weak team — only Meslet and Martin had managed to keep at his side today — and it was not his business to tow his riders up to Delisle. So nobody made a move. Moreover nobody at the finish feels any need to excuse his inaction. To Merckx, or to Ocana in 1973, it would have been unthinkable to surrender the yellow jersey without a struggle at this stage of the Tour. But to Van Impe it is simply consistent with his strategy of limited war.

The collective wisdom of the Press Room — which has taken a few hard knocks over the past twenty-four hours — is that Delisle's escapade was just a diversion. In itself it was a brave effort — 'Well played' reads the headline of Jacques Goddet's editorial next day — but in terms of the race it is irrelevant. But less irrelevant, perhaps, is the fact that the ages of the two leading Frenchmen in the Tour total seventy-three years.

Saint-Gaudens, 9 JULY

A brief gallop by Poulidor towards the finish, gaining him seven seconds; otherwise none of the leaders has raised his head over the 188 kilometres from Bourg-Madame. With Régis Ovion, a minor matinée idol of French cycling taking the seven-man sprint, stage 13 simply adds a third victory to Peugeot's list of successes and a couple of wistful footnotes to the Tour.

The first concerns the two Rolands, Berland and Smet, until to-day anonymous members of the poor bloody infantry. After the second-category col de Puymorens, where the road was being resurfaced and the tyres began popping like Rice Crispies, and with sixty-one kilometres covered, one Roland followed the other out of the pack. It was Berland's initiative, but Smet already had the same plan in mind. He comes from the region and the previous evening his supporters had phoned to tell him they would be waiting at the top of the second prime, the col de Port. To please them Smet had decided to try and cross it ahead of giants. This wasn't just a sentimental gesture, however. Last year his inconspicuous efforts had brought him only seven contracts for the post-Tour races. A long, well-publicised attack might improve his billing.

Smet took the mountain prime, Berland the Hot Spot after the descent, and the two worked together companionably, relaying each other and increasing their distance (the roadside posters '*Vas-y Roland*' did for both of them). When Smet punctured, Berland waited. With forty-five kilometres to go to the finish, their lead had risen to 4-10, and with a flat road ahead, so had their hopes of reaching Saint-Gaudens ahead of the rest. Berland, who is thirty-one and has never won a stage in the Tour, says afterwards: 'The years pass. The primes and the flowers don't interest me. It's only victory that counts.'

That victory eluded them. Behind them the *peloton* began to pick up speed, and seventeen kilometres from home they were caught. Apart from the prime that each had won on the way, Berland was left with the most aggressive rider's prize of the day, and Smet with the award for the No. 1 escape. 'Why have Flandria been so hard on us?' asks Berland. 'To give Maertens a win, I suppose . . .' Again the fieldmice have been caught in the threshing machine.

The other man who tried and failed was Kuiper. It was his parents' fortieth wedding anniversary and he badly wanted to make them a present of a stage win. He survived the final selection on the run-in to Saint-Gaudens, getting away with six others for the deciding sprint, and then just as he wound up fifty metres from the line he was catapulted to the ground. He thought Tierlinck had nudged him. The television replay showed that almost certainly he had pulled his own front wheel over in his effort. He was half-helped across the finish, but he cannot bear anyone to touch his back. It is hard to believe that he will start again tomorrow.

Saint-Lary-Soulan, 10 JULY

Hennie Kuiper is at the start after all, and looking reasonably well for a man who has scarcely slept. The summons to the line is not for another fifteen minutes, and he is leaning against the Raleigh team car while the morning rations are collected and doled out. But Peter Post, who has already taken Kuiper out for an hour's trial run, says he's not going at all well. We'll see. . . . He breaks off, uncoiling like a spring, because a Press car is about to back into Kuiper's unattended bike (you'd know it anywhere because the taping on the handlebars is trimmed in the rainbow colours of the world championship jersey). Post rescues it and is at once engaged by a Dutch journalist.

There's the usual disorder with pockets of calm and ceremony. On the steps of the announcer's caravan, Goddet and Lévitan are presenting the mayor of Saint-Gaudens, a dark-complexioned, navy-suited man who looks as though he can't wait to get back to the fields, with the *médaille de la reconnaissance* of the Tour. Goddet makes a speech which only the three can hear, but from the gestures looks ex-tremely eloquent. The mayor in return presents the other two with the *médaille d'honneur* of the town and a gift-wrapped parcel.

Because the Tour has been running late the start is put for-ward twenty minutes. The whistle blows, setting off the statutary panic to reach the Press cars. A brief downward stretch, and we are climbing once again into the mountains. This fourteenth stage is — or so we've been promising ourselves — the cherry on the cake, the pint of Guinness at the end of the frog-march. It begins with two second-category primes, the col de Menté (thirty-five kilometres) and col du Portillon (seventy-four kilometres). This quickly dissolves into the first-category col de Peyresourde (ninety-eight kilometres) and at the finish comes another, the uphill slog to the ski resort of Pla-d'Adet. It's not long, only 139 kilometres, but it has a profile like the Needles. Something must come of it.

As we start going up we meet the drizzle coming down and there is cloud spreading like a gorse fire across the tops of the hills. All the same, although mist hides the view as often as not, the Pyrenees seem to me much more attractive than the Alps. They are on a more human scale and less inclined to look like bad oil paint-ings. The trees grow further up the slopes, the roads aren't marvels of civil engineering, nor are the houses consciously built to look picturesque (although they are). Anyway, who's arguing? Particularly since the sun breaks through once more and the day becomes progressively hotter.

There is an early exchange of hostilities, but nothing of consequence to report until the doleful news comes through that Kuiper has fallen again. It's not a crash; he has simply keeled over. The team wait for him, hoping that he can continue, but he has cut the back of his head and is concussed. After some minutes' persuasion he abandons the race and takes an ambulance back to Saint-Gaudens. Unaware of this, the other riders are tackling the col de Menté, a series of short twists and turns, not sinuous alpine curves, leading up to a summit still below the tree-line. Here all the front-runners are recaptured, and it's Van Impe who takes the prime — but no further advantage. Behind, the field is beginning to struggle, with Thévenet one of those in difficulty.

What follows is complicated, as all hard-fought mountain stages are, with the riders constantly changing partners and positions. But in its simplest form this is the sequence of events. On the descent from the col there is a big regrouping as the Tour heads for the eighteen kilometre sector where it will race on Spanish soil. Then a dozen men break away, in two groups of six, mostly Spaniards and Italians, good climbers but not an immediate threat to the leaders. Ocana, too, feels that he must put on some sort of show on his own home territory and sets out in pursuit; he takes four others with him including — of all the people who will surrpise us — the sprinter, Maertens. So at sixty-five kilometres, when the Hot Spot is contested at Bosost on the Spanish side of the Pyrenees, there are sixteen men and 160 seconds between the winner, De Witte, and the group which contains Delisle and all the other leaders.

Meanwhile Van Impe is playing a rather childish but more devious game than you would expect from him. On the way up the col de Menté he has been hanging back in the bunch, rubbing his legs from time to time and calling up his team-mates to help him. This has its effect on Zoetemelk and Poulidor who notice his apparent discomfort and begin talking together. Soon one of Van Impe's team, René Dillen, who has been keeping his ears tuned in the bunch, comes up to warn him that the two Gan-Mercier riders are going to push up the pace and make things hard for him. Which is exactly what Van Impe hoped for. His plan is to make his attack on the final climb to Pla-d'Adet, and it will have more chance of succeeding if his two main opponents have worn themselves out by riding aggressively through the stage.

This is not what Cyrille Guimard, Van Impe's team-manager, expects from him, however. He wants his man to make a frontal attack in the middle of the stage and win back the yellow jersey by minutes, not seconds. When Dillen drops back to the team car for water bottles on the Spanish section, he returns with a message for Van Impe. 'Guimard,' he says in Flemish, 'asks you to attack.' Van Impe whistles through his teeth and says it's mad. Nor does be budge when Ocana strikes away.

Then Raymond Martin arrives with a more emphatic message: 'Guimard says you must attack now.' 'If he wants me to attack,' says Van Impe, 'he must come and tell me himself.' And that is what Guimard does, driving up the narrow road beside the *peloton*, klaxon going, to deliver his ultimatum. It was that moment, or never, to win the Tour. Van Impe still has no faith in the move, but reluctantly he obeys. He attacks on the climb to the Portillon, and at the second attempt gets clear away with roughly seventy kilometres covered and still the same distance to go.

The curious factor in the relationship between rider and manager is that Guimard — one-time leader in the Tour and even now, in spite of his administrative job, cyclo-cross champion of France — is three months younger than Van Impe. Of a contrasting temperament, far more bustling and decisive, and of a different nationality, Guimard seems to have an impatient liking for his rider, but far more respect for his talent as a rider than for his attitude towards racing.

The following week Guimard is interviewed in *L'Équipe* and describes his task as making Van Impe do what he has never dared to do before. 'He is a boy who makes sure of everything, who never takes risks. And it must be said that there are others like him in the *peloton*, some of the big men among them. Above all he's a big schoolboy who has never taken initiatives or accepted responsibilities. . . . He likes life, for it has been very kind to him. In fact he behaves in the *peloton* as in life, like a child. You have to understand that in Belgium the cyclist, especially if he is a champion, is a sort of little god to whom everything is allowed.'

The yellow jersey has made Van Impe more aware of his obligations to his team, 'but where tactical initiatives are concerned, let us say that his behaviour is still a bit evasive. I don't think he understands racing particularly well, mainly because he has never tried to understand it.

'To improve on his previous level he has had to accept that he must give more of himself. He is afraid of collapsing, and dreads a prolonged effort. When I ask him to attack on the Portillon, I was forcing him to go against his nature. Then he discovered that the effort was not beyond his strength, he was capable of doing things he hadn't done before.'

Having accepted his orders and made his move, Van Impe does so wholeheartedly. He goes off like a train chasing its runaway coaches, and those who have simply been passengers are left standing. By now Ocana, who was sixth over the Portillon as the forward group began to shed its weaker members, has reached the front. Van Impe is still 4–20 down and the *peloton* at 5–50.

By the foot of the next climb, the Peyresourde, Van Impe has further closed the gap. To freeze the fluid situation once again at eighty-five kilometres, and give some idea of the fragmentation of the stage, Ocana is in a group of eleven (still including the dogged Maertens) in the lead; at fifty-five seconds are Talbourdet and Menéndez; at 1–20 Martinez; at 1–45 Maingon; at 3–45 Van Impe and Conati; at 4–10 Lasa; at 4–25 Bourreau; and at 5–55 what remains of the *peloton*. This contains Delisle, Zoetemelk, Poulidor and Thévenet but is now down to twenty-one members. So this still accounts for only forty of the ninety-eight riders who set out from Saint-Gaudens. Two more (Cigana and Casas) have abandoned, apart from Kuiper, which means that somewhere back along the road are fifty-five dusty, sweaty riders trying to cling somehow to the coat-tails of the race.

On the Peyresourde, a vast figure-Z tacking back and forward across the face of a green hill, the leading eleven break up and Van Impe, in a majestic show of strength, overtakes them and the intervening riders, and discards them one by one. At three kilometres from the summit he is at the head and in control with only Ocana and Riccomi for companions. With appropriate generosity he allows Ocana, the animator of the stage, to take the prime. Then the three of them (Riccomi is dropped but gets back when Van Impe punctures) set off on the long, flat bridging passage which leads to the foot of the finishing climb.

Meanwhile, back at the bunch things are also stirring. Shortly after Van Impe had finally submitted to his orders, Zoetemelk received a similar command to attack from his manager, Maurice de Muer. 'It is too soon, much too soon,' he said, and sat tight. That was his fatal error, but on the Peyresourde he does his best to repair it. He leaves the *peloton*, dropping Delisle and Pollentier, the two men who try to fasten onto him, and producing a climb which is — but too late, much too late — as notable as Van Impe's. He crosses the summit in eighth place only 2–25 down on Ocana and Van Impe, having cut his losses by three and a half minutes, and continues the pursuit along the valley in a group of seven which has Maertens as its driving force.

On the cliff-hanging ledges leading up to the Pla-d'Adet, where the crowds are massed among the chalets and ski-lifts, Van Impe and Zoetemelk both '*dynamite*' their little groups and take up their personal duel, though never within sight of one another. Van Impe soars ahead, undoing his toe-straps as he crosses the line, with no hint that he has exceeded his powers or done any more than he expected to do. He has already put on the yellow jersey when Zoetemelk arrives in second place after another 3 mins 12 secs have passed. After him, at decent intervals, come Riccomi, Ocana, Torres, Pessarodona, Maertens and the rest, leading a dishevelled procession that takes precisely 46 min 23 sec to reach its conclusion.

What the Tour has done today is play a colossal game of snakes and ladders in the Pyrenees. Up the ladder, three rungs at a time, goes Van Impe, who now leads overall by 3–18 and must surely win the race if he keeps out of trouble. Zoetemelk, failing with the last dice, lies second with only two mountain stages and one uphill finish, the Puy-de-Dôme, on which to exercise his special talents.

Up, too, at least in everyone's estimation, goes Luis Ocana with fourth place and the prize for the No. 1 escape of the day. Super Ser once again have something to publicise. Also Maertens, back to eighth overall after beating a dozen celebrated climbers. He has no chance of winning this Tour, but in future he can't be dismissed as a sprinter who will drop out of sight at the first hump-backed bridge.

Down the snakes, by more than twelve minutes, go Delisle, race leader for only two days, and Poulidor, still fifth overall but scarcely within hailing distance at 11–42. Thévenet, who has lost 13–15, is practically off the board.

The final scene is enacted in an office off the Press Room in the ski school where the international jury — a Belgian, an Italian and a Spaniard — sit to settle a perplexing problem. If any is needed, the last convincing testimony to the strength of Van Impe's effort is that only fifty-two of the riders have finished within the time limit. The latitude they were allowed, given an average speed for the stage of 31.974 kph, was ten per cent of Van Impe's time. And that — after a little by-play with slide rule and scrap paper — works out at, give or take, twenty-eight minutes.

Well, that's perfectly clear. The figures can't be challenged. But can the Tour afford to face the last eight days' racing with a pitiful field of fifty-two? With riders demoralised, and some teams reduced to two or three men, probably no more than forty would reach Paris. So as a compromise the organisers want to draw the line between those who finished up to forty minutes late, and the nine riders who came in six minutes later. And that's what the argument in the jury room is about. Five of those nine are Raleigh men who stayed behind with their fallen leader (the bulletin on Kuiper is that he has cuts and concussion, but no fracture, and will probably be released from hospital after forty-eight hours) and were unable to regain contact with the race. All things considered they did well to finish the stage at all, but only Pronk has beaten the amended deadline. Peter Post, a QC among dressing room lawyers after his years as head man of the Six Day races, pleads their special case. He threatens to withdraw his team if it amounts only to Pronk. He bangs the table and is asked to leave. But he prevails; ninety-five riders live to pedal another day.

12

– A Diamond Frame with
Titanium Lugs –

Cyclists are far from indifferent to what they ride. I have seen Ocana throw his bike to the ground in a rage like a golfer with a putter that (he thinks) has let him down. Merckx is another man who's as restless in the saddle as a princess with a pea beneath her mattress; he may change his bike half a dozen times in the course of a stage until everything from the fit of the pedal clips to the smoothness of the brakes is just so. And at the start and finish of a race you will see the real buffs counting the teeth on a sprocket or the spokes in a wheel to try and discover the secret of success. All the same, cycle racing shows nothing to compare with motor sport's devouring interest in the car, and for very obvious reasons. A fast car is a fast car whoever is at the wheel, which isn't to deny the driver's contribution. But on a bike the cyclist is both the driver and the engine. Take him away and what's left is no more (though admittedly no less) significant than the chassis, gears and wheels of a motor-less motor car.

It is *the* bicycle, not any particular bicycle, which is the marvel. As simple, and as beautiful in its simplicity, as a gyroscope. Practically a laboratory model for illustrating certain laws of movement. And for that reason it has gone for ninety years without being plunged into any of these design revolutions which periodically affect the racing car.

Until the mid-1880s the bicycle makers pursued each other down the blind alley of the Ordinary or penny-farthing. This was more absurd in appearance than in concept. The pedal cranks were attached directly to the front axle — the farthing was just there for balance — which meant that one complete turn of the pedal equalled one complete turn of the wheel. It also followed that the bigger you made the front wheel the further and faster you went as you pedalled. On an Ordinary in 1882 an Englishman, H. L. Cortis, became the first cyclist to cover twenty miles in an hour. But the machine was cumbersome and precarious (the higher you were the harder you fell), exposed to every gust of wind and finally limited in its possibilities by a single uncontrollable factor: the length of the rider's leg.

Then between 1885 and 1888 nearly a century of fanciful experiment with hobbyhorses and boneshakers, tricycles and quadricycles, treadles and hand-operated ratchets fell into place when John Kemp Starley's Rover safety bicycle came on the market in a series of rapidly improved versions. With two wheels of almost the same size at either end of a diamond-shaped frame, and with a chain drive from centrally-positioned pedals to the rear wheel, the Rover settled the future shape of the bicycle right up to the present day. The Moulton small-wheel bike of 1963 has been the only serious challenger; but though you might ride it up to the shops you wouldn't choose to race it over the Tourmalet.

Since then successors to the safety have been considerably lightened (the first Rover racer weighed thirty-three pounds). They have also been made vastly more efficient. From 1888 pneumatic tyres began to replace solid rubber. Variable gears (which date back to 1889), freewheels and cable brakes have been introduced. The angles of the diamond, too, have been adjusted. But during this gradual evolution, in essence Starley's design has never been improved upon.

Even the refinements have tended to become more marginal. Above a certain level of quality, the difference in performance between makes of bike (which in effect means makes of frame) resides mainly in the wishful thinking of the advertisers. It is not a detectable factor in the racing. If an established rider transfers between, say, Mercier, Raleigh, Gitane, Flandria, Peugeot or Lejeune, it will not be in order to ride one bike rather than another. What will weigh with him are the terms of his contract, his status in the team and his relations with the team-manager. His new machines will be built to his specifications and to a standard almost indistinguishable from his rivals'. So much he can take for granted. He is in a very different position from the racing driver who, for purely technical reasons, will find his prospects transformed by switching from one car maker to another.

At this point, although I don't take back a word I've said, I must admit that the family resemblance is pretty slim between any of the bikes in Merckx's stable and the conventional black Raleigh with North Road handlebars and without even three-speed which was the best present of my life. Not the least difference is the price. Mine, if I remember, cost just under £20. Even if you could buy the love and labour that went into assembling one of Merckx's machines, which you can't, it would not come to less than £500. And you would have to pay almost as much for any bike ridden by one of the favourites in the Tour de France.

A racing bike is stripped down to essentials. (A cherished story from the Tour of Britain is of the mayoress who heard that the race would pass her house next morning. 'Don't forget,' she told the riders, 'to all ring your bells as you go by.') Yet when an American trade magazine published a feature on the bike which Thévenet rode to win the 1975 Tour it ran to ten pages and dealt with contributions made by fourteen different manufacturers.

Often the sponsor's livery and transfers will cover a frame made by a craftsman outside the company, but Thévenet's Peugeot was 'practically a stock PY 10 . . . that anyone can buy for a current US retail of $725'. After that there came separate credits for brakes and brake levers (Mafac), chains (Sedis), crank and chainwheel set and headset (Stronglight), *dérailleurs* (Simplex), freewheel (Maillard), handlebars and stem (Atax), lugs (Nervex), rim tape (Velox), rims (Pellet), saddle (Tron & Berthet), toe clips, straps and pump (Poutrait-Morin), and tools (Var). Even that list omitted such items as pedals, spokes, tubulars and *bidon* holder.

The frame is the starting point since its size and its angle provide the essential balance; if they are wrong the rider will find his position contorted and the bike unsafe as he corners or throws it around in the sprint. It is tailored like a suit, beginning with the inside-leg measurement and working through the other dimensions of limb and trunk and body weight as well as the rider's normal position in the saddle (a good frame-maker works from action pictures as well as a set of figures). The frame is also an area where a good deal of weight can be saved. This is done by further hollowing out the tubes, by intricate fretwork on the lugs which hold them together at the corners, and by using basic materials like aluminium and titanium. In every case, though, there's a complicated equation with lightness on one side and strength and rigidity on the other, and the very lightest bike is kept only for the short, critical efforts of the time trial on the flat. Van Impe, for instance, had five machines at his disposal during the 1976 Tour. Two of them weighed nine kilogrammes (19.84 lbs); two with thinner tubing were eight kilogrammes (17.64 lbs) and were the bikes he generally rode; and the fifth had been built specially for the time trial in Paris. This had carbon fibre tubes and titanium lugs and the frame weight of only 1.200 kilogrammes (2.64 lbs) brought the total weight of the bicycle down to seven kilogrammes (15.43 lbs). In fact Willy Tierlinck, acting as a guinea-pig, rode an identical model on the hilly time trial between Fleurance and Auch, and was impressed by it, but Van Impe decided not to risk it on the Champs-Élysées.

Van Impe's wheels had twenty-eight spokes compared with the conventional thirty-six (or thirty-two front, forty rear which used to be the British practice), and these would have been drawn to narrow the gauge in the centre. In fact his bike, like everyone else's, was an anthology of all the standard weight-reducing methods: alloy wheel rims, chainsets and handlebars, tape instead of chunky handlebar grips, hubs and chainwheel cut to a delicate tracery, flimsy 'rat-trap' pedals, brake levers bored out like a slice of gruyère, narrow streamlined saddle of fine leather over latex foam. And, of course, no mudguards — or bells.

By closing up the space which the mudguard would have occupied and making the angle of the seat tube steeper, the frame and therefore the wheelbase of a racing bike is shortened. This, for once, has nothing to do with weight. It simply makes the machine livelier to handle and quicker to corner.

Tubular tyres *are* chosen for their lightness. They usually weigh only six to nine ounces and in cross-section are narrower than the conventional tyre with its separate outer cover and inner tube, and are slightly oval in cross-section. They are made up of two complete layers and one half-layer. Working outward, the first is a very thin rubber inner tube. This is completely encased in a flimsy sleeve of silk or cotton which has the valve from the inner tube poking through it. On the inside, where it rests against the rim of the wheel, this fabric cover is left bare. But on the outside, where it runs along the road, it is protected by the semi-layer of rubber which provides the tread.

Unlike the tyre on an everyday bike, the tubular has no wire stiffening to keep it in place. Instead it is held in the rim — which on a racing bike is a good deal shallower — by a coat of rubber cemeht. It's not a flawless system. A badly glued tubular may roll out, though this seems to happen more often on a cambered track than on the road. And the lighter the tubular (which may be nothing more than a three to four ounce circular puff of air), the more liable it is to puncture. All the same, these are inconveniences, or sometimes worse, that riders willingly accept for the sake of a wheel which has less weight to drag around and therefore helps them to go faster.

By far the most sophisticated aid on a racing bike, however, is the *dérailleur* gear. We'll take it slowly from the top. As a cyclist rides along his power is transmitted by a continuous chain which runs between the chain wheel attached to his pedals and a sprocket attached to the hub of his rear wheel. So far, so obvious. It then follows that how far he will travel with each turn of the pedals must depend on the number of teeth on both the chain wheel and the rear sprocket. Say that there are forty-four teeth on the chain wheel and twenty-two on the sprocket. In that case the rear wheel will go round twice for every complete revolution of the pedals. In Britain we have a formula to express this which relates back to the gearing of a penny-farthing, and is decidedly quaint of us. On the Continent it's given simply as 44×22 (i.e. chain wheel first).

That particular ratio may suit some purposes, but it is too high for the very hardest climbing and far too low either for sprinting or time trialling. Fortunately the *dérailleur* solves the problem. When it is used, instead of the single gear sprocket of the ordinary utility bike, five or six sprockets of graded size are mounted side by side in a block on the rear hub. What the *dérailleur* does — when the rider moves a small lever on the down-tube (the front, sloping tube) or at the end of his handlebars — is literally to derail the chain, lifting it from one sprocket and transferring it to another. So now the rider gets the choice of six different gear ratios.

He can, and invariably does, go further. He can fit a double chain wheel, with one ring bigger than the other, and another *dérailleur* mechanism to move the chain backward and forward between them. He can now take his pick from twelve different ratios, which ought to satisfy anyone. But it doesn't, at least from one day to the next. But there's nothing to stop the rider, or rather his mechanic, fitting a different variation of back sprockets for a mountain stage and a flat stage. He's only in trouble when a piece of grit gets into the mechanism and he finds he can't get into his chosen gear.

On the first mountain stage of 1976, finishing at Alpe d'Huez, Zoetemelk and Poulidor used a double chain wheel of 42–53 and six rear sprockets of from thirteen to twenty-three teeth. Van Impe and Romero, on the other hand, had chain wheels of 44–52, and when Romero made his attack to chase the leaders he used a ratio of 44 × 21, or 44 × 19 in the harder sections. I'm not suggesting that I counted the teeth as I passed; this information was contained in an advertisement by Maillard, maker of the most fashionable freewheel in the Tour. (Freewheels are compulsory; if a fixed rear wheel were used the pedals might touch the ground in cornering and cause dreadful carnage.) Nor do I think that in themselves the gear ratios are of any interest except to a specialist. But to the kind of person who just rides a bike to get somewhere, it might come as a surprise that cycling can even be considered in these terms.

In fact the racing bike, for all that it has retained the basic simplicity of Starley's design, is an instrument of high refinement: a single lens reflex compared with the box cameras most of us grew up with. For all that its chief fascination remains, that it's the only form of transport with an engine that can think for itself, act on impulse, show courage and alarm and suffer from loss of morale.

13

– Thévenet will not Climb the Puy-de-Dôme –

Pau, II JULY

Tomorrow starts a five-day meander through the provinces of Aquit-aine and Limousin ending at the summit of the Puy-de-Dôme. Then a train journey to Montargis, the brief stage to Versailles, and the last laps on the Champs-Élysées until the clockwork finally runs down. In principle it can be argued (and in print it invariably is) that these last days might very well see a daring escape on the flat, a prodigious ride in one of the two remaining time trials, or a combination of one man's physical resurgence with another's breakdown on the Puy throwing the whole race into disorder. In private we know that these things rarely happen, that the level roads of south-west France will probably deliver the race back to the sprinters, that the seconds won and lost in the time trial won't count for all that much, and that Van Impe and Zoetemelk will be matched like twins on the finishing climb. The reporters would love a great *bouleversement,* the cart on its side, the apples spilling in all directions. But that requires more than strength and ability on some rider's part. It needs a stubborn, impatient, destructive will. Merckx has it, Ocana used to have it, Thévenet displayed it once last year, on the 14th of July. Today, on the last stage in the Pyrenees, there was little sign of it, more a spirit of resignation.

Most of the riders came down by cable-car from Pla-d'Adet to begin the stage from the square at Saint-Lary-Soulan. It was warm but damp, and some of the riders were putting newspapers under the front of their jerseys as a protection against the cold of the descents. Today's section of the Pyrenees are famous for their mist and drizzle. An Italian paper, meant to be read not worn, was shown to Maertens and translated to see how he would react; in it Bergamo accused him of behaving like a bandit in the sprint. Maertens offered no quotes; he simply put his right hand on his left elbow, and brought his left forearm up with the fist clenched. The Italians needed no interpreter for that.

The middle portion of the 195 kilometre stage was slung like a hammock between two of the classic cols, the Tourmalet and the Aubisque. The non-climbers could see no joy in it, but neither could the climbers see any gain, for the last seventy-five kilometres were a long descent to the flat and a finish which was no more than hilly. With small expectations they slowly approached the first obstacle, the second-category col d'Aspin at twenty-four kilometres, and with no perceptible change of pace, began climbing it like a column of coloured soldier ants.

One pleasure of the race is that on any day you can look out of the car window and see the makings of a photograph by Cartier-Bresson: a wedding procession walking back from the church between the banks of Tour spectators; a flock of nuns beneath a banner which says, 'Poulidor, you are the strongest'; four generations of one family sitting on kitchen chairs in a doorway. Today's picture was of a woman in her eighties, dressed in dark blue overall, black stockings and black headscarf, lying on her side in a high field on the Aspin and watching the approach of the riders through high-powered binoculars. They came by her in tight formation, and it told its own story that the man who won the mountain prime was the Raleigh sprinter, Karstens.

The Tourmalet, however, is not a climb that anyone can take in his stride. It is gaunt and grey (as the sky was, too, today), a seventeen kilometre drag to almost 7,000 feet across what might just as well be the face of a quarry. Even if nobody tried to make the crossing any harder by attacking, the simple difference between the pace of the born climbers and the rest was bound to leave behind a trail of discarded riders. Even at the first count their number included Thévenet, who appears to have no heart for the race any longer.

In fact there was an attack of sorts, by Galdós, immediately marked by Van Impe, the two men crossing the summit together forty seconds ahead of the next man. But they didn't persist, and on the flat before the Aubisque they allowed a group of forty men to form around them, and with equal indulgence let eight of these escape. They included some familiar names but none with a sinister ring — Bellini, runner-up in the Mountain Grand Prix, Ovion, the winner at Saint-Gaudens, Sibille, the French national champion, and the little Polish-Italian sprinter, Wladimiro Panizza, who lay fourth on the points table.

The Aubisque is eighteen kilometres long, rising first to the col du Soulor — last year a first-category prime in its own right — then after a shallow dip, lifting once more along a moorland road with precipitous edges to 5,900 feet. It was on this second section, as rain began to drive across the bare mountain, that Panizza left his little group, greatly increasing his seven second lead at the summit by a recklessly fast descent, and at Laruns, eighteen kilometres on, took one and a half minutes out of the chasers. The other seven were caught, but Panizza covered the last seventy-five kilometres to Pau alone, winning on the motor racing track beneath the Casino by over two minutes.

Van Impe, who arrived in the same group as Zoetemelk, Poulidor and Delisle, could regard Panizza's rise from sixteenth to twelfth overall with a certain complaisance. He had got out of the Pyrenees with the shirt still on his back. But why was it only Galdós who gave him any concern at all? Thévenet, thoroughly demoralised, lost over thirteen minutes on the day; the ex-champion can only just hold on to the ropes, and looks as though he would like to sleep for a month. Poulidor has never been a man to take risks, and it would be absurd to expect him to start to do so at forty. But Zoetemelk, who has said that he did not enter the Tour just to take second place again, and who reproached himself for his prevarication yesterday, why did he let another chance slip today? The Dutch journalists go to his hotel and put the question to him directly. They and their readers have little patience left. The reason, he says, is that he has a boil which not only prevented him attacking, but may even prevent him reaching Paris. They make sceptical noises, so he pulls down his track suit trousers, and there on the inside of his thigh is a boil the size of an egg. That is evidence they have to accept.

Unlike most athletes, cyclists rarely suffer from pulled muscles or strained tendons; this is because, unless they fall, there is nothing to wrench or jerk them out of the rhythm of their movements. But there are two ailments to which they are particularly prone. One is what they all-embracingly call bronchitis, by which they mean any inflammation short of pneumonia. This is due to sudden changes of temperature on a sweat-soaked body: the heat of climbing followed by the chill of cutting through the air on the way down. It's to protect themselves against these changes that, even on the hottest day, they wear woollen vests and jerseys instead of the silk which, for aerodynamic reasons, they adopt in time trials.

The other, and less romantic complaint, is boils in the area of the seat and groin. To prevent their shorts chafing they smear lanolin onto a chamois gusset in the crutch of their racing shorts. This is sensible enough, but this cream also attracts grit and dust from the road which can work into the open pores of their skin. Although most of them scrupulously wash themselves in these areas with surgical spirit, or their *soigneur* does it for them, inevitably at some time some dirt penetrates and causes boils. Even the most carefully protected riders, like Merckx himself, are laid low with the complaint. It is painful, debilitating and tiring, not least because it makes the rider sit awkwardly in the saddle (sometimes they wear steaks inside their shorts to ease the discomfort). Almost certainly Zoetemelk's trouble will stop him giving any to Van Impe.

Two items in the legal small print at the end of the day. Bernard Labourdette, a random choice for the dope test, has been caught attempting that old trick, substituting someone else's sample of urine for his own. It's not only taken as proof of guilt, but more heavily punished than a positive analysis. He receives a fine of 5,000 Swiss francs (getting on for £1,000), demotion to last place on the stage, and a ten-minute penalty on general classification. In addition four riders — Thévenet's man, Molineris, the two Flandria riders, Van Springel and Tabak, and the Italian, Bellet — are disqualified for accepting an excessive number of pushes from spectators on the climbs. After ten pushes the commissaires stopped counting.

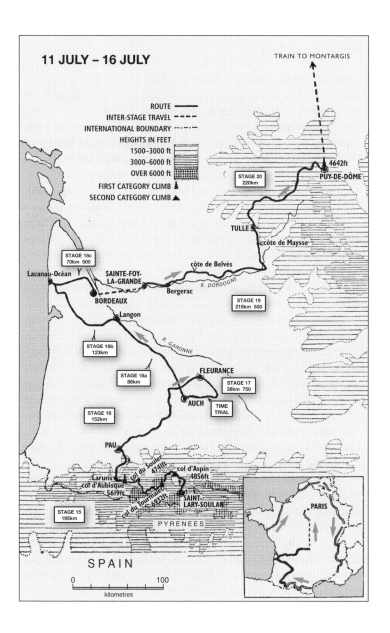

11 JULY – 16 JULY

TRAIN TO MONTARGIS

ROUTE
INTER-STAGE TRAVEL
INTERNATIONAL BOUNDARY
HEIGHTS IN FEET
1500–3000 ft
3000–6000 ft
OVER 6000 ft
FIRST CATEGORY CLIMB
SECOND CATEGORY CLIMB

4642ft
PUY-DE-DÔME

STAGE 20
220km

TULLE

côte de Maysse

côte de Belvès

STAGE 18c
70km 500

Lacanau-Océan

SAINTE-FOY-
LA-GRANDE

Bergerac

R. DORDOGNE

BORDEAUX

STAGE 19
218km 500

Langon

R. GARONNE

STAGE 18b
123km

STAGE 18a
86km

FLEURANCE

STAGE 17
38km 750

AUCH

TIME
TRIAL

STAGE 16
152km

PAU

col du Soulor
4741ft

col d'Aspin
4856ft

Laruns
col d'Aubisque
5619ft

col du Tourmalet
6932ft

SAINT-
LARY-SOULAN

STAGE 15
195km

PYRENEES

SPAIN

PARIS

0   100
kilometres

Fleurance, 12 July

A ride of 152 kilometres through a rolling garden of Indian corn, small patches of wheat, green vegetables and plots of sunflowers. It's an area where, as the roadside notices remind us, eating and drinking aren't exactly out of favour. There is one splendid series: Foi Gras: Jambon du Pays: Confits: Confitures: Armagnac: Fruits à l'Armagnac. Bringing up the rear in sorry anticlimax is 'Ravitaillement TUC à 12km', which is a different *musette* of sandwiches altogether.

The incidents of the stage won't detain us long. The optimistic Bellini nips ahead to pick up the top points at each of the two fourth-category hill primes along the route; provided that Van Impe is prepared to waive his interest in the mountain jersey, now that he has a lien on the yellow, there are enough small primes before Paris to allow a vigilant Bellini to snatch the crown of King of the Mountains for himself. In fact he is one of the few riders who continue to have a daily purpose in life.

Otherwise the flock moves gently on, shepherded by the Flandria team, to the finish at Fleurance. This centre of the great natural gourmet larder of the south-west is a rosy, overgrown village with high ambitions, headquarters of the National Group for the Defence of Nature and exporters of fine potted pâtés, canned *cassoulets* and *canard sauvage aux olives,* and herbal cosmetics to the best-kept tables and dressing-tables of Europe. As part of its programme of self-promotion it has made a successful bid to be selected as the starting point for next year's Tour, and it has organised the finish of the stage with a suitable concern for the money it is laying out.

An entrance fee of one pound has been charged to a five kilometre circuit of roads which run through its industrial garden suburb, in return for which the spectators are able to watch the riders pass three times. What they see is Roger Legeay unjustly robbed of victory, and Michel Pollentier unexpectedly rewarded for his loyalty to Maertens. Flandria harrass every would-be escaper until, at the approach to the circuit, Legeay gets away with Pollentier in his slipstream. Legeay has his head down over the handlebars; Pollentier sitting up is constantly looking back over his shoulders to see whether Maertens is coming up for the kill. At the first crossing of the line they have twelve seconds lead, and are increasing their distance when suddenly Legeay punctures and falls. Pollentier's work for Maertens has been beyond reproach so far, but there is nothing in the code of chivalry to say that he must pass up an opportunity like this. He heads for home, while Flandria switch to blocking the pursuit as best they can, and wins the stage by ten seconds. Maertens simply demonstrates what might have been by leading the bunch in behind him.

Auch, 13 JULY

The 38.75 kilometre time trial between Fleurance and Auch, a hilly rural ride with one severe climb towards the finish, was critical last year. Merckx won it, but by only nine seconds from Thévenet who, for the first time, declared himself as the rider who would dog the leader to the end of the race. This year the trial comes later in the Tour, and too much has been already decided. The winner is Ferdinand Bracke, and when the announcement is made the tears stream down his pointed face which, with its mat of grey hair and its furrow around the mouth, might belong to a garden gnome. He is thirty-seven, and his best days, when he took the world pursuit title on the track, are long past. He has not won a stage in the Tour since 1967. But it isn't so much the nine years' wait to win again that brings the tears, it is the two and a half hours to kill at the finish while seventy-seven other riders try to beat the time he has set.

As is usual, the riders went off at two-minute intervals in the reverse order of their standing in the race. And since Bracke had had an indifferent Tour, he was eleventh man away. It was still lunchtime when his 52–41.6 went up on the blackboard at the athletics cinder track at Auch. Had he only known it, his nearest rival, the Norwegian Knut Knudsen, arrived only twenty minutes later and eight seconds slower. In fact Knudsen might well have taken the stage if, on passing his two-minute man, Lazcano, he hadn't wasted his time and temper shaking off the Spaniard who tried to steal a tow at his rear wheel. Knudsen zig-zagged across the road. Then his team car intervened — there are never enough commissaires to police every rider on the road — and Knudsen lost his rhythm and composure. However, Bracke wasn't to guess that the main danger was over, and since the early riders are normally submerged by the race leaders at the end, his suspense was dragged out unbearably through the hot afternoon. The man he most feared was Maertens who, again, would certainly have won but for a puncture in mid-course; he lost twenty seconds in the wheel change yet finished only eleven seconds outside Bracke's time. But even when Maertens's bid had failed, it was not until Van Impe rode in to take fourth place that Bracke knew he was safe and broke into tears of relief.

Van Impe can consider his ride quite sufficient for its purpose. Zoetemelk, his boil compressed beneath a bandage but not yet ready to lance, has finished tenth, his deficit on Van Impe lengthening from 3–18 to 4–33. And the only significant gain among the leaders is Poulidor's 1–45 on Delisle, which puts him only half a minute from third place overall. There is still some life left in the struggle to be the leading Frenchman, but little admiration lost between them. The other day when Poulidor was asked if he really meant to make this his last Tour, he confirmed it vigorously — then added that he supposed he could manage one more if he rode on other people's rear wheels like Delisle.

For Thévenet, the Frenchman left out of every calculation, it is another day of humiliation. He is fortieth, thirty-three minutes slower than Bracke, and rides the last lap on the track with distressing listlessness. Having heard the result he stands breathing heavily at the trackside, ignoring the reporters who come up to him, neither he nor they knowing what to say. He doesn't break the silence. He pushes his bike into the shade of a yellow post office van, and stands there with blobs of sweat breaking out and running down like rain on a window. Some older French journalists try to catch him as he moves towards the exit, but he mumbles only a few words, brushes off an autograph collector, mounts and follows Danguillaume out of the stadium. In no position to contest the race, and in no shape to make a last gesture of defiance, he seems to have no reason to continue.

Bordeaux, 14 July

Bastille Day, the longest of the Tour, though not as long as had been planned. The programme of three separate stages starting at seven-twenty in the morning, finishing at six-thirty in the evening and covering 362 kilometres has been unpopular with the riders since they first learnt of it. Back in May Kuiper complained in a Rotterdam paper that 'the organisers tell us they are meeting the wishes of the public, but we will be exhausted'. In reply the organisers reminded him that the triple stage would mean triple prizes, and these would bring the total over three weeks to more than a million francs. 'Let it be understood,' they wrote in *L'Équipe*, 'that Kuiper is free to participate or not.'

Now they have relented. 'Following the difficult stages in the Pyrenees and the testing effort in the time trial', and taking into account 'the general fatigue of the riders', they have agreed to lop forty-seven kilometres off the opening section and give everyone an extra hour in bed. It makes little difference except to those spectators who miss the announcement, get up early to see the heroes in the saddle, and instead see them ride past in a fleet of buses making for the new starting point.

If the organisers are able to call the tune, the riders can always blow the last raspberry, which is what they do. Without actually staging a strike, they reach a tacit agreement to keep in line until the last twenty kilometres before each finish: then it's a free for all. So the day passes in a blur of impressions: the small, neat flowery farms on the way to Langon; the Sauternes vineyards giving way to the well-drilled pine forests of the Gironde (like travelling through the bristles of a hairbrush) on the westward leg to Lacanau-Océan; the return through the trees and the Margaux vineyards to the exhibition site at the lake of Bordeaux; the dense crowds bored with waiting; the excited announcement of a demonstration at Lacanau, which turns out to be a jolly parade of students who sign themselves on their leaflets protesting at the Tour's commercialism, The Revolutionary Teachers of l'École Émancipée.

Only Bellini, with his eye on the hill prime points, takes any interest in the mid-stage racing, and only Maertens and the other thoroughbred sprinters in the finishes. Now back in *super-form* — this year's vogue word — Maertens wins at Langon and Lacanau, in both cases looking back to check his lead and easing on the line. And it is only the pugnacious Gerben Karstens who stops him winning at Bordeaux-le-Lac as well. Karstens leads out, twice takes him almost into the curb, and when he spurts forward again Maertens, for his own safety, leaves him to it. After two wins and a second place, and £800 in prizes, Maertens is enraged by this final and, to his mind, unjust defeat.

Régis Ovion is no better pleased to find that the laboratories have confirmed the positive result of his dope test at Saint-Gaudens. Apart from the usual penalties, it means that he has forfeited his stage win. He protests his innocence, and offers one plausible argument: if he had taken dope, would he have tried to win, knowing that the winner is always tested? But come to that, why does anyone take dope except to improve his performance — and make himself more liable to be caught out?

Tulle, 15 JULY

Today the *peloton* agrees on how best to check the repeated successes of Maertens. It is to release one rider, like a hare from a trap, at a reasonable distance from the line. This isn't to the liking of the other sprinters who cling to the idea that one day — like Esclassan at Divonne and Karstens at Bordeaux — they will get the better of Maertens at the finish, but the leaders overrule them. A strong resentment against Maertens is building up, particularly among the rank and file who find Flandria blocking the route and Maertens picking up a disproportionate share of the daily prizes. They can see themselves finishing the Tour without cash or credit.

The man picked out for favour is Hubert Mathis, a twenty-five-year-old second-year professional from northern France. *Centre-Presse*, which shares the national taste for playful coincidences and anomalies, affects to find it odd that a man named after the patron saint of hunters should make his attack in the anglers' reserve of the Dordogne, the Lot and the Corrèze, and have his triumph at Tulle, 'the veritable paradise of those who dream of catching trout, pike and gudgeon'. The more prosaic fact of the matter is that Mathis is 61–3 down on general classification, and belongs to the Miko-De Gribaldy team, leaderless since Laurent retired and reduced to only three men. He is therefore a proper object for charity if anyone is feeling charitable which, it must be admitted, Maertens is not. It's he who puts up the strongest resistance to Mathis's escape after 153 of the 220 kilometres, but he can't keep the race tied down for ever, and over the last twenty-five kilometres, when it's clear that Mathis will take the stage (which he does by exactly seven minutes), he makes no effort to stop another ten men moving ahead. Maertens is not interested in coming second, since his points lead is now unassailable, and he simply makes the gesture, which is second nature to him, of winning the bunch sprint.

Otherwise the stage, lacing back and forward across the Dordogne valley in constant sunlight, has the now familiar end-of-term air, only Bellini doing any work to improve his prospects on Prize Day. He takes the côte des Belvès on a detour into this small hill-top village, and then comes second to Mathis at the côte de Maysse; this puts him six points clear of Van Impe in the Mountain Grand Prix. He has done all he can. The rest depends on whether Van Impe by force of habit attacks, or by force of circumstances has to counter-attack tomorrow on the Puy-de-Dôme, the last first-category climb and the last uphill finish of the Tour.

Thévenet Will Not Ride the Puy-de-Dôme. Understandably the French papers make headlines of his retirement, but it comes as no surprise. There have been reports that a recent blood test on Thévenet revealed traces of hepatitis, and his doctors told him that by persisting with the Tour he would delay his recovery. He wasn't a hospital case, but the only place for a sick champion was home and in bed. What persuaded him to follow their advice was a bout of vomiting two-thirds of the way through the stage. He got off and in tears stood leaning against his bicycle at the side of the road until the Aspro ambulance drew up and he got aboard. Raymond Delisle paid his captain the tribute of staying at his side until he had officially abandoned the race. Then he rode off to regain his place in the *peloton* and take up with Poulidor one of the few live issues still to be decided in the race.

Puy-de-Dôme, 16 July

The riders can see the Puy-de-Dôme, at least its slightly rounded tip and its television mast, when they are still ninety kilometres away (as the Tour winds) from the finish. At 4,600 feet it is the highest of the puys — the chain of peaks to the west of Clermont-Ferrand — a sacred mountain to Gauls (Lug), Romans (Mercury), Christians (Saint Barnabus) and now the Tour (Coppi, Bahamonte and others). Oddly it was not until 1952 that the Tour first recognised its possibilities, not least of them being that here was a climb of great severity with a toll-gate at its entrance and a town of 170,000 inhabitants at its foot. This will be its eighth appearance in the Tour, and it is already famous for its run of dramatic successes. Each evening the *Spectacle du Tour* at the stage-town ends with an outdoor cinema show featuring the shoulder-to-shoulder struggle of Anquetil and Poulidor on the Puy in 1964 (today it could be repeated in duplicate: Van Impe and Zoetemelk; Poulidor and, this time, Delisle). This piece of film is the French equivalent of the Stanley Matthews Cup Final. Even the Puy's great anticlimax of 1969 had a magnificent irrelevance about it; first to the top ahead of Merckx was not simply an obscure rider but the *lanterne rouge* himself, Matignon.

Today is warm and overcast, the stage 220 kilometres long, rising with the first fourth-category prime to a section of the Auvergne plateau which gradually shelves upward from 2,000 to 3,000 feet. Bellini, still prudently taking out insurance against defeat on the Puy, makes sure that he wins this climb and another of equally small value, but for the leaders, as for most of the led, the first 209 kilometres are simply a preamble to the final climb. This is eleven kilometres long, the first section an approach with a steady incline of 1–14. Then the road levels out for a kilometre, passing through a gate at which spectators pay two pounds to walk the final five kilometres to the summit. Only accredited cars are allowed to pass.

The Puy can never be used except as a stage finish, since there is only one way up and down. Beyond the toll-gate the mountain becomes almost perfectly conical, and the road spirals upward around it like a helter-skelter in reverse. It begins with a kilometre of 1–7.5, then continues to rise at nearly 1–8 for the final four kilometres to the summit. It's here that the riders begin to suffer with every turn of the screw. Of all the climbs on the Tour it seems to attract the most commitedly partisan crowd. The climbs in the Alps and Pyrenees are free, and spectators can afford to look generously on the whole cavalcade. Here on the Puy, having paid to climb the narrow mountain road on foot while the privileged official and Press cars hoot past them, they look hot, weary and fractious. Last year as Merckx struggled up the climb a man jumped out of the crowd and punched him, an incident still the subject of a legal action. If it had to happen anywhere, the Puy seemed the likeliest place.

Two men try to get ahead of the queue for the climb, Labourdette who breaks away at 186 kilometres, and Mariano Martinez who chases and catches him at the toll-gate. Both, however, are swallowed up by the leaders when Zoetemelk makes his move four kilometres from the summit, and the only five who can keep up with him are Van Impe, Poulidor, Galdós, Delisle and Riccomi; in fact the leading group coincides precisely with the first six names on general classification. Delisle is the first to fail two and a half kilometres from the line, then Riccomi at just over a kilometre, Poulidor at 800 metres and Galdós at 500 metres. This leaves just Van Impe and Zoetemelk at each other's shoulder until, 250 metres from the line, Zoetemelk attacks and in that short distance gains twelve seconds. At extended intervals their other four companions join them — Galdós at twenty-five seconds, Poulidor at thirty-two seconds, Riccomi at forty-two seconds and Delisle at 1–2. The last climb is over, the last predictable chance of any big gains and losses. The ledger can at least be pencilled in.

First to dispose of Bellini and his dogged quest for the mountain title, he came fifteenth and so just failed to pick up any points. Van Impe is back in the mountain lead by four points, and to get ahead again, Bellini must win five out of a possible nine on tomorrow's little climbs.

The battle for third place overall is even closer. Poulidor gained exactly half a minute on Delisle, and the two are now tied on precisely the same second. To separate them the officials have added up their finishing positions at every stage, making Poulidor third overall with 468 and Delisle fourth with 963. Which will please Poulidor's supporters, but certainly won't satisfy them. They want their hero to be unequivocally the top Frenchman.

Last but not least, there's Zoetemelk's win, remarkable for a man disabled only a few days before, but doing no more than reduce Van Impe's lead from 4–33 to 4–21. The Dutchman has won three of the four mountain finishes — at Alpe d'Huez, Montgenèvre and now the Puy-de-Dôme — but the fact remains that it has gained him, in total, only sixteen seconds on Van Impe. He lost only one, at Pla-d'Adet — and 3–12 in the process. By now Zoetemelk must have seen some moral in it.

14

– J'Adore Poulidor –

It was no new experience for Poulidor to find himself in 1976 battling to become the top Frenchman in the Tour with the whole population of race followers ranged like an invisible host of angels at his back. It was simply gratifying to experience it once more at forty: *Poupou tu es le papa* indeed. Meanwhile a more celebrated adversary of his was also with the Tour, an energetic man with longish blond hair who looked younger than his forty-two years and was employed as a TV and newspaper reporter. On one stage in the south he stopped at a country bar and was chatting to an elderly farmer about crops and stock when the subject of the Tour came up. No, said the farmer, he didn't follow it any longer. It wasn't like the old days when Poulidor and Anquetil used to fight it out on the climbs.

Even then nobody told the farmer that it was Anquetil he was talking to, and it was understandable that he had failed to recognise him. Anquetil had filled out a little. His eyes no longer had the sunken look of a man who had just emerged from the trenches. He was dressed like a businessman on holiday, which in effect he was. He talked like a successful farmer, which he also was. During the heat and drought of the Tour he was constantly concerned about the 200 cattle on his ranch in Normandy, whether he could continue to feed them, whether he ought to send them to slaughter. Yet it was only seven years since he had retired as a professional cyclist, and only twelve since he had last won the Tour, beating Poulidor by fifty-five seconds.

As constant rivals through the sixties the pair were as famous as Tom and Jerry, though how far their competition was charged with genuine dislike of each other, and how far it was a figment of the Press is difficult to establish. 'Contrary to what people think,' Poulidor wrote in his first book of memoirs, *Glory Without the Yellow Jersey*, 'I have never detested Anquetil.' And in turn Anquetil protested that he felt no personal animosity towards Poulidor. 'Of course I would like to see Poulidor win the Tour de France in my absence,' he told a reporter in

1965, adding drily, 'I have beaten him so often that his victory could only add to my reputation.' Never a man to hide the profit motive, he went on to talk of the money they could make out of a series of revenge matches.

Beyond their common agricultural background, there is a marked contrast in personality, style of life, and certainly in physical appearance. Anquetil, the fair-haired, fair-skilled Norman has always been at ease among the businessmen on the fringes of the sport, and has diversified into property and farming as well as the natural extensions of the bike game like equipment manufacture, publicity and journalism. Poulidor, with swarthy complexion and dark, regimentally short hair, is reserved, even secretive, much attached to the privacy of his family life and the familiar surroundings of his native department of La Creuse to the north-east of Limoges. He has few commercial interests, and though he, too, is now thinking of setting up as a cattle farmer, it will only be after he finally retires, at which point he is determined to cut completely his connections with cycle racing.

You get the impression that, in their racing days, Anquetil looked on Poulidor as a bit of a yokel. For three years Vin Denson, an amiable, adaptable Cheshire man, found himself riding as *domestique* to Anquetil. 'They weren't always quarrelling,' he says. 'I've seen them at the table together, joking and drinking. But Anquetil often used to remark that he found Poulidor uninteresting, and not at all good company.'

These differences in character were also expressed in their approach to racing. Anquetil was subtle and calculating; he used his head. Poulidor used his physical strength, forcing a confrontation in which he would gain minutes or perish. It was often the latter; a perpetual Most Unfortunate Rider's trophy might well have been struck for him. So, too, they drew their support from separate sections of the public. Anquetil was admired by other racing cyclists for the pure speed, the sheer mechanical efficiency of his riding, and by urban young men for his shrewdness and habit of winning. But he never excited the same warmth of feeling as Poulidor, especially in the countryside. All along the route there were, and still are, banners reading *Courage Poupou, Allez Poupou, Poupou tu es le plus fort.* He would have preferred to be called *Pouli,* as he was early on, but he came to accept his absurd nursery nickname as a compliment. Nobody ever devised an affectionate diminutive of Anquetil's name.

'Poulidor's one of the peasants, one of the boys,' says Denson. 'A farm worker who found an old bike in the hedge, jumped on it and tried to beat the big champion.' And the legend survived both Poulidor's growing fortune and, at least in the Tour, his repeated failure even to draw blood from the champion, let alone kill him. 'Dear Monsieur Poupou,' wrote a six-and-a-half-year-old boy in a letter quoted in Poulidor's book, 'All the family, papa, maman, Xavier, Édith, Brigitte and myself, love you very much.'

All these contrasts were played up by the Press and cherished in the minds of the fans who created the kind of hero they wanted. Anquetil was never as circumspect as he was made out to be; no great climber, he nevertheless rode with courage and whole-heartedness in the mountains. A man who was stingy with his effort could never have won five Tours. If Anquetil was given less than his due, Poulidor was sentimentalised. He is certainly not uninterested in money (a trait, of course, which country people wouldn't hold against him; quite the reverse). And in his later Tours he developed a strain of cautious in-decision which is not in the authorised version of the legend.

Whether or not their natural rivalry was exaggerated by the riders themselves for the sake of publicity, they often behaved (as Maertens and De Vlaeminck, for instance, continue to do) as though it were more important to beat each other than to win the race. Denson recalls a Tour of Lombardy in which they were both competing: 'I was riding near the front and trying to control the bunch with one or two of my team-mates when I noticed that Tommy Simpson looked very fit, very dangerous. So I dropped back to Anquetil and said, "I know Simpson very well, and when he's in for a good day. If you keep with Tommy, you'll be in the first three, or not far off."

'And he said, "To hell with Simpson, just keep your eye on Poulidor." Well Simpson did escape in a break with Motta and a few others later on, and Jacques could easily have gone with them. But Poulidor also missed the break and Anquetil stayed with Poulidor. It was only when Poulidor attacked to pursue this little group that we really had to chase eyeballs out. We had to drag Anquetil up from the back of the bunch, and he really made a tremendous effort to close the gap on Poulidor. But once he'd done it, he was ready to let Simpson and the others ride on to take the race.'

It was in the Tour de France, though, that the two men struggled most bitterly together. Anquetil had a head start. He was two years older than Poulidor, and also an earlier developer. By nineteen he had turned professional and won the first of his nine Grands Prix des Nations; already he was able to earn more in a week than his father, a strawberry grower, did in three months. The Nations is the one classic run as a time trial, and it suited Anquetil's pure athletic ability and self-sufficient nature. And since the Tour de France included three or four time trials he exploited this same ability to destroy the opposition. What he lost in the mountains, which wasn't all that much, he would count on regaining in the trials, and if it wasn't magnificent, it was a highly effective means of waging war.

Poulidor's background was that much humbler. His parents, unlike Anquetil's, were not even small proprietors, they were agricultural labourers (the mother as well as the father) on a great domaine, Les Gouttes, in the commune of Masbarraud-Merignat. Raymond was their fourth son. In his book there is a marvellously evocative photograph taken of Poulidor during the early days of his success in the kitchen of his family home. He is sitting at the end of the oilcloth-covered table sifting through a drawerful of fan letters. One of his brothers and his father (with cap on) are at the side of the table reading the newspapers spread out in front of them. His mother, wearing a headscarf, sits looking on from a corner of the room. There are two silver cups on a wireless set which is curtained off with a frill of cloth, a list of cycle races and a calendar pinned to the wall, a black stove with a metal stock pot on top and a chimney pipe climbing up behind it, an open wood fire with a vest drying on a line below the mantlepiece, and electric flex trailing dangerously around — 'all the decor of my childhood'. Although he never felt deprived, there was nothing to spare in that home, and when at fourteen Raymond said that more than anything he would love to have a racing bike, 'my father raised his hands in the air as if I had asked for a Ferrari'. Instead he had to ride his mother's old, heavy lady's bike with twanging spokes, and it was not until he had made a local name for beating the other boys on this clumsy machine that he found a patron; a cycle dealer gave him a blue semi-racer of his own.

He was twenty-three before he turned professional with Mercier cycles, a team he has never left, and twenty-five when he entered his first Tour de France, by which time Anquetil had already won it twice, and was to win it three more times in successive years. This was 1962 and Poulidor, who started with a broken finger after a training accident, won the nineteenth stage at Aix-les-Bains alone and with a lead of more than three minutes. He finished third overall, on the strength of which he was made favourite for 1963. But that year Anquetil, who seemed anxious to live down his lopsided reputation as a time trialist, carried two mountain stages while Poulidor, who over-reached himself, finished eighth.

It was in 1964 that he ran Anquetil closest, narrowing the gap to only fourteen seconds on the Puy-de-Dôme in that famous cheek-by-jowl battle in which he first subdued Anquetil and then drew away from him between the ranks of *Poulidoristes*. In his own region he had lived out the slogan of *Poulidor le plus fort*, but as usual the Tour ended in a time trial, and against the clock Anquetil was able to lengthen his lead to fifty-five seconds.

From there on Poulidor managed only to preserve his titles as the eternal second and France's favourite loser. In 1965, with Anquetil absent, he came second in the Tour to a first-year Italian professional, Felice Gimondi. And in 1966, on Anquetil's return, the unbreakable habit of mutual distrust was resumed. While each did his best to destroy the other, one of Anquetil's more gifted *domestiques*, Lucien Aimar, ran away with the race. Pleading illness Anquetil retired from the Tour for ever remarking, 'I have done what I could for Lucien; I would only be in his way from now on.' Even in the moment of abandoning, Anquetil could claim the moral victory, while Poulidor rode on in dignity to take third place.

In the autumn of 1968 there was an attempt to bring the two riders together as team-mates for Mercier. 'The disappearance of an antagonism that has lasted many years,' said the team-manager, Antonin Magne, himself a double winner of the Tour, 'would not be a bad thing for cycling and for a public perhaps wearied of the Anquetil-Poulidor rivalry.' But in the event the deal fell through, and in any case the rivalry had already begun to die from natural causes. Anquetil, at thirty-four, was now riding only a few picked races and devoting more time to becoming *un gentleman farmer*. At the end of 1969 he rode his last professional event after a round of operatic farewells at the vélodromes of France and the Low Countries. And in the Press photographs, as Anquetil cut an iced cake or received a flowery tribute, Poulidor could often be seen smiling shyly in the background. The two men treated each other courteously if without any noticeable warmth.

Meanwhile Poulidor had continued his pursuit of glory — without the yellow jersey. In the 1967 Tour, after falling on the 3,850 foot Ballon d'Alsace, he worked humbly for the victory of another Frenchman, the tall, heron-like Roger Pingeon: *Poupou le fidèle* it was now. And next year it was understood that Pingeon would repay the compliment of having had France's second highest-paid rider working for him as a *domestique*. For fifteen days Pingeon waited for Poulidor to make a decisive move against the minor riders who were taking too much upon themselves. But Poulidor, winner of classics and one-time champion of France, with thirty-five major victories to his name, seemed paralysed by caution, a reluctance to risk what he already had for the sake of what he might gain. Losing patience Pingeon struck out on his own, and in the hectic pursuit that followed Poulidor crashed into one of the motorcycle outriders: *Poulidor le malchanceux* once more. Poulidor came in at the end of the stage with his face caked in blood, and didn't even look towards Pingeon in the crowd at the finishing line. Two days later, when it was discovered that he had broken his nose as well as suffered more obvious injuries, he left the race. 'Without Poulidor the Tour will still go on,' he announced solemnly from his hotel bed, which of course it did, the Dutchman, Janssen, winning on the last half-stage and Pingeon, not the most popular rider in France, finishing in fifth place.

From that point it was simply as a courtesy that Poulidor was listed among Tour favourites every June. There were people who argued that, relieved of the pressure of public expectation, a more relaxed and carefree Poulidor would now take the Tour. But a new hero had arrived, the twenty-four-year-old Eddy Merckx. He could climb like Poulidor in his prime and ride a time trial with the chilling speed of Anquetil — which made him potentially a better rider than either had been. So it proved. At the first attempt he won the Tour by eighteen minutes from Pingeon and twenty-two minutes from Poulidor, third. Going over the race in his mind afterwards Poulidor reflected with growing fatalism, 'Perhaps if I had pushed a little harder I could have finished second.'

He was to do so once more in 1974, but though he took the stage at the Pla-d'Adet summit in splendid isolation, he lost the race to Merckx by over eight minutes. The people of the French countryside never abandoned Poulidor, but now they would have been thankful to see him leave the stage before he made himself ridiculous. In 1975 it looked as though he had stayed on a year too long. He was unfit at the start of the race, regretted his decision to ride after a couple of days, and finished nineteenth, his worst placing ever. And by that time France had found a new champion in Thévenet. It was to try and prove that illness, not age, had disarmed him the year before that Poulidor presented himself at Saint-Jean-de-Monts for his fourteenth Tour. Now he had been vindicated. He was back in his familiar role contending for the place of top Frenchman. The banners were right, Poulidor was the strongest — of the French riders.

15

– La Boucle est Bouclée –

Versailles, 17 July

The Grande Boucle is almost over; the big buckle is about to be buckled. What makes up the last Saturday is a long train journey to Montargis and a short race of 145 kilometres through rain and adverse winds to Versailles. A chance for Bellini to regain the mountain jersey, Poulidor to earn some measurable fraction of time on Delisle, and Maertens to win another stage. These three have something to ride for in the twenty-first stage; for the rest it's just the means of achieving an end to the race. Unknown to them, too, it's also the occasion for another demonstration by the printers in their sixteen-months' dispute with M. Amaury, proprietor of *Le Parisien-Libéré.* The riders would have to read *l'Humanité*, the Communist Party paper, to discover that 260 workers' cars had followed the caravan for 120 kilometres to cries from the roadside of, 'Keep it up boys, you must go on.'

Much the same advice might have been given to the tired, slow-moving and now largely motiveless *peloton* of eighty-seven riders which shows only occasional signs of breaking ranks. Bellini, however, has an anxious, restless day since he needs five points from the three remaining fourth-category primes to overtake Van Impe. He makes a healthy start by winning three points at the top of the côte de Dourdan, but then complications set in. Bellini finds himself in conflict with the interests of Maertens who, after setting out to retrieve the errant Bracke, decides to form an alliance with him. The two men earn, and for six kilometres maintain, a lead of one minute, and Bellini knows that if they stay ahead they will leave behind only one point to secure at the last two hill primes. They're wretchedly small pickings after the dozens of points on offer in the Alps and Pyrenees, but Bellini must be sure of winning both of them to become King of the Mountains.

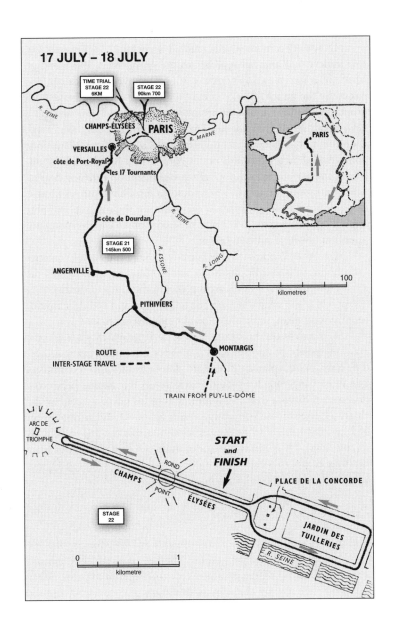

17 JULY – 18 JULY

TIME TRIAL
STAGE 22
6KM

STAGE 22
90km 700

R. SEINE

CHAMPS-ÉLYSÉES

PARIS

R. MARNE

VERSAILLES

côte de Port-Royal

les 17 Tournants

côte de Dourdan

R. SEINE

STAGE 21
145km 500

R. ESSONE

R. LOING

ANGERVILLE

0   100
kilometres

PITHIVIERS

ROUTE
INTER-STAGE TRAVEL

MONTARGIS

TRAIN FROM PUY-LE-DÔME

PARIS

ARC DE
TRIOMPHE

START
and
FINISH

ROND
POINT

CHAMPS

ÉLYSÉES

PLACE DE LA CONCORDE

STAGE
22

JARDIN DES
TUILLERIES

R. SEINE

0   1
kilometre

His anxiety is momentarily relieved when, at 123 kilometres, the two leaders skid and fall together to the greasy road. But although Maertens is forced to stop with mechanical trouble, and is caught and passed by the bunch, Bracke is able to continue alone and take both primes. So Bellini's problems are merely halved, and now he faces a new threat. At the crest of Les Dix-sept Tournants, an Italian rival, Antonini, spitefully takes second place and leaves Bellini with just one point. And shortly afterwards on the côte de Port-Royal it is Danguil-laume, impervious to Bellini's feelings but intent on catching Bracke, who goes into the attack. In a fit of desperation Bellini thrusts himself forward, beats the Frenchman in the sprint for the summit, and puts himself out of his agony. Men have suffered more to win the mountain prize, but few have suffered longer.

Meanwhile Bracke's lead has been dwindling, and eight kilometres from home he is caught. Soon afterwards Maertens, too, regains the *peloton* and sixty-seven riders are together at the entry to the finishing circuit where the stage times are taken. Poulidor and Delisle are num-bered among them, so that little matter remains unresolved.

The finish is on the broad Avenue de Paris which leads grandly up to the palace of the Sun King but today, after more heavy drizzle, is fit only for aquaplaning. There are almost two circuits to complete and three dangerous hairpins to navigate on the avenue before the final sprint. But not in the least unnerved by his fall or wearied by the chase, Maertens is back in charge. With his now familiar impression of a bolt from the blue, he presses forward across the line to take his seventh stage. He is still two victories short of a new record, but since the Tour comes to a close with a double bill on the Champs-Élysées tomorrow, who's to say that it's beyond him?

Paris, 18 July

And still it's raining. At ten o'clock on this Sunday morning the tri-colors are hanging down like washing. The cafe tables which optimistic waiters have set up on the pavements are turning to bird baths. What few people are already about loiter in arcades and doorways and are outnumbered by the black-uniformed police from the Compagnie

Républicaine de Sécurité. Their grey vans, without which no social event in Paris is complete, are parked in every side street with riot helmets stacked in the rear windows. Apart from the CRS contribution, it's a very different scene from a year ago when, for the first time, this splendid but shop-soiled avenue was turned into a racing circuit for the Tour's final stage. Half a million people — to take an average of the newspaper estimates — turned out to see Thévenet return in triumph on a gleaming day to receive the ultimate yellow jersey from the hands of President Giscard d'Estaing. It was the biggest popular fête in the city centre since the Liberation.

This year there are two parts to the entertainment: a six kilometre individual time trial and a fifteen-lap, ninety kilometre criterium or circuit race. The anti-clockwise course is the same for both. It starts almost opposite the Élysée Palace and heads towards the Arc de Triomphe, crossing the Rond Point and climbing the hill to the turn, an island of traffic cones just short of what used to be the Étoile and is now the Place Charles de Gaulle. Then down the other carriageway, past the start, bearing right across the Place de la Concorde and into the Quai des Tuileries. On this 300 metres stretch the organisers once again hope to maintain some privacy in which the riders can relieve themselves, if they wish, as they pass through; but last year this spectacle, if not exactly an attraction, was no deterrent, and the sector was almost as crowded as the rest of the circuit. Rounding the Tuileries gardens, the course comes back along the arcaded shop fronts of the Rue de Rivoli, cuts across the other side of the Place de la Concorde, and so through to the finishing line — a route as privileged, and normally as busy on a summer Sunday, as the Mall and a loop around Trafalgar Square would be.

You don't think of the lower end of the Champs-Élysées being lined with dirt paths until the rain turns them into mud and puddles. Just before eleven we slide and splash our way down to the start of the time trial and the overcrowded Press Room and riders' changing quarters which have been set up in the Pavilion Gabriel, one of the chic little park buildings built in the Élysée gardens.

The rain is easing, but the road is still slippery as the trial is opened by Raleigh's Aad Van den Hoek who, nearly three minutes clear at the bottom of the table, has no need to ride particularly slowly to protect his title of *lanterne rouge*. It hardly needs saying that Maertens, with his deftness on the glassy corners, wins by eleven seconds in 7–46, covering the course at 46.27 kph. He is now on a level with Merckx and Pelissier in the records. But what the French are more concerned with is the outcome of the Poulidor-Delisle struggle for third place overall; like any other chauvinists (Titanic Disaster: Aunt of Bideford Man Feared Lost) they find a French bronze far more absorbing than a Belgian victory. There has been a rather stagey reconciliation between the two men; last night's *France Soir* carried a photograph of them shaking hands in a hotel bedroom: 'the peace of the brave'. And the International Association Against Violence in Sport has already announced its award to Delisle for valour combined with perfect correctness. In its citation it particularly commends Delisle's remark after the ascent of the Puy-de-Dôme, 'Ce Raymond Poulidor, c'est un Monsieur.' It never did anyone's reputation any harm in France to be valorous but correct in opposition to Poulidor.

The time trial settles the matter beyond reasonable doubt. Poulidor, in another tireless ride, puts up the third best time: eleven seconds behind Maertens but only fourteen-hundredths of a second behind Zoetemelk. After Pollentier and Van Impe comes Delisle in sixth place, nine seconds slower than his indignant siamese twin in the classification. The French have been accorded their dearest wish. Provided that he keeps out of trouble in the criterium, Poulidor has reserved his place on the podium.

This has also made things a little easier for France Inter. According to last night's bulletins, the French radio service — 'to render homage to Raymond Poulidor's exceptional career and celebrate his fourteenth and last Tour de France' — has arranged to present him at the finish with a gold bust of himself sculpted by Daniel Druet, winner of the (artistic) Prix de Rome. At the ceremony the veteran singing star Henri Salvador is due to direct the Fanfare des Marmousets de la Croix St Ouen in a first performance of 'Poulidor, that's health'. Delisle's presence on the platform as the third man might have diminished the effect.

By the afternoon the clouds, as well as the suspense, have lifted and the scene is much like last year's. The *casquette* and back-number sellers have drawn their vans up on the pavement. Another Tour de France special, this time the sandwich Matignon, is being pressed on the customers. And hucksters are offering cardboard periscopes: five francs plain, 7.50 with football pictures on them. Although they are about as much use for following the race as opera glasses for tracking a satellite, they gave latecomers a fleeting contact with events. Loud-speakers strung along the avenue do the rest. The crowds are cheerful and undemanding, with no apparent dissenters apart from the collectors who keep their eyes down on the albums in the open-air philatelists' market and a young man with a cardboard breastplate which reads, '*Tour de France — Tour des Flics*'.

Apart from Maertens, all the leaders are now satisfied, or at least resigned to, what they have already achieved, and the spectators expect no more from them than fifteen energetic laps of honour with a sprint at the finish. All the same, to give a little animation, each lap carries a £100 prime, and a £650 first prize for the man (it is Raleigh's Jan Raas) who takes the most lap points. With the final circuit all the escapes, which have never reached more than forty seconds, are at an end, and Flandria are setting up the sprint for Maertens's *coup de grace*. But as at Bordeaux the job is botched at the very last moment, and the man who makes him lose his concentration is Raleigh's little Dutch sprinter, Gerben Karstens. He sees Karstens lead out just after the bunch comes round from the Place de la Concorde, unaccountably misjudges his effort and has to follow him across the line several lengths behind. His final victory on points is a prodigious 293 to Gavazzi's 140, but the record has eluded him.

The tide of people swells up towards the platform, another printers' demonstration forms on the Champs-Élysées ('where', according to *l'Humanité*, 'supporters of Poulidor in yellow tee-shirts raise their thumbs in a signal of support'), and as Van Impe pushes through the crowd, embracing his team-mates on the way, the only clear view of the closing moments is offered by the television sets in the Press Room. Van Impe is in tears on the podium. So is his big

Belgian mother wearing a print dress with a fish-scale pattern. So is his slim, ash-blonde wife, Rita.

Van Impe receives from M. Alain Poher, president of the Senate, his final yellow jersey, which tomorrow at noon he will give to King Baudouin and Queen Fabiola in an audience at the royal palace of Laeken (though of course he is less familiar than Merckx with the King of the Belgians; after Merckx's crash last year, they were in regular touch by telephone in the evenings). M. Guy Merlin presents him with a large symbolic key to his prize apartment at Merlin-Plage-Aquitaine. As the Marseillaise dies out, one by one Maertens, Zoetemelk and Poulidor come up to congratulate him, and then the ceremony breaks up in disorder as the great men are buttonholed and hustled along to the television stand.

By now Poulidor has had enough of it (tomorrow night he is contracted to ride his first post-Tour race, a criterium at Caen). The camera picks him out as he gets on his bicycle once more and begins weaving through the fringes of the crowd. A man carrying a microphone tries to waylay him, but with unaccustomed roughness Poulidor mouths something and then pushes him away. Leaving the surprised, disgruntled interviewer behind, he pedals off up the Champs-Élysées, his figure diminishing. *Fin*. Fade. Titles.

– Stage by Stage Winners 1976 –

		STAGE PLACINGS		OVERALL PLACINGS		MOUNTAIN LEADER
Thursday 24 June Prologue	Merlin-Plage, Saint-Jean-de-Monts, Indiv. time trial, 8 km	1 Maertens 2 Manzanèque 3 Thévenet	11'03" 11'20" 11'23"	1 Maertens 2 Manzanèque 3 Thévenet	11'03" 11'17" 11'20"	
Friday 25 June Stage 1	Merlin-Plage, Angers, 173 km	1 Maertens 2 Delépine 3 Gualazzini	4h43'37" same time st	1 Maertens 2 Manzanèque 3 Thévenet	4h54'40" @17" @20"	Legeay, Kuiper = 1st
Saturday 26 June Stage 2	Angers, Caen, 236.5 km	1 Battaglin 2 Gavazzi 3 Raas	6h43'49" @10" st	1 Maertens 2 Manzanèque 3 Thévenet	11h38'39" @17" @20"	Caverzasi by 2pts from Kuiper
Sunday 27 June Stage 3	Le Touquet (Paris-Plage), Indiv. time trial, 37 km	1 Maertens 2 Pollentier 3 Schuiten	47'08" 48'45" 49'09"	1 Maertens 2 Pollentier 3 Manzanèque	12h26'47" @1'58" @2'29"	
Monday 28 June Stage 4	Le Touquet, Bornem, 258 km	1 Kuiper 2 Loder 3 Gavazzi	7h31'25" st @9"	1 Maertens 2 Pollentier 3 Manzanèque	19h57'26" @1'58" @2'29"	Caverzasi, Kuiper = 1st
Tuesday 29 June Stage 5A	Louvain, Team time Trial, 4.3 km	1 TI-Raleigh 2 Flandria 3 Peugeot	26'49" 26'54" 27'09"			

		STAGE PLACINGS		OVERALL PLACINGS		MOUNTAIN LEADER
Stage 5B	Louvain Verviers 144 km	1 Lasa 2 Sibille 3 Périn	3h51'17" st @8"	1 Maertens 2 Pollentier 3 Kuiper	23h49'10" @2'04" @3'16"	Caverzasi, Kuiper = 1st
Wednesday 30 June Stage 6	Bastogne Nancy 209 km	1 Parecchini 2 Paolini 3 Knetemann	5h22'32" @4'29" st	1 Maertens 2 Pollentier 3 Kuiper	29h16'23" @2'04" @3'16"	Caverzasi, Kuiper = 1st
Thursday 1 July Stage 7	Nancy Mulhouse 207.5 km	1 Maertens 2 Esclassan 3 Gavazzi	5h41'12" st st	1 Maertens 2 Pollentier 3 Kuiper	34h57'35" @2'04" @3'16"	Kuiper by 6pts from Bellini
Friday 2 July Stage 8	Beaulieu-Valentigney Divonne-les-Bains 220.5 km	1 Esclassan 2 Maertens 3 Gavazzi	5h54'11" st st	1 Maertens 2 Pollentier 3 Kuiper	40h51'46" @2'04" @3'16"	Bellini by 3pts from Kuiper
Saturday 3 July	Divonne-les-Bains	REST DAY				
Sunday 4 July Stage 9	Divonne-les-Bains Alpe d'Huez 258 km	1 Zoetemelk 2 Van Impe 3 Galdós	8h31'49" @3" @58"	1 Van Impe 2 Zoetemelk 3 Maertens	49h27'32" @8" @54"	Bellini by 17pts from Kuiper and Van Impe
Monday 5 July Stage 10	Bourg d'Oisans Montgenèvre 158 km	1 Zoetemelk 2 Thévenet 3 Van Impe	5h02'20" @1 st	1 Van Impe 2 Zoetemelk 3 Poulidor	54h29'53" @7" @1'36"	Van Impe by 10pts from Zoetemelk

		STAGE PLACINGS		OVERALL PLACINGS		MOUNTAIN LEADER
Tuesday 6 July Stage 11	Montgenèvre Manosque 224 km	1 Viejo 2 Karstens 3 Maertens	5h42'34" @22'50" st	1 Van Impe 2 Zoetemelk 3 Poulidor	6oh35'34" @7" @1'36"	Van Impe by 13pts from Bellini
Wednesday 7 July	Port-Barcarès	REST DAY				
Thursday 8 July Stage 12	Port-Barcarès Pyrénées 2000 205.5 km	1 Delisle 2 Menendez 3 Panizza	6h47'32" @4'59" @5'14"	1 Delisle 2 Van Impe 3 Zoetemelk	67h27'23" @2'41" @2'47"	Van Impe by 3pts from Bellini
Friday 9 July Stage 13	Font-Romeu (Bourg-Madame) Saint-Gaudens 188 km	1 Ovion* 2 Tierlinck 3 Panizza	4h57'50" st st	1 Delisle 2 Van Impe 3 Zoetemelk	72h24'53" @2'41" @2'47"	Bellini by 4pts from Van Impe
Saturday 10 July Stage 14	Saint-Gaudens Saint-Lary-Soulan 139 km	1 Van Impe 2 Zoetemelk 3 Riccomi	4h20'50" @3'12" @3'45"	1 Van Impe 2 Zoetemelk 3 Delisle	76h48'24" @3'18" @9'27"	Van Impe by 25pts from Bellini
Sunday 11 July Stage 15	Saint-Lary-Soulan Pau 195 km	1 Panizza 2 Paolini 3 Pollentier	6h01'37" @2'16" st	1 Van Impe 2 Zoetemelk 3 Delisle	82h55'45" @3'18" @9'27"	Van Impe by 11pts from Bellini

* Ovion was demoted from 1st place after a positive dope test.

			STAGE PLACINGS	OVERALL PLACINGS	MOUNTAIN LEADER
Monday 12 July Stage 16	Pau Fleurance 152 km		1 Pollentier 4h38'33" 2 Maertens @16" 3 Karstens st	1 Van Impe 87h34'34" 2 Zoetemelk @3'18" 3 Delisle @9'27"	Van Impe by 5pts from Bellini
Tuesday 13 July Stage 17	Fleurance Auch Indiv. time trial, 38.75 km		1 Bracke 52'41" 2 Knudsen 52'49" 3 Maertens 52'52"	1 Van Impe 88h28'06" 2 Zoetemelk @4'33" 3 Delisle @11'25"	
Wednesday 14 July Stage 18A	Auch Langon 86 km		1 Maertens 2h34'37" 2 Karstens st 3 Gavazzi st		
Stage 18B	Lacanau-Océan 123 km		1 Maertens 3h27'00" 2 Esclassan st 3 Paolini st		
Stage 18C	Bordeaux 70.5 km		1 Karstens 1h42'13" 2 Maertens st 3 Paolini st	1 Van Impe 96h11'56" 2 Zoetemelk @4'33" 3 Delisle @11'25"	Bellini by 1pt from Van Impe
Thursday 15 July Stage 19	Sainte-Foy-la-Grande Tulle 219.5 km		1 Mathis @7'00" 2 Paolini st 3 Vianen	1 Van Impe 103h06'20" 2 Zoetemelk @4'33"	Bellini by 6pts from Van Impe

		STAGE PLACINGS		OVERALL PLACINGS		MOUNTAIN LEADER
Friday 16 July Stage 20	Tulle Puy-de-Dôme 220 km	1 Zoetemelk 2 Van Impe 3 Galdós	6h52'52" @12" @25"	1 Van Impe 2 Zoetemelk 3 Poulidor 4 Delisle	109h59'24" @4'21" @12'15"	Van Impe by 4pts from Bellini
Saturday 17 July Stage 21	Montargis Versailles 145.5 km	1 Maertens 2 Gavazzi 3 Paolini	4h16'07" st st	1 Van Impe 2 Zoetemelk 3 Poulidor 4 Delisle	114h15'31" @4'21" @12'15"	Bellini by 1pt from Van Impe
Sunday 18 July Stage 22A	Champs-Élysées Indiv. time trial, 6 km	1 Maertens 2 Zoetemelk 3 Poulidor	7'46".85 7'57".74 7'57".88			
Stage 22B	Circuit race 90.7 km	1 Karstens 2 Maertens 3 Gavazzi	1h58'48" st	1 Van Impe 2 Zoetemelk 3 Poulidor 4 Delisle	116h22'23" @4'14" @12'08" @12'17"	Bellini by 1pt from Van Impe

General Classification: 1. Van Impe, 116h22′23″; 2. Zoetemelk, at 4′14″; 3. Poulidor, 12′08″; 4. Delisle, 12′17″; 5. Riccomi, 12′39″; 6. Galdós, 14′50″; 7. Pollentier, 14′59″; 8. Maertens, 16′06″; 9. Bertoglio, 16′36″; 10. Lopez-Carril, 19′28″. Among other notable riders, Ocana was 14th at 25′08″; Bellini, winner of the Mountain Grand Prix, 16th at 26′43″; De Witte, leader of Brooklyn, 18th at 34′21″; Viejo, hero of the long escape on stage 11, 31st at 55′16; Romero, leader of Jobo-Wolber, 39th at 1h07′37″; Martinez, leader of Lejeune, 42nd at 1h25′34″; Gavazzi, runner-up in the points competition, 63rd at 2h05′05″.

Out of 130 starters, 87 finished the Tour. The *lanterne rouge* was Van Den Hoeck, who was 3h12′54″ slower than Van Impe. The corrected official distance of the race was 4,018km 950m, and was covered at an average speed of 34.822 kph. Van Impe's average speed was 34.535 kph.

Mountain Grand Prix: 1. Bellini, 170pts; 2. Van Impe, 169pts; 3. Zoetemelk, 119pts; 4. Galdós, 85pts; 5. Poulidor, 81pts; 6. Torres, 65pts.

Points competition: After winning the Prologue, Maertens was points leader throughout the Tour, although naturally he didn't wear the green jersey until after he had lost the yellow. 1. Maertens, 293pts; 2. Gavazzi, 140pts; 3. Esclassan, 128 pts; 4. Paolini, 122pts; 5. Karstens, 108pts; 6. Pollentier, 92pts.

Hot Spot Sprint: 1. Mintkewicz, 54pts; 2. Maertens, 31pts; 3. Osler, 24pts; 4. Torres, 14pts; 5. Tierlinck, 13pts; 6. Gavazzi, 12pts.

Team competitions: On time: 1. Kas; 2. Gan-Mercier; 3. SCIC-Fiat-France. On points: 1. Gan-Mercier; 2. SCIC-Fiat-France; 3. Peugeot-Esso.

Young Riders GP: 1. Martinez-Heredia (23rd overall); 2. Meslet (24th); 3. Pronk (26th).

– 1977: Prodigy's Arrival,
Prodigal's Return –

It was the smallest field since 1947 — only a hundred riders — but it contained the full complement of those past Tour winners still getting around on two wheels. There was Van Impe, the defender, who must surely have passed a new vote of confidence in himself. Merckx, who hadn't put in a challenge since his defeat by Thévenet in 1975. Thévenet himself, a diminished, even pathetic figure when he retired from the race in 1976. And the quixotic Ocana. There were also two Englishmen: the veteran Barry Hoban, looking for a ninth-stage win, and the novice Bill Nickson with the British-sponsored, Dutch-based TI-Raleigh team. Missing were Maertens, the new world champion; his side-kick, Pollentier, who had just won the Tour of Italy; De Vlaeminck, yet again; and Moser, the most glamorous of the Italians.

According to the form book the race was between Van Impe, Merckx, Thévenet and that perpetual best man at other people's weddings, Zoetemelk. But how reliable was past form when Thévenet was on the threshold of his thirties, and the other three were already through the door and looking for somewhere to sit down? Wasn't it time for them to be pushed aside by a younger man? Not a *much* younger man, of course. Except for precocious exceptions like Merckx, road riders tend to mature slowly. But maybe the Dutchman, Kuiper. Until his injury he had a good, solid Tour in 1976, and at twenty-eight might just be coming into his prime.

At any rate that was roughly how the odds were being called before the start of the sixty-fourth Tour at Fleurance, that prosperous little market town in the south-west of France lying roughly half-way between the Atlantic and the Mediterranean and about the same distance north of the Spanish border.

Obviously the route of any Tour is largely dictated by the position of the start town, but the choice of Fleurance, tucked away in the corner of the map, restricted the options more than most. For one thing, if the race was to pass through the Pyrenees — and not to do so was unthinkable — then this had to be done in the first few days. Normally the organisers wouldn't think of sending the riders up the great cols until they had spent at least five days warming up on the flat.

Instead, the flat section of the race was to *follow* the first attack on the mountains. And it was to be inordinately long. It was Brittany's turn for a visit: and by winning six of the last eight Tours, the Belgians, too, had established some sort of prescriptive right to see their men in action. There was only one means of reconciling these two demands — a long, clockwise sweep around the western and northern coasts of France. This was not a cheering prospect. The sprinters would struggle for the daily prizes, and the ultimate battle to win the Tour itself would be held in suspense.

Again, there was the problem of sheer distance. To reach Charleroi in Belgium within a fortnight, and yet keep the daily stages inside the maximum length that the rules allowed, they couldn't simply be laid end-to-end. There had to be repeated hops by bus and team-car from one day's finish to the next day's start.

Even then only ten working days were left for getting from Charleroi to the Vosges and the Alps for the last, critical bout of mountaineering, and then turning north-west to Paris for the ceremonial finish on the Champs-Élysées. Clearly it couldn't all be done by bike. The organisers' solution was to fly the riders to Freiburg in Germany for a rest day and a circuit race, then transport them back to France by bus. And on the penultimate day of the Tour they were to be taken by train from Dijon to within striking distance of the capital.

Altogether it was a route devised to meet various obligations, some sentimental, most of them commercial. It was not the route that anyone with a free hand would have planned. But only the next three weeks would show what effect this would have on the racing.

The Good German

It was one of the more fancied outsiders, twenty-two-year-old Dietrich Thurau from Frankfurt, who won the eight kilometres time trial

Prologue in 6–16. This made him the first German to wear the yellow jersey since 1969, when Rudi Altig also took the prologue, as well as being the first member of the TI-Raleigh team to do so. Indeed it was a promising start to Raleigh's second Tour. Their time-trial specialist, Gerrie Knetemann, was runner-up, only four seconds behind. Kuiper was thirteenth and Bert Pronk fourteenth.

Merckx came third, at eight seconds. Since he prefers a longer race against the clock, and since, anyway, he had beaten all his supposed rivals, this was a perfectly good result. Thurau, however, was talking confidently of defending his yellow jersey against all comers. He believed that if he still had it on at Pau in two days' time, when the heaviest climbing in the Pyrenees was over, there was every chance that he would wear it at least until the Tour paid its brief visit to Germany. He could hardly ask for more.

Next day, in a roundabout stage through the Armagnac country — which took 237 kilometres to reach Auch, only fifty kilometres away — Thurau kept his word and his jersey. He finished sixth, losing no time on the winner of the bunch sprint, a Cyrille Guimard discovery called Raymond Villemiane. But this was simply a preparation for the first big test when the Tour moved on from Auch to Pau, circling to take in three celebrated climbs, the Aspin, Tourmalet and Aubisque.

The second stage was as decisive as it promised to be. By the end of the day it had created a short list of fourteen possible winners and condemned the other eighty-four (there were two retirements) to nothing more than a supporting role in the race. But Thurau was not displaced. Far from it, he strengthened his moral claim to be leader by beating the other thirteen front-runners in the sprint at the end of the stage.

Not that he had an easy ride. The big attack was launched on the Tourmalet, where Van Impe led a breakaway of fifteen men from which Thurau, Merckx, the young Frenchman, Michel Laurent, and Ocana dropped away on the climb. That could well have been the end for Thurau, but discarding Ocana he joined up with the other two on the descent and they got stuck into the chase. At the foot of the Aubisque they rejoined the leaders and that group stayed intact to the finish on the Pau motor circuit. There, by inches from the previous day's winner, Villemiane, Thurau took his second stage.

All the group (except Delisle who lost five seconds) were credited with the same time, but the fifteenth man home, Pronk, did not arrive until over seven minutes later, and the rest came straggling in at intervals over the next forty minutes or so. What the day's racing proved above all else was that the majority of the riders had not been physically prepared to meet the mountains so soon; that Thurau was a rider of great courage as well as versatility; and that we needn't look further for the race winner than to the fourteen men who had put seven minutes between themselves and the rest of the field. The stage was that conclusive.

These fourteen, in order of appearance on the new general classification, were: Thurau, Merckx, Laurent, Van Impe, Rouxel, Zoetemelk, Thévenet, Villemiane, Kuiper, Meslet, Aja, Galdós, Delisle and Andiano. And though four of them subsequently dropped behind or out of the Tour altogether, the others, on the strength of that one day's ride, were to occupy the first ten places when the final results were published in Paris.

For a time this had a disastrous effect on the race. The favourites had now removed themselves from any risk of being caught unawares by lesser men. They knew exactly who their enemies were. And at this early point in the Tour they were disposed to play for safety. Their strategy was to control and damp down the race on the flat stages, and to confine their effort to making gains or limiting their losses in the time trials at Bordeaux and Angers. There were still some 3,500 kilometres to go, and unless an unforeseeable chance occurred they wanted to postpone hostilities until the final week when the Alps appeared on the horizon.

As for the rest of the riders, they recognised that they had nothing left to compete for except the daily prizes.

Stage 3, ending at Vitoria in Spain, also crossed the Pyrenees, but by a route which offered only one second-category and two third-category climbs. There was a little by-play during which Van Impe took back the lead in the mountain prize from Kuiper, but then by consent the leaders allowed the lowly-placed Spaniard, José Nazabal, to ride away and take the stage by over five minutes. Appropriately the finish was outside the factory of Nazabal's sponsors, Kas.

The fourth stage, which brought the Tour back to France, was similarly uneventful except for the victory at Seignosse of thirty-one-year-old Régis Delépine, his first in eight Tours. So was stage 5A, won by Jacques Esclassan in a perilous bunch sprint on the Bordeaux track. But this was just a prelude to the afternoon's 30.2 kilometre time trial at the Bordeaux exhibition centre where Thurau produced his most astonishing performance. Riding with an almost unchanging rhythm he beat Merckx, the old grand master of this discipline, into second place by fifty seconds. Almost as surprisingly, remembering his uneven style and his previous year's embarrassments, was Thévenet's fourth place, behind Knetemann, at 1–6. He had clearly found something like his 1975 form.

After a rest day at Bordeaux there was a little more action on the road to Limoges, where Jan Raas won, and Thurau had to act decisively in the chase to head off a strong attack by Meslet (now sixth overall), abetted by Merckx's team-mate, Sercu. These two were in action again the following morning, on stage 7A, and this time it was Sercu who crossed the line first at Angers. Thurau survived this sniping, however, and it was not until the afternoon, when a four kilometre team time trial was staged, that his lead was clipped. And then by only seven seconds. This was the one event in which time bonuses were awarded, the Fiat team gaining ten seconds for Merckx by taking first place while Raleigh, coming third, won Thurau only three seconds.

So the Tour moved at the pace of a club outing into Brittany and then back eastward through Normandy and towards the Belgian border. At Lorient, Santambrogio took the first stage for Italy; at Rennes, Klaus-Peter Thaler added to West Germany's successes. But more significant on that latter day was a pile-up near the finish which cost Zoetemelk and Laurent 1–30 — and effectively any real hope of winning the Tour.

The next three stages were won in lone attacks — by Den Hertog at Rouen, by Danguillaume at Roubaix, and by Sercu at Charleroi. Sercu's win in his own country showed how far this one-time world sprint champion had developed as an all-rounder. Without support he covered 170 kilometres, including the stiff climb of the Mur de Grammont, at an average speed of forty-two kph, and he won this twelfth stage by over six minutes. Despite the negative pattern of the racing, there was still room for private initiative — provided that it didn't cut across the interests of the major powers. But what worried the reporters was that for ten days they hadn't had a serious story to tell.

Frenchman on the Climb

The Press had to keep its patience for a few more days. The morning circuit race at Freiburg was little more than an opportunity for Thurau to show his yellow jersey to his fellow-countrymen and Sercu to win his second successive stage. The afternoon canter from Altkirch to Besançon similarly brought Danguillaume his second victory in three days' racing. But next day, surely, with a long second-category climb, the col de Cou, only twenty kilometres from the finish at Thonon-les-Bains, the leaders would surely go into action.

Well, they did and they didn't. They split the field by forcing the pace, but they did not attack each other. All but one of the top twenty-five riders reached Thonon together, having allowed the obscure Bernard Quilfen to ride ahead and take the stage by over three minutes.

There was another lone win, by Paul Wellens, the following morning at Morzine, but this time the leaders' reluctance to give chase was totally forgivable. They wanted to save themselves for the afternoon's short ride — a fourteen kilometre time trial that ran straight up the side of a first-category mountain climb to the Avoriaz ski station.

It was here that the lid blew off the Tour, and a fortnight's suppressed ambitions came bubbling to the surface. Fastest to the summit was Zoetemelk in 33–4, which helped cut his losses in the crash on stage 9 (in fact a dope test taken at Avoriaz proved positive, although we were not to know that for a week). Second, as consistent in his riding but forty-five seconds slower, was Van Impe. And third, at 1–5, was Thévenet. Thurau, starting well but flagging badly, was well down in fifteenth place, losing 2–38 and the yellow jersey he had defended for nearly 3,000 kilometres. Merckx, too, had wilted on the hill and was beaten by just over two minutes. So the order of the first six overall now read Thévenet, Thurau (at 11 seconds), Merckx (25 seconds), Van Impe (33 seconds) Kuiper (51 seconds) and Zoetemelk (1–13). Still not much in it, but riders like Thurau and Merckx who fail on the first big climb can't be given much chance on the rest of the mountain section. It looked very much as if the real battle over the next few days would be confined to Thévenet, Van Impe and Kuiper, the men in form.

Immediately the young German entered a vigorous objection to that particular reading of the race. Stage 16 was another heavy climbing day, taking in the first-category col de la Forclaz on the way to Chamonix — and Thurau won it in the finishing sprint. True, he regained none of his lost time, for Thévenet was close behind in the leading group. But on a day when Merckx's fortunes slumped still further—by 2–37, to be exact, which demoted him to seventh overall — Thurau showed that he still saw himself as a natural winner.

It was the hot, grim seventeenth stage that settled everything, a 185 kilometre ride with two first-category climbs — the col de la Madeleine and the col du Glandon — in the middle and another at Alpe d'Huez, the summit finish.

There was an early attack by five middle-rank riders, and a pursuit led by Merckx until, suffering from stomach pains, he faltered on the Madeleine. But by the time the foothills of the Glandon were reached, the race leaders had reasserted their control and, in rounding up the escapers, had shattered the rest of the field. Eight kilometres from the summit of the Glandon, the leaders, too, began to break up. Van Impe danced away to reach the top 1–25 ahead of Thévenet and Zoetemelk and 1–30 ahead of Kuiper. The rest were strung out far behind with Thurau at 4–40 and Merckx at an incredible 10–30.

On the descent and over the flat towards the final ladder of tight hairpin bends leading up to Alpe d'Huez, Van Impe managed to increase his lead. Five men had come together behind him — Thévenet, Zoetemelk, Kuiper, Galdós and Lopez-Carril — and were working anxiously together, but it looked as if Van Impe had taken control just as he did at Saint-Lary-Soulan the year before. But this time the little Belgian really had done too much too soon. He began to lose ground as first Thévenet, then Kuiper, stirred up the counter-attack. And then, with desperately bad luck, Van Impe was baulked by a car and fell. Before he could change bikes Kuiper was past him; and while he was trying to get back his rhythm after remounting, so was Thévenet. And that was their finishing order at the ski resort. Kuiper took the stage with Thévenet at forty-one seconds and Van Impe at 2–6. The rest were stragglers.

Thévenet only just succeeded in protecting his yellow jersey by eight seconds from Kuiper who moved up into second place overall ahead of Van Impe (1–58). Thurau had now dropped to sixth and Merckx to ninth, though that was only one aspect of the great upheaval. No fewer than thirty riders were eliminated for finishing outside the time limit. They included the two British entrants, Hoban and Nickson, past stage-winners like Sercu, Thaler, Delépine and Quilfen, and the one-time points leader, Van Linden (Esclassan now had this prize in his pocket).

Only fifty-six riders were left to take the still mountainous road next morning to Saint-Étienne, and though the race had, in effect, been decided there were still a few scores to settle. The thirty-four-year-old Portuguese, Joaquim Agostinho, won this eighteenth stage by over three minutes (a feat put into a different perspective later when the dope test results were announced), while Merckx pulled back 4–40 on Thévenet by setting out in pursuit, and so took his place once more in the first six.

Dijon gave Knetemann another win for Raleigh at the end of the nineteenth stage, but more importantly it offered the last credible opportunity for overturning the race result. On the next day a hilly fifty kilometre time trial was staged there. Kuiper gave it everything, but in the end Thévenet proved to have more to give. He won by twenty-two seconds from Thurau, with Kuiper third at twenty-eight seconds. His overall lead was now thirty-six seconds, and that was that.

Knetemann was first across the line again at Versailles, while the Champs-Élysées time trial gave Thurau his fifth and Raleigh their eighth stage win of the Tour. Otherwise the final day belonged to the French. In the afternoon's criterium the last victory went to Alain

Meslet, while Thévenet escaped a pile-up, the one stroke of ill-luck which might have cost him his second Tour.

If Thévenet was a hero once more, six men ended the Tour in disgrace. Dope tests had proved positive for Zoetemelk, Agostinho, Ocana, Antoine Menéndez, Fernando Mendez and Sebastien Pozo. A race which, against the odds, had found some greatness in the Alps, deserved a better ending than this.

– Figures of the Past –

YEAR	Starters	Finishers	DIST. (KM.)	No. of stages	AVGE. SPEED (KPH)	WINNER AND NATIONALITY
1903	60	21	2,428	6	25.29	Maurice Garin (Fr.)
1904	88	23	2,428	6	24.29	Henri Cornet (Fr.)
1905	60	24	2,975	11	27.28	Louis Troussellier (Fr.)
1906	82	14	4,637	13	24.46	René Pottier (Fr.)
1907	93	33	4,488	14	28.47	Lucien Petit-Breton (Fr.)
1908	114	36	4,487	14	28.74	Lucien Petit-Breton (Fr.)
1909	150	55	4,507	14	28.66	François Faber (Lux.)
1910	110	41	4,474	15	28.68	Octave Lapize (Fr.)
1911	84	28	5,344	15	27.32	Gustave Garrigou (Fr.)
1912	131	41	5,319	15	27.89	Odile Defraye (Belg.)
1913	140	25	5,387	15	27.63	Philippe Thys (Belg.)
1914	145	54	5,405	15	27.03	Philippe Thys (Belg.)
1919	69	10	5,560	15	24.95	Firmin Lambot (Belg.)
1920	113	22	5,519	15	24.13	Philippe Thys (Belg.)
1921	123	38	5,484	15	24.72	Léon Scieur (Belg.)
1922	120	38	5,375	15	24.20	Firmin Lambot (Belg.)
1923	139	48	5,394	15	24.43	Henri Pélissier (Fr.)
1924	157	60	5,425	15	23.96	Ottavio Bottecchia (It.)
1925	130	49	5,430	18	24.78	Ottavio Bottecchia (It.)
1926	126	41	5,745	17	24.07	Lucien Buysse (Belg.)
1927	142	39	5,320	24	26.84	Nicolas Frantz (Lux.)
1928	162	41	5,377	22	27.83	Nicolas Frantz (Lux.)
1929	155	60	5,286	22	28.32	Maurice Dewaele (Belg.)
1930	100	59	4,818	21	27.98	André Leducq (Fr.)
1931	81	35	5,095	24	28.76	Antonin Magne (Fr.)
1932	80	57	4,520	21	29.22	André Leducq (Fr.)
1933	80	40	4,395	23	29.70	Georges Speicher (Fr.)

WINNING MARGIN	SECOND	THIRD
2hr 49min	Pothier (Fr.)	Augereau (Fr.)
2hr 16min 14sec	Dortignac (Fr.)	Jousselin (Fr.)
26pts	Aucouturier (Fr.)	Dortignac (Fr.)
28pts	Passerieu (Fr.)	Trousselier (Fr.)
19pts	Garrigou (Fr.)	Georget (Fr.)
32pts	Faber (Lux.)	Passerieu (Fr.)
20pts	Garrigou (Fr.)	Alavoine (Fr.)
4pts	Faber (Lux.)	Garrigou (Fr.)
41pts	Dubose (Fr.)	Georget (Fr.)
59½pts	Christophe (Fr.)	Garrigou (Fr.)
8min 37sec	Garrigou (Fr.)	M. Buysse (Belg.)
1min 49sec	Pélissier (Fr.)	Alavoine (Fr.)
1hr 42min 45sec	Alavoine (Fr.)	Christophe (Fr.)
57min	Heuseghem (Belg.)	Lambot (Belg.)
19min	Heuseghem (Belg.)	Barthélémy (Fr.)
41min 15sec	Alavoine (Fr.)	Sellier (Belg.)
30min 41sec	Bottecchia (It.)	Bellenger (Fr.)
35min 36sec	Frantz (Lux.)	L. Buysse (Belg.)
54min 20sec	L. Buysse (Belg.)	Aymo (It.)
1hr 22min 25sec	Frantz (Lux.)	Aymo (It.)
1hr 48min 21sec	Dewaele (Belg.)	J. Vervaecke (Belg.)
50min 7sec	Leducq (Fr.)	Dewaele (Belg.)
32min 7sec	Demuysère (Belg.)	Pancera (It.)
14min 19sec	Guerra (It.)	Magne (Fr.)
12min 56sec	Demuysère (Belg.)	Pesenti (It.)
24min 3sec	Stoepel (Germ.)	Camusso (It.)
4min 1sec	Guerra (It.)	Martano (It.)

YEAR	Starters	Finishers	DIST. (KM.)	No. of stages	AVGE. SPEED (KPH)	WINNER AND NATIONALITY
1934	60	39	4,363	23	29.46	Antonin Magne (Fr.)
1935	93	46	4,338	21	30.62	Romain Maës (Belg.)
1936	90	43	4,442	21	31.07	Sylvère Maës (Belg.)
1937	98	46	4,415	20	31.74	Roger Lapébie (Fr.)
1938	96	55	4,694	21	31.56	Gino Bartali (It.)
1939	79	49	4,224	18	31.97	Sylvère Maës (Belg.)
1947	100	53	4,640	21	31.38	Jean Robic (Fr.)
1948	120	44	4,922	21	33.40	Gino Bartali (It.)
1949	120	55	4,775	21	32.12	Fausto Coppi (It.)
1950	116	51	4,808	22	32.78	Ferdinand Kubler (Switz.)
1951	123	66	4,697	24	32.98	Hugo Koblet (Switz.)
1952	122	78	4,807	23	31.60	Fausto Coppi (It.)
1953	119	76	4,479	22	34.61	Louison Bobet (Fr.)
1954	110	69	4,855	23	34.64	Louison Bobet (Fr.)
1955	130	69	4,495	22	34.43	Louison Bobet (Fr.)
1956	120	88	4,528	22	36.51	Roger Walkowiak (Fr.)
1957	120	56	4,686	22	34.51	Jacques Anquetil (Fr.)
1958	120	78	4,319	24	36.91	Charly Gaul (Lux.)
1959	120	65	4,363	22	35.24	Federico Bahamontes (Sp.)
1960	128	81	4,173	21	37.21	Gastone Nencini (It.)
1961	136	72	4,397	21	36.28	Jacques Anquetil (Fr.)
1962	147	94	4,274	22	37.56	Jacques Anquetil (Fr.)
1963	130	76	4,137	21	36.66	Jacques Anquetil (Fr.)
1964	132	81	4,504	22	35.59	Jacques Anquetil (Fr.)
1965	130	96	4,188	22	36.09	Felice Gimondi (It.)
1966	130	82	4,303	22	36.74	Lucien Aimar (Fr.)
1967	130	88	4,696	22	35.02	Roger Pingeon (Fr.)
1968	110	63	4,684	22	35.19	Jan Janssen (Neth.)
1969	130	86	4,110	22	35.44	Eddy Merckx (Belg.)
1970	150	100	4,359	23	36.57	Eddy Merckx (Belg.)
1971	130	94	3,578	20	37.16	Eddy Merckx (Belg.)
1972	132	88	3,730	20	35.49	Eddy Merckx (Belg.)
1973	132	87	4,150	20	33.93	Luis Ocana (Sp.)
1974	130	105	4,090	22	35.66	Eddy Merckx (Belg.)
1975	140	86	4,000	22	34.94	Bernard Thévenet (Fr.)
1976	130	87	4,019	22	34.82	Lucien Van Impe (Beige.)

WINNING MARGIN	SECOND	THIRD
37min 31sec	Martano (It.)	R. Lapébie (Fr.)
17min 52sec	Morelli (It.)	F. Vervaecke (Belg.)
26min 55sec	Magne (Fr.)	F. Vervaecke (Belg.)
7min 17sec	Vicini (It.)	Amberg (Switz.)
18min 27sec	F. Vervaecke (Belg.)	Cosson (Fr.)
30min 38sec	Vietto (Fr.)	Vlaemynck (Belg.)
3min 58sec	Fachleitner (Fr.)	Brambilla (It.)
26min 16sec	Schotte (Belg.)	G. Lapébie (Fr.)
10min 55sec	Bartali (It.)	Marinelli (Fr.)
9min 30sec	Ockers (Belg.)	Bobet (Fr.)
22sec	Géminiani (Fr.)	Lazaridès (Fr.)
28min 17sec	Ockers (Belg.)	Ruiz (Sp.)
14min 18sec	Malléjac (Fr.)	Astrua (It.)
15min 49sec	Kubler (Switz.)	Schaer (Switz.)
4min 53sec	Brankart (Belg.)	Gaul (Lux.)
1min 25sec	Bauvin (Fr.)	Adriaenssens (Belg.)
14min 56sec	Janssens (Belg.)	Christian (Austria)
3min 10sec	Favero (It.)	Géminiani (Fr.)
4min 1sec	Anglade (Fr.)	Anquetil (Fr.)
5min 2sec	Battistini (It.)	Adriaenssens (Belg.)
12mm 14sec	Carlesi (It.)	Gaul (Lux.)
4min 59sec	Plankaert (Belg.)	Poulidor (Fr.)
3min 35sec	Bahamontes (Sp.)	Perez-Frances (Sp.)
55sec	Poulidor (Fr.)	Bahamontes (Sp.)
2min 40sec	Poulidor (Fr.)	Motta (It.)
1min 7sec	Janssen (Neth.)	Poulidor (Fr.)
3min 40sec	Jimenez (Sp.)	Balmanion (It.)
38sec	Van Springel (Belg.)	Bracke (Belg.)
17min 54sec	Pingeon (Fr.)	Poulidor (Fr.)
12min 41sec	Zoetemelk (Neth.)	Pettersson (Swed.)
9min 51sec	Zoetemelk (Neth.)	Van Impe (Belg.)
10min 41sec	Gimondi (It.)	Poulidor (Fr.)
15min 51sec	Thévenet (Fr.)	Fuente (Sp.)
8min 4sec	Poulidor (Fr.)	Lopez-Carill
2min 47sec	Merckx (Belg.)	Van Impe (Belg.)
4min 14sec	Zoetemelk (Neth.)	Poulidor (Fr.)

Winners of the Mountain Prize

1933	Vincent Trueba (Sp.)	1958	Federico Bahamontes (Sp.)
1934	René Vietto (Fr.)	1959	Federico Bahamontes (Sp.)
1935	Felicien Vervaecke (Belg.)	1960	I. Massignan (It.)
1936	J. Berrendero (Sp.)	1961	I. Massignan (It.)
1937	Felicien Vervaecke (Belg.)	1962	Federico Bahamontes (Sp.)
1938	Gino Bartali (It.)	1963	Federico Bahamontes (Sp.)
1939	Sylvère Maës (Belg.)	1964	Federico Bahamontes (Sp.)
1947	P. Brambilla (It.)	1965	Julio Jiménez (Sp.)
1948	Gino Bartali (It.)	1966	Julio Jiménez (Sp.)
1949	Fausto Coppi (It.)	1967	Julio Jiménez (Sp.)
1950	Louison Bobet (Fr,)	1968	Aurelio Gonzales (Sp.)
1951	Raphaël Géminiani (Fr.)	1969	Eddy Merckx (Belg.)
1952	Fausto Coppi (It.)	1970	Eddy Merckx (Belg.)
1953	J. Lorono (Sp.)	1971	Lucien Van Impe (Belg.)
1954	Federico Bahamontes (Sp.)	1972	Lucien Van Impe (Belg.)
1955	Charly Gaul (Lux.)	1973	Pedro Torres (Sp.)
1956	Charly Gaul (Lux.)	1974	Domingo Perurena (Sp.)
1957	Gastone Nencini (It.)	1975	Lucien Van Impe (Belg.)

1976 Giancarlo Bellini (It.)

Winners of the Points Prize

1953	Fritz Schaer (Switz.)	1965	Jan Janssen (Neth.)
1954	Ferdi Kubler (Switz.)	1966	Willy Planckaert (Belg.)
1955	Stan Ockers (Belg.)	1967	Jan Janssen (Neth.)
1956	Stan Ockers (Belg.)	1968	Franco Bitossi (It.)
1957	Jean Forestier (Fr.)	1969	Eddy Merckx (Belg.)
1958	Jean Graczyk (Fr.)	1970	Walter Godefroot (Belg.)
1959	André Darrigade (Fr.)	1971	Eddy Merckx (Belg.)
1960	Jean Graczyk (Fr.)	1972	Eddy Merckx (Belg.)
1961	André Darrigade (Fr.)	1973	Herman Van Springel (Belg.)
1962	Rudi Altig (Germ.)	1974	Patrick Sercu (Belg.)
1963	Rik Van Looy (Belg.)	1975	Rik Van Linden (Belg.)
1964	Jan Janssen (Neth.)	1976	Freddy Maertens (Belg.)

STARTING POINTS

Up to 1951 the Tour began as it ended — and still ends — in Paris, with the exception of the 1926 race which set off from Evian on its longest route of all, 5,745 km. Since then the Tour has all but once (1963) started outside Paris, and on live occasions outside France:

1951	Metz	1965	COLOGNE
1952	Brest	1966	Nancy
1953	Strasbourg	1967	Angers
1954	AMSTERDAM	1968	Vittel
1955	Le Havre	1969	Roubaix
1956	Reims	1970	Limoges
1957	Nantes	1971	Mulhouse
1958	BRUSSELS	1972	Angers
1959	Mulhouse	1973	THE HAGUE
1960	Lille	1974	Brest
1961	Rouen	1975	CHARLEROI
1962	Nancy	1976	Saint-Jean-de-Monts
1964	Rennes		

SUPERLATIVE EFFORTS

Most Tour wins
Up to the end of 1976 the record — five — was held jointly by Jacques Anquetil (Fr.) and Eddy Merckx (Belg.). They also shared the record of four consecutive wins. There have been two triple-winners: Philippe Thys (Belg.) and, in successive years, Louison Bobet (Fr.).

On the basis of the individual winners' nationality, France, after 63 Tours, led with 28 victories from Belgium (18), Italy (8), Luxemburg (4), Switzerland and Spain (2 each) and the Netherlands (1).

Winning margins

The biggest has been 2 hr 49 min for Maurice Garin (Fr.) in the opening Tour of 1903; the smallest, 22 sec for Hugo Koblet (Switz.) in 1950.

Most Tours completed

André Darrigade (Fr.) completed 13 of the 14 Tours he started in the fifties and sixties, riding a total of 57,750 km. In 1976 Raymond Poulidor (Fr.) finished for the twelfth time in fourteen starts, having missed only one Tour (1971) since 1962. In that period he was three times second overall and five times third.

Longest time-span

Eugène Christophe (Fr.), known as 'le vieux Gaulois', completed the Tour for the first time in 1906, and for the eighth and last time in 1925, a span of nineteen years. Ten years is the widest gap between the victories of any one rider — those of Gino Bartali (It.) in 1938 and 1948.

Winners from first to last

Four riders have taken the lead on the first day and held it to the finish. They are:

Ottavio Bottecchia (It.) in 1924. He won the initial stage from Paris to Le Havre, and kept ahead with two more stage victories before taking the final sprint at Paris.

Nicolas Frantz (Lux.) in 1928. Since he had won the Tour the year before, he was entitled to wear the yellow jersey on the opening day, when he won at Caen. This makes him the only rider to have literally been in yellow from start to finish.

Romain Maës (Belg.) in 1936. Built his success on a piece of good luck during the stage from Paris to Lille when a level crossing closed between himself and his pursuers.

Jacques Anquetil (Fr.) in 1961. Qualifies only on a technicality. It was André Darrigade (Fr.) who won the opening morning's half-stage, Rouen–Versailles, and therefore the first yellow jersey. But Anquetil had taken it over by the end of the day as winner of the afternoon's time trial.

Winners on the final day

Two post-war riders have won the Tour without ever leading the race, receiving their first and only yellow jersey on the podium at Paris. In 1947 Jean Robic (Fr.) was 2 min 58 sec down on the Italian race leader, Brambilla, before the start of the final stage from Caen to Paris. Instead of allowing it to be treated as a procession, Robic made a surprise attack to win the Tour by 3–58 and beat Brambilla by 10–07. In 1968 Jan Janssen (Neth.) began the final half-stage, a time trial from Melun to Paris, 16 sec behind Van Springel (Belg.) who had taken the yellow jersey on stage 19. Janssen won the 55 km trial beating Van Springel by 54 sec.

Most stage wins

After 63 Tours, Merckx leads with 34 stage wins, far outstripping André Leducq (Fr.), 25; André Darrigade (Fr.), 22; Nicolas Frantz (Lux.), 20; François Faber (Lux.), 19; Jean Alavoine (Fr.), 17; Charles Pélissier (Fr.) and René le Grève (Fr.), 16; Jacques Anquetil (Fr.), 15.

The record of eight stage wins in a single Tour is shared by Pélissier (1930) and the two Belgians, Merckx (1970 and 1974) and Freddy Maertens (1976).

Biggest stage wins

The more significant breakaway stage wins belong to the early days of the Tour. The two longest were made by François Faber (Lux.), who took the 1909 Tour after winning stage 2 at Metz and stage 3 at Belfort by the same margin of 33 min. A lead of 25 min 48 sec at Luchon also gave the 1926 Tour to Lucian Buysse (Belg.). In post-war Tours the big stage wins have rarely been important except to the man concerned — often a minor figure given his head since he can do the race leaders no harm. During this period the longest leads built up by the end of a stage have been 22–50 by Viejo (Sp.) at Manosque, 1976; 21–48 by Baffi (It.) at Bordeaux, 1957; 20–31 by De Groot (Neth.) at Albi, 1955; and 20–06 by Brian Robinson (GB) at Chalon-sur-Saône, 1959

Mountains and Points

Federico Bahamontes (Sp.) holds the climbers' record with five victories in the mountain grand prix within the space of seven years. Curiously only three Frenchmen — René Vietto, Louison Bobet and Raphaël Géminiani — have been King of the Mountains. Jan Janssen (Neth.) and Merckx lead the points table with three victories each. Merckx's name is the only one which appears on both lists; he has won the mountain competition twice. In 1969 he performed the remarkable feat of carrying off both the points and mountain prize in the same Tour — as well as winning the race itself.

– Index –